MUNCHKIN®

VOLUME SIX

BOOM! BOX™
STEVE JACKSON GAMES

STEVE JACKSON GAMES

MUNCHKIN Volume Six, September 2017. Published by BOOM!
Box, a division of Boom Entertainment, Inc. **Munchkin**, the **Munchkin**
characters, and the names of all products published by Steve Jackson
Games Incorporated are trademarks or registered trademarks of
Steve Jackson Games Incorporated, used under license by Boom
Entertainment, Inc. All rights reserved. The **Munchkin** comic is copyright
© 2017 by Steve Jackson Games Incorporated. All rights reserved.
Originally published in single magazine form as MUNCHKIN No. 22-
25. ™ & © 2016, 2017 Steve Jackson Games. All rights reserved.
BOOM! Box™ and the BOOM! Box logo are trademarks of Boom
Entertainment, Inc., registered in various countries and categories. All
characters, events, and institutions depicted herein are fictional. Any
similarity between any of the names, characters, persons, events, and/or
institutions in this publication to actual names, characters, and persons,
whether living or dead, events, and/or institutions is unintended and
purely coincidental. BOOM! Box does not read or accept unsolicited
submissions of ideas, stories, or artwork.

BOOM! Studios, 5670 Wilshire Boulevard, Suite 450, Los Angeles, CA
90036-5679. Printed in China. First Printing.

ISBN: 978-1-68415-015-1, eISBN: 978-1-61398-686-8

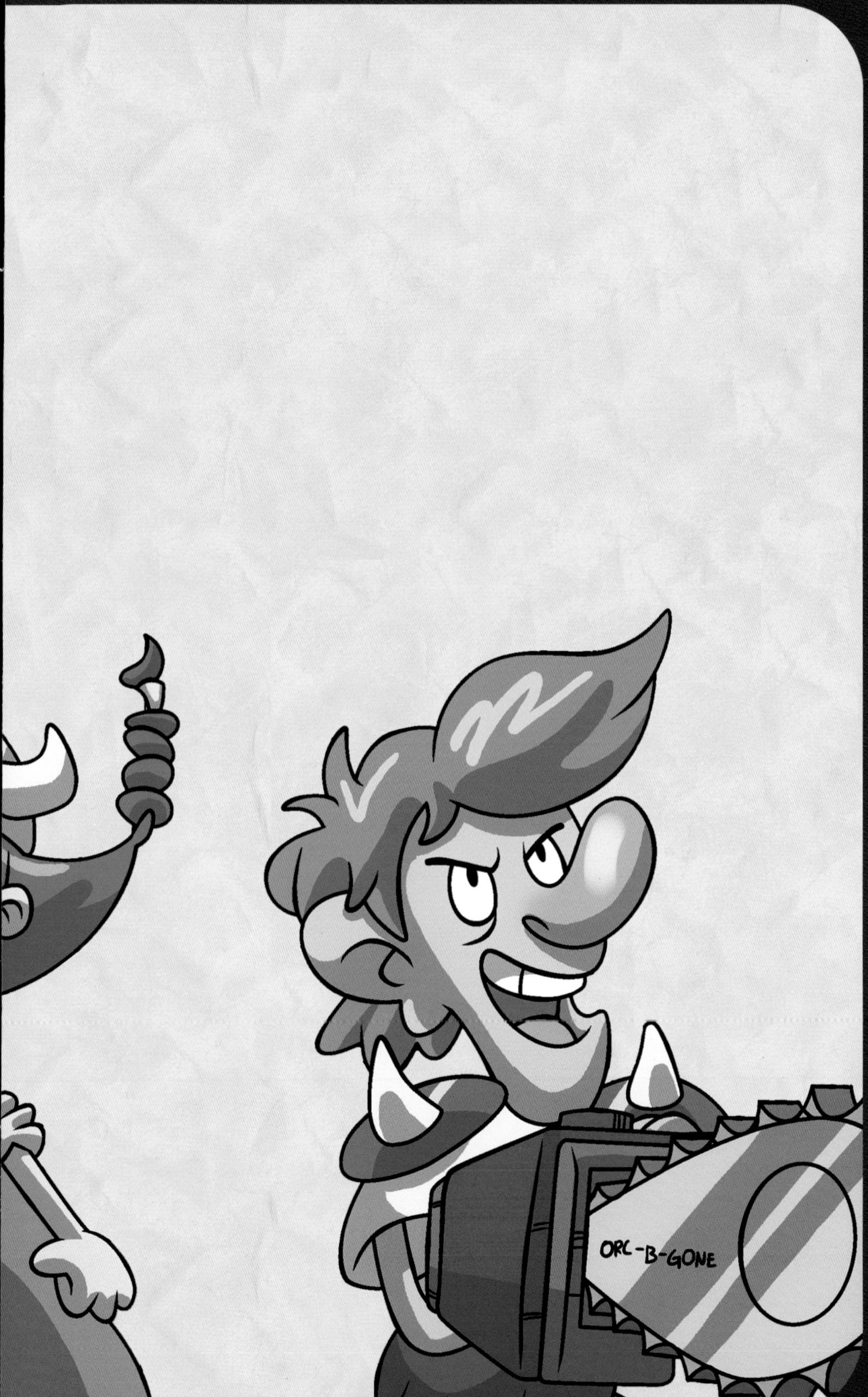
ORC-B-GONE

MUNCHKIN

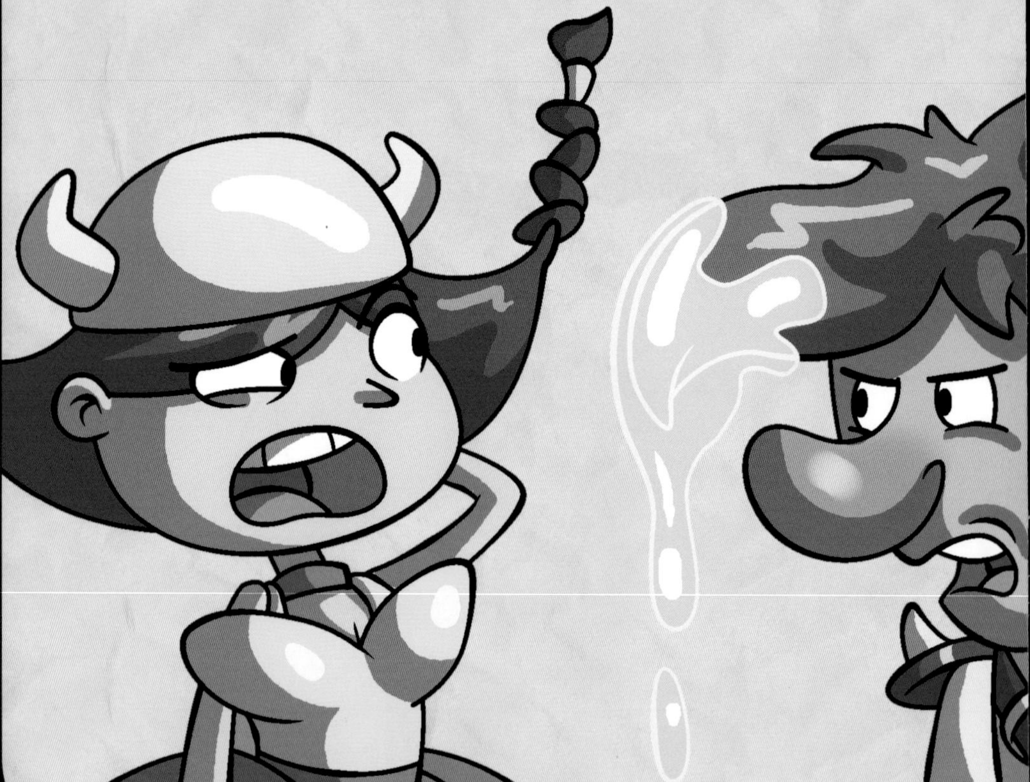

WRITTEN BY
SAM SYKES
(CHAPTER 21)
NICOLE ANDELFINGER
(CHAPTER 22)
AND ANDREW HACKARD
(CHAPTERS 23, 24)

ILLUSTRATED BY
IAN MCGINTY
(CHAPTER 21)
LEN PERALTA
(CHAPTERS 22, 24)
AND PHIL MURPHY
(CHAPTER 23)

COLORS BY
MEG CASEY

"MUNCHKIN MINIS"

"WE'RE SAFE HERE—THIS IS A BOWLING ALLEY"
WRITTEN BY
DAVE SCHEIDT
ILLUSTRATED BY
GREG HYLAND
COLORS BY
FRED STRESING

"THE MARK OF THE GAZEBO"
WRITTEN BY
SAM SYKES
ILLUSTRATED BY
MADDI GONZALEZ

"THE ECOLOGY OF THE GAZEBO"
WRITTEN BY
ANDREW HACKARD
ILLUSTRATED BY
PHIL MURPHY

LETTERS BY
SIMON BOWLAND

COVER BY
MIKE LUCKAS

DESIGNER
GRACE PARK

EDITORS
JASMINE AMIRI & SHANNON WATTERS

SPECIAL THANKS TO STEVE JACKSON, PHIL REED, ANDREW HACKARD, ALAIN H. DAWSON AND ALL OF THE AMAZING FOLKS AT STEVE JACKSON GAMES.

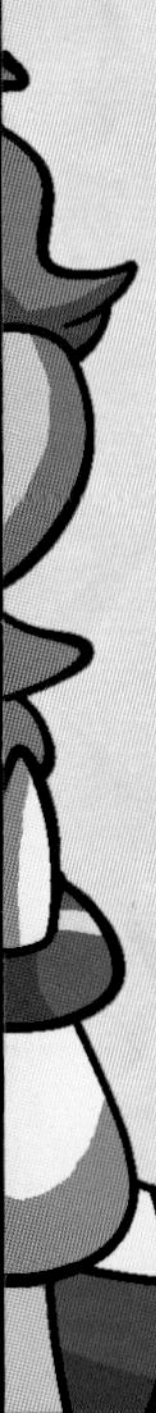

CHAPTER
TWENTY-ONE

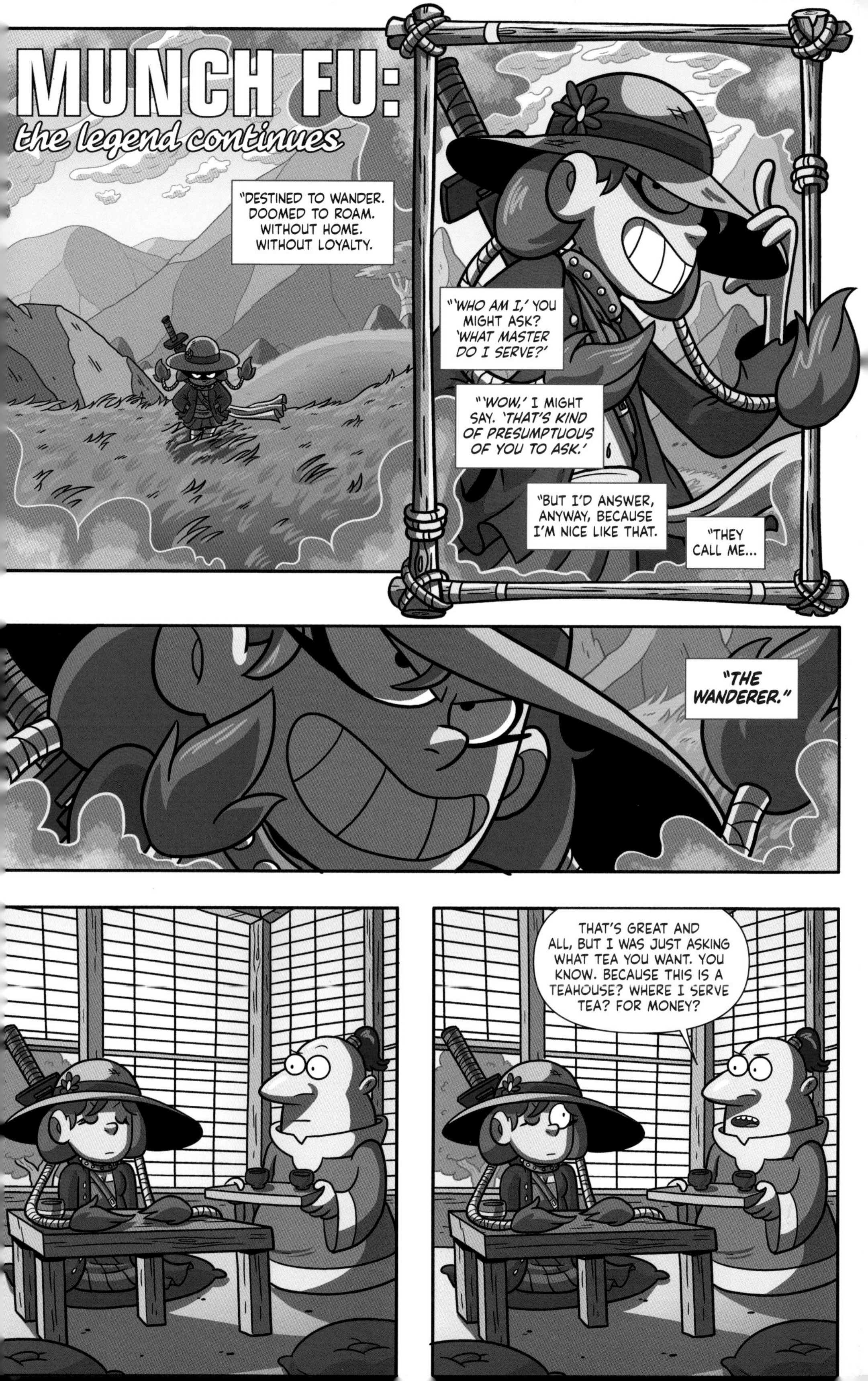
MUNCH FU:
the legend continues
"DESTINED TO WANDER. DOOMED TO ROAM. WITHOUT HOME. WITHOUT LOYALTY.
"'WHO AM I,' YOU MIGHT ASK? 'WHAT MASTER DO I SERVE?'
"'WOW,' I MIGHT SAY. 'THAT'S KIND OF PRESUMPTUOUS OF YOU TO ASK.'
"BUT I'D ANSWER, ANYWAY, BECAUSE I'M NICE LIKE THAT.
"THEY CALL ME...
"THE WANDERER."
THAT'S GREAT AND ALL, BUT I WAS JUST ASKING WHAT TEA YOU WANT. YOU KNOW. BECAUSE THIS IS A TEAHOUSE? WHERE I SERVE TEA? FOR MONEY?

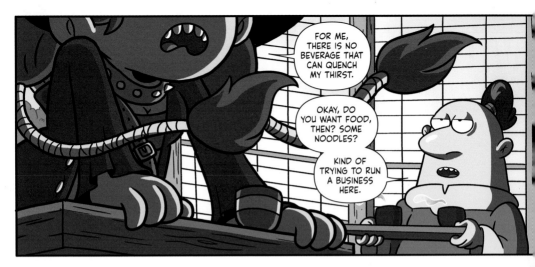

FOR ME, THERE IS NO BEVERAGE THAT CAN QUENCH MY THIRST.

OKAY, DO YOU WANT FOOD, THEN? SOME NOODLES?

KIND OF TRYING TO RUN A BUSINESS HERE.

I THIRST...FOR *VENGEANCE!*

THAT'S NOT A THING WE SELL HERE. LISTEN, IF YOU'RE NOT GOING TO BUY ANYTHING, YOU NEED TO--

MY QUEST BEGAN THREE WEEKS AGO...

WAIT! WHAT'S THIS STUFF? WHAT'S GOING ON?!

WITH THE DEATH OF MY MASTER...

IT ITCHES! IS IT SUPPOSED TO ITCH? HELP! *HELP!*

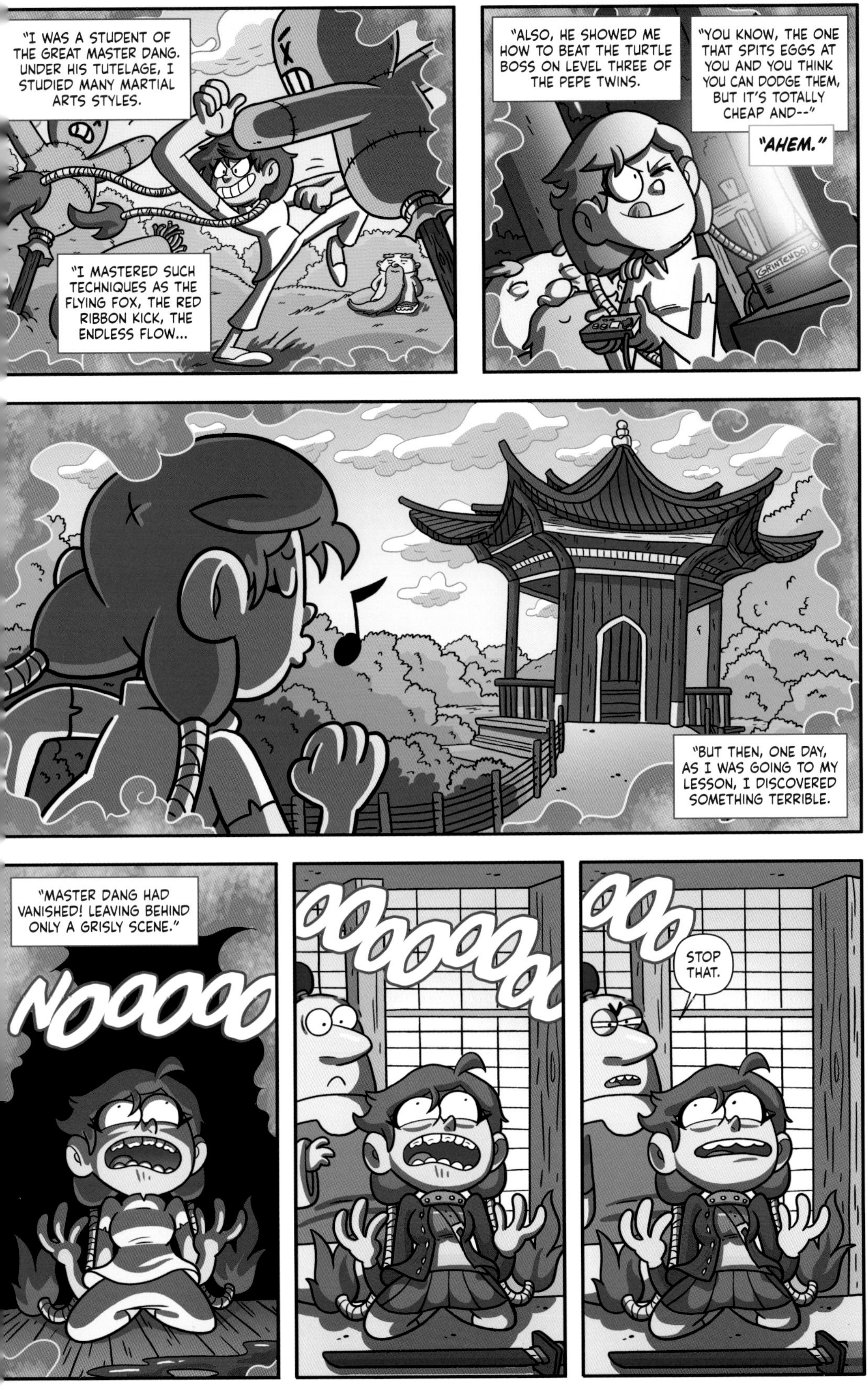
"I WAS A STUDENT OF THE GREAT MASTER DANG. UNDER HIS TUTELAGE, I STUDIED MANY MARTIAL ARTS STYLES.
"I MASTERED SUCH TECHNIQUES AS THE FLYING FOX, THE RED RIBBON KICK, THE ENDLESS FLOW...
"ALSO, HE SHOWED ME HOW TO BEAT THE TURTLE BOSS ON LEVEL THREE OF THE PEPE TWINS.
"YOU KNOW, THE ONE THAT SPITS EGGS AT YOU AND YOU THINK YOU CAN DODGE THEM, BUT IT'S TOTALLY CHEAP AND--"
"AHEM."
GRINTENDO
"BUT THEN, ONE DAY, AS I WAS GOING TO MY LESSON, I DISCOVERED SOMETHING TERRIBLE.
"MASTER DANG HAD VANISHED! LEAVING BEHIND ONLY A GRISLY SCENE."
NOOOOO
OOOOOOOOO
OOO
STOP THAT.

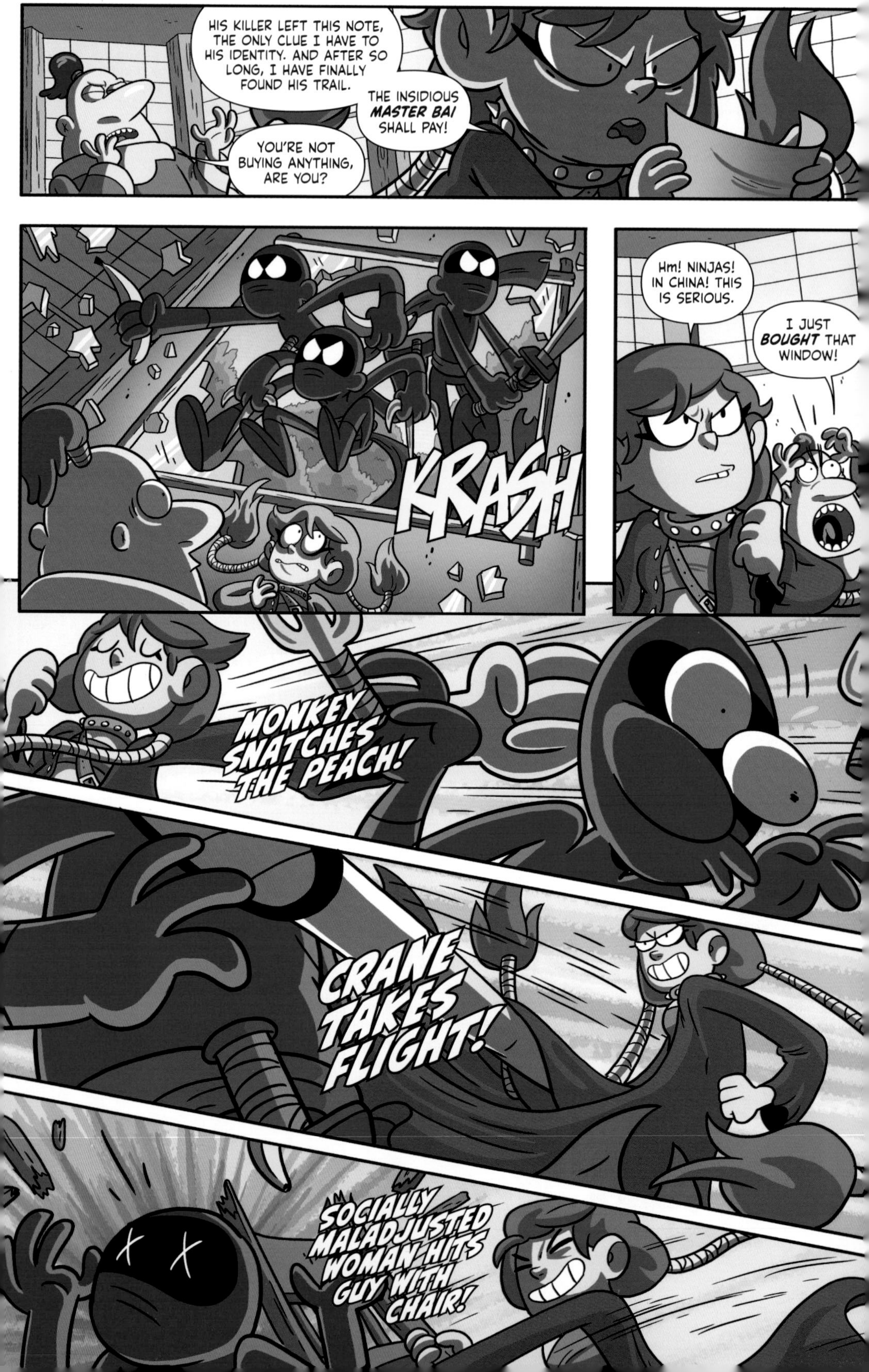
HIS KILLER LEFT THIS NOTE, THE ONLY CLUE I HAVE TO HIS IDENTITY. AND AFTER SO LONG, I HAVE FINALLY FOUND HIS TRAIL.
THE INSIDIOUS MASTER BAI SHALL PAY!
YOU'RE NOT BUYING ANYTHING, ARE YOU?
KRASH
Hm! NINJAS! IN CHINA! THIS IS SERIOUS.
I JUST BOUGHT THAT WINDOW!
MONKEY SNATCHES THE PEACH!
CRANE TAKES FLIGHT!
SOCIALLY MALADJUSTED WOMAN HITS GUY WITH CHAIR!

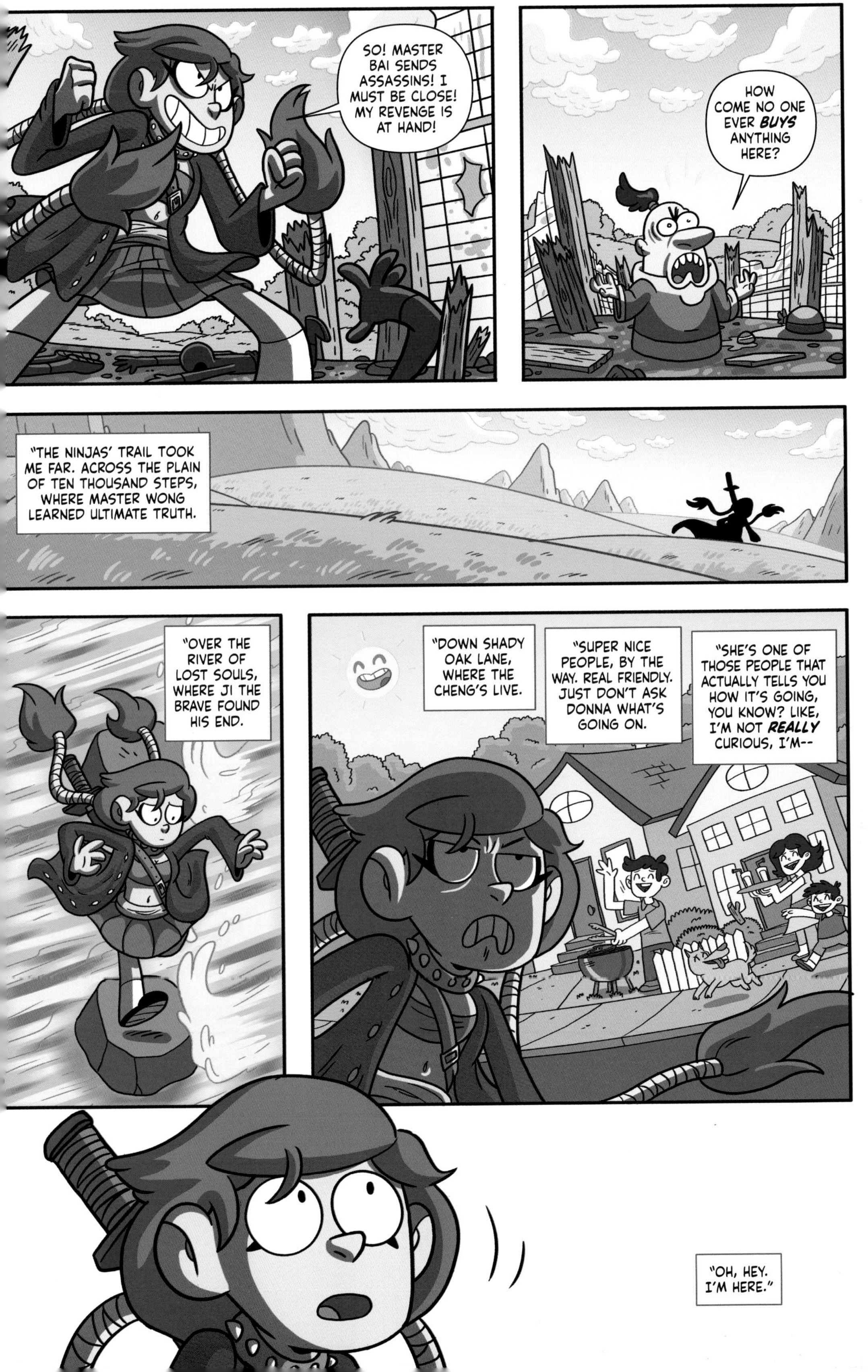
SO! MASTER BAI SENDS ASSASSINS! I MUST BE CLOSE! MY REVENGE IS AT HAND!
HOW COME NO ONE EVER **BUYS** ANYTHING HERE?
"THE NINJAS' TRAIL TOOK ME FAR. ACROSS THE PLAIN OF TEN THOUSAND STEPS, WHERE MASTER WONG LEARNED ULTIMATE TRUTH.
"OVER THE RIVER OF LOST SOULS, WHERE JI THE BRAVE FOUND HIS END.
"DOWN SHADY OAK LANE, WHERE THE CHENG'S LIVE.
"SUPER NICE PEOPLE, BY THE WAY. REAL FRIENDLY. JUST DON'T ASK DONNA WHAT'S GOING ON.
"SHE'S ONE OF THOSE PEOPLE THAT ACTUALLY TELLS YOU HOW IT'S GOING, YOU KNOW? LIKE, I'M NOT ***REALLY*** CURIOUS, I'M--
"OH, HEY. I'M HERE."

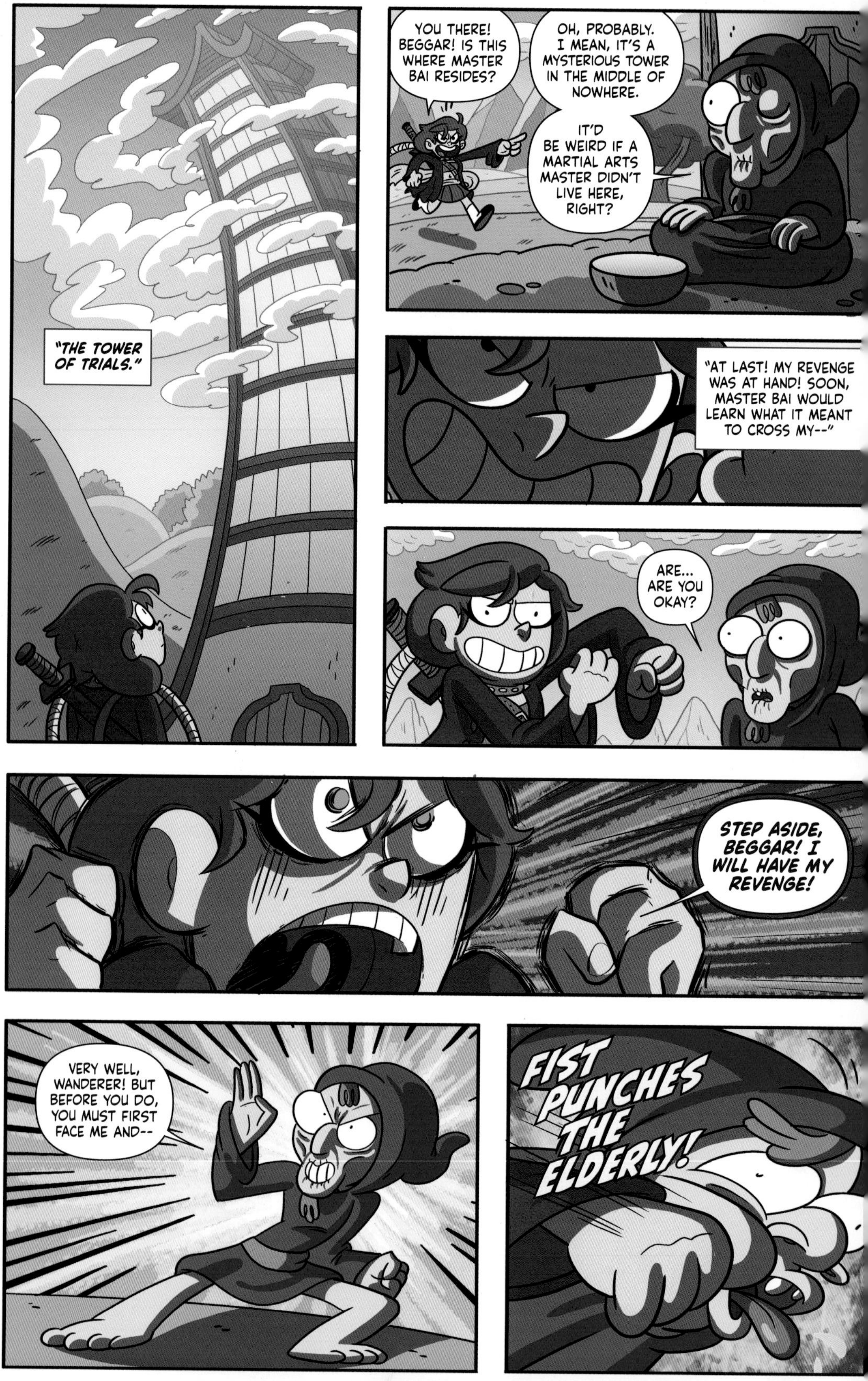

"THE TOWER OF TRIALS."
YOU THERE! BEGGAR! IS THIS WHERE MASTER BAI RESIDES?
OH, PROBABLY. I MEAN, IT'S A MYSTERIOUS TOWER IN THE MIDDLE OF NOWHERE.
IT'D BE WEIRD IF A MARTIAL ARTS MASTER DIDN'T LIVE HERE, RIGHT?
"AT LAST! MY REVENGE WAS AT HAND! SOON, MASTER BAI WOULD LEARN WHAT IT MEANT TO CROSS MY--"
ARE... ARE YOU OKAY?
STEP ASIDE, BEGGAR! I WILL HAVE MY REVENGE!
VERY WELL, WANDERER! BUT BEFORE YOU DO, YOU MUST FIRST FACE ME AND--
FIST PUNCHES THE ELDERLY!

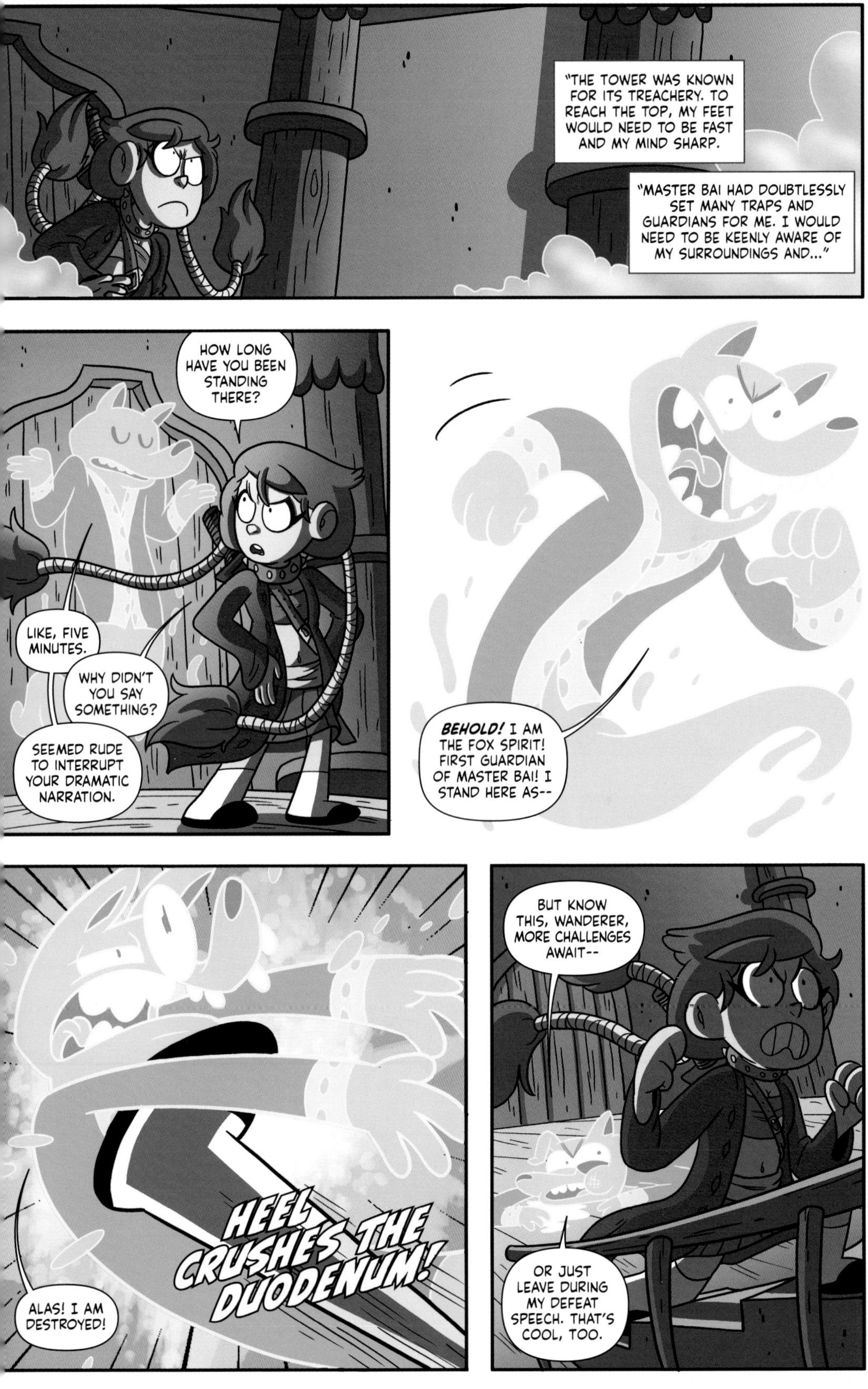

"THE TOWER WAS KNOWN FOR ITS TREACHERY. TO REACH THE TOP, MY FEET WOULD NEED TO BE FAST AND MY MIND SHARP.
"MASTER BAI HAD DOUBTLESSLY SET MANY TRAPS AND GUARDIANS FOR ME. I WOULD NEED TO BE KEENLY AWARE OF MY SURROUNDINGS AND..."
HOW LONG HAVE YOU BEEN STANDING THERE?
LIKE, FIVE MINUTES.
WHY DIDN'T YOU SAY SOMETHING?
SEEMED RUDE TO INTERRUPT YOUR DRAMATIC NARRATION.
BEHOLD! I AM THE FOX SPIRIT! FIRST GUARDIAN OF MASTER BAI! I STAND HERE AS--
HEEL CRUSHES THE DUODENUM!
ALAS! I AM DESTROYED!
BUT KNOW THIS, WANDERER, MORE CHALLENGES AWAIT--
OR JUST LEAVE DURING MY DEFEAT SPEECH. THAT'S COOL, TOO.

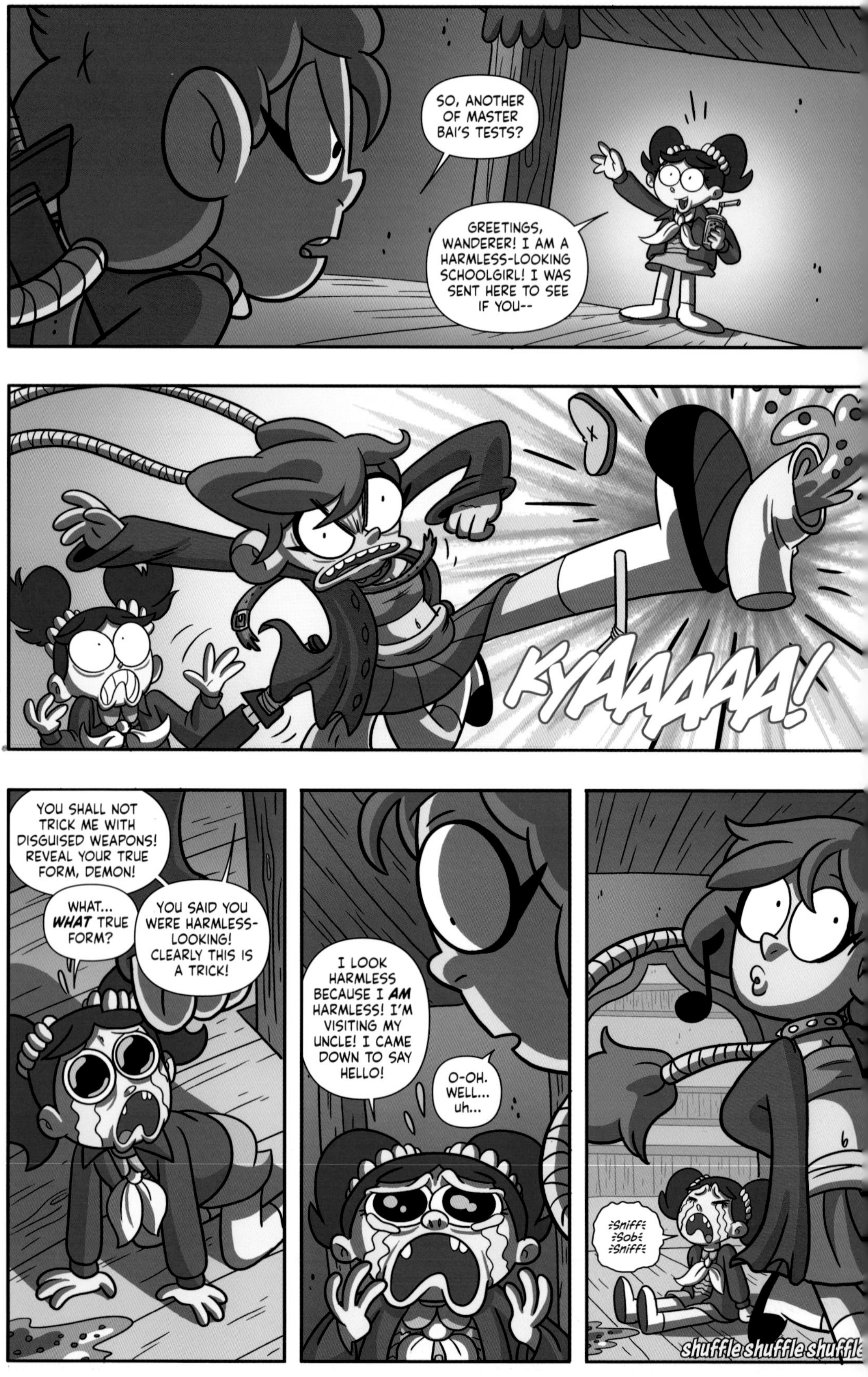
SO, ANOTHER OF MASTER BAI'S TESTS?
GREETINGS, WANDERER! I AM A HARMLESS-LOOKING SCHOOLGIRL! I WAS SENT HERE TO SEE IF YOU--
KYAAAAAA!
YOU SHALL NOT TRICK ME WITH DISGUISED WEAPONS! REVEAL YOUR TRUE FORM, DEMON!
WHAT... WHAT TRUE FORM?
YOU SAID YOU WERE HARMLESS-LOOKING! CLEARLY THIS IS A TRICK!
I LOOK HARMLESS BECAUSE I AM HARMLESS! I'M VISITING MY UNCLE! I CAME DOWN TO SAY HELLO!
O-OH. WELL... uh...
Sniff Sob Sniff
shuffle shuffle shuffle

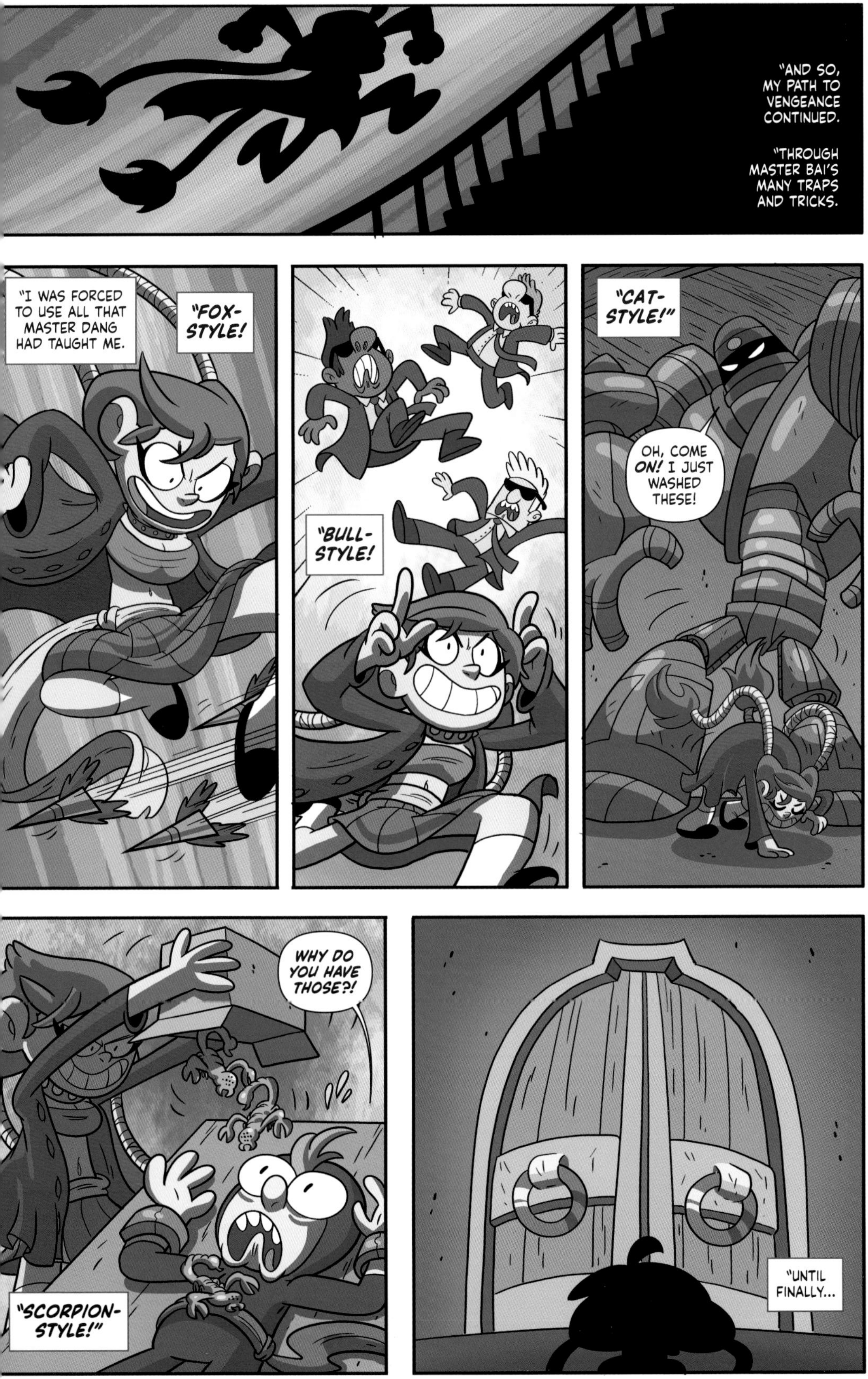
"AND SO, MY PATH TO VENGEANCE CONTINUED.
"THROUGH MASTER BAI'S MANY TRAPS AND TRICKS.
"I WAS FORCED TO USE ALL THAT MASTER DANG HAD TAUGHT ME.
"FOX-STYLE!
"BULL-STYLE!
"CAT-STYLE!"
OH, COME ON! I JUST WASHED THESE!
WHY DO YOU HAVE THOSE?!
"SCORPION-STYLE!"
"UNTIL FINALLY...

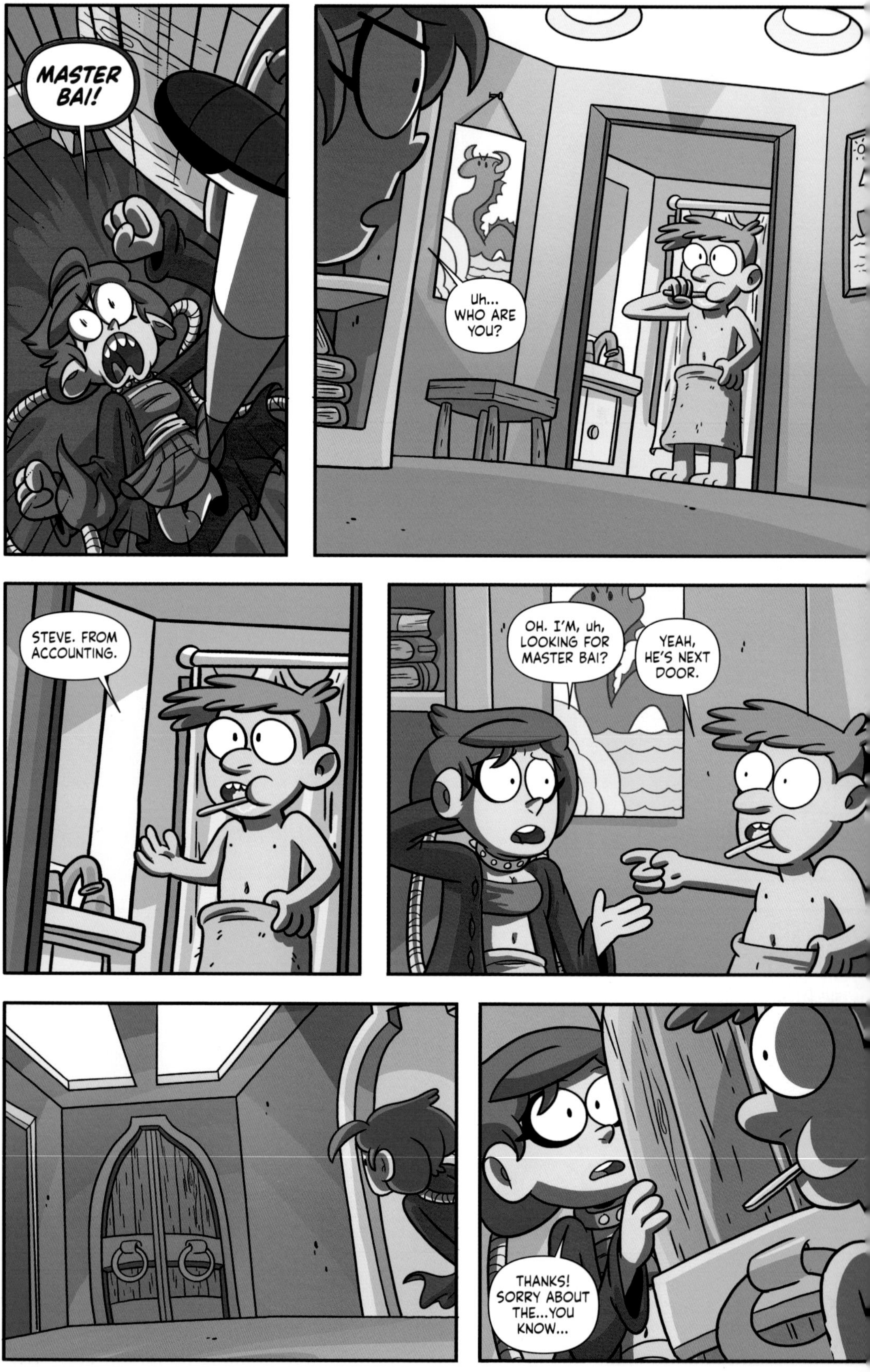
MASTER BAI!
Uh... WHO ARE YOU?
STEVE. FROM ACCOUNTING.
OH. I'M, uh, LOOKING FOR MASTER BAI?
YEAH, HE'S NEXT DOOR.
THANKS! SORRY ABOUT THE...YOU KNOW...

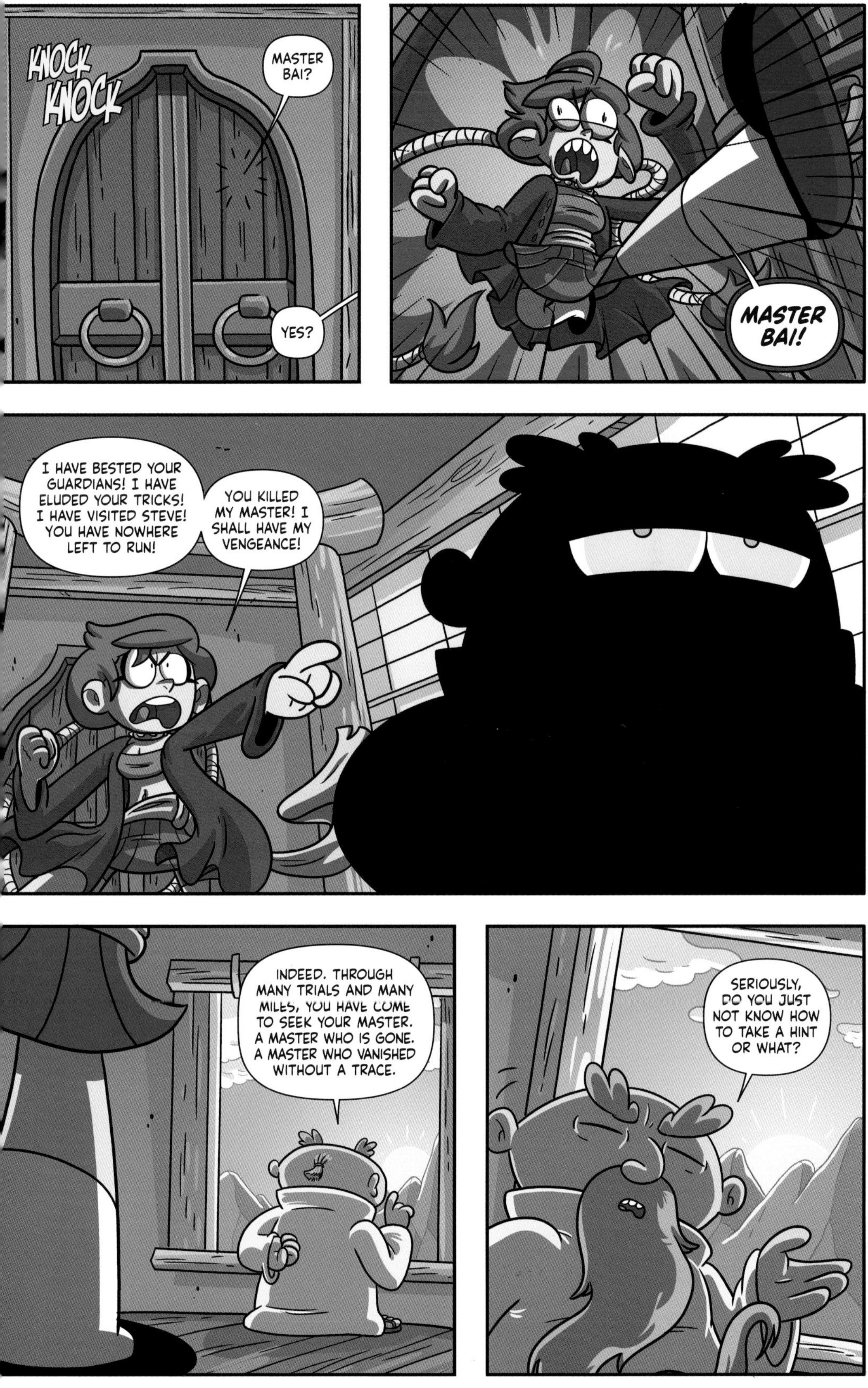
KNOCK KNOCK
MASTER BAI?
YES?
MASTER BAI!
I HAVE BESTED YOUR GUARDIANS! I HAVE ELUDED YOUR TRICKS! I HAVE VISITED STEVE! YOU HAVE NOWHERE LEFT TO RUN!
YOU KILLED MY MASTER! I SHALL HAVE MY VENGEANCE!
INDEED. THROUGH MANY TRIALS AND MANY MILES, YOU HAVE COME TO SEEK YOUR MASTER. A MASTER WHO IS GONE. A MASTER WHO VANISHED WITHOUT A TRACE.
SERIOUSLY, DO YOU JUST NOT KNOW HOW TO TAKE A HINT OR WHAT?

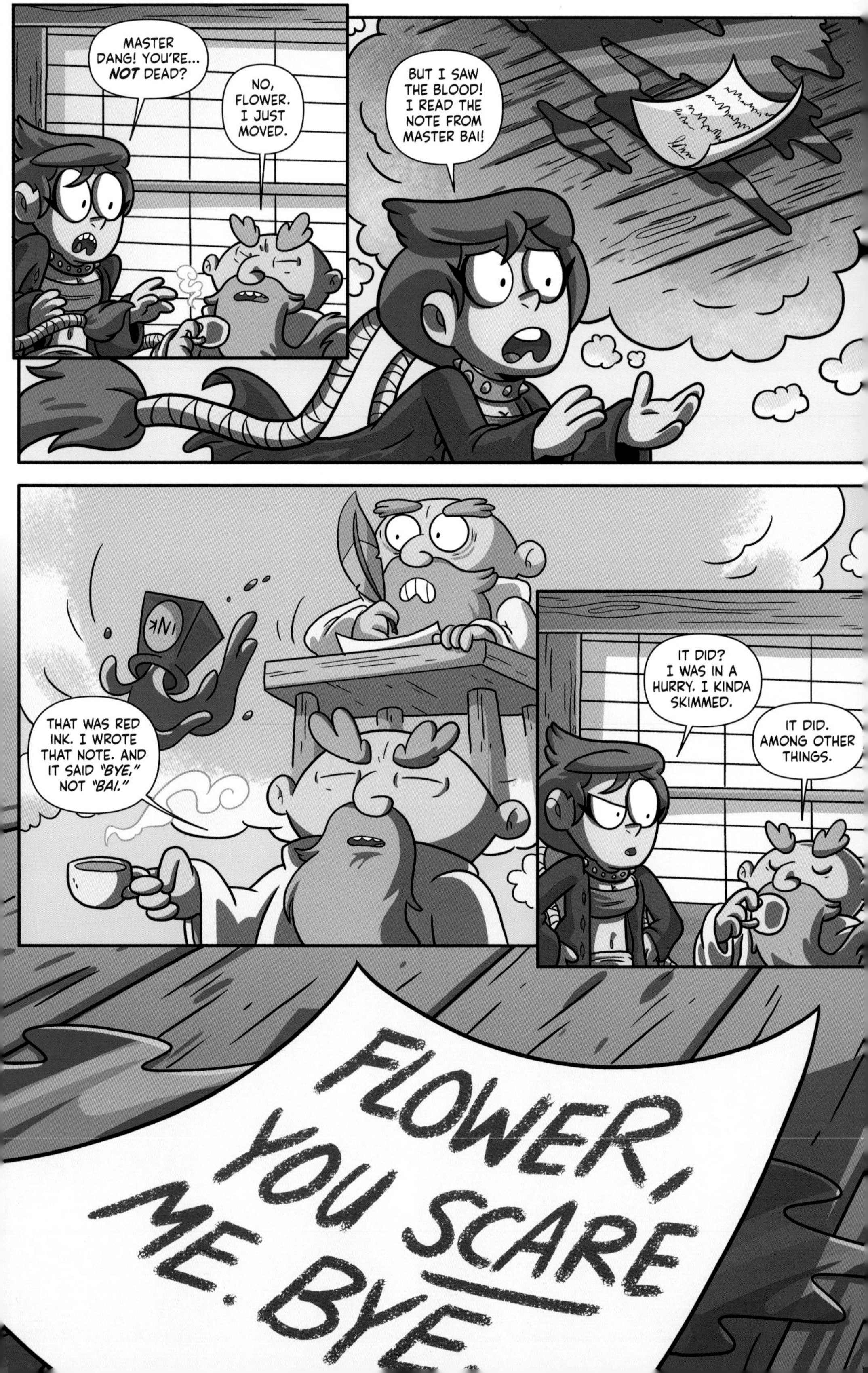
MASTER DANG! YOU'RE... *NOT* DEAD?
NO, FLOWER. I JUST MOVED.
BUT I SAW THE BLOOD! I READ THE NOTE FROM MASTER BAI!
INK
THAT WAS RED INK. I WROTE THAT NOTE. AND IT SAID *"BYE,"* NOT *"BAI."*
IT DID? I WAS IN A HURRY. I KINDA SKIMMED.
IT DID. AMONG OTHER THINGS.
FLOWER, YOU SCARE ME. BYE.

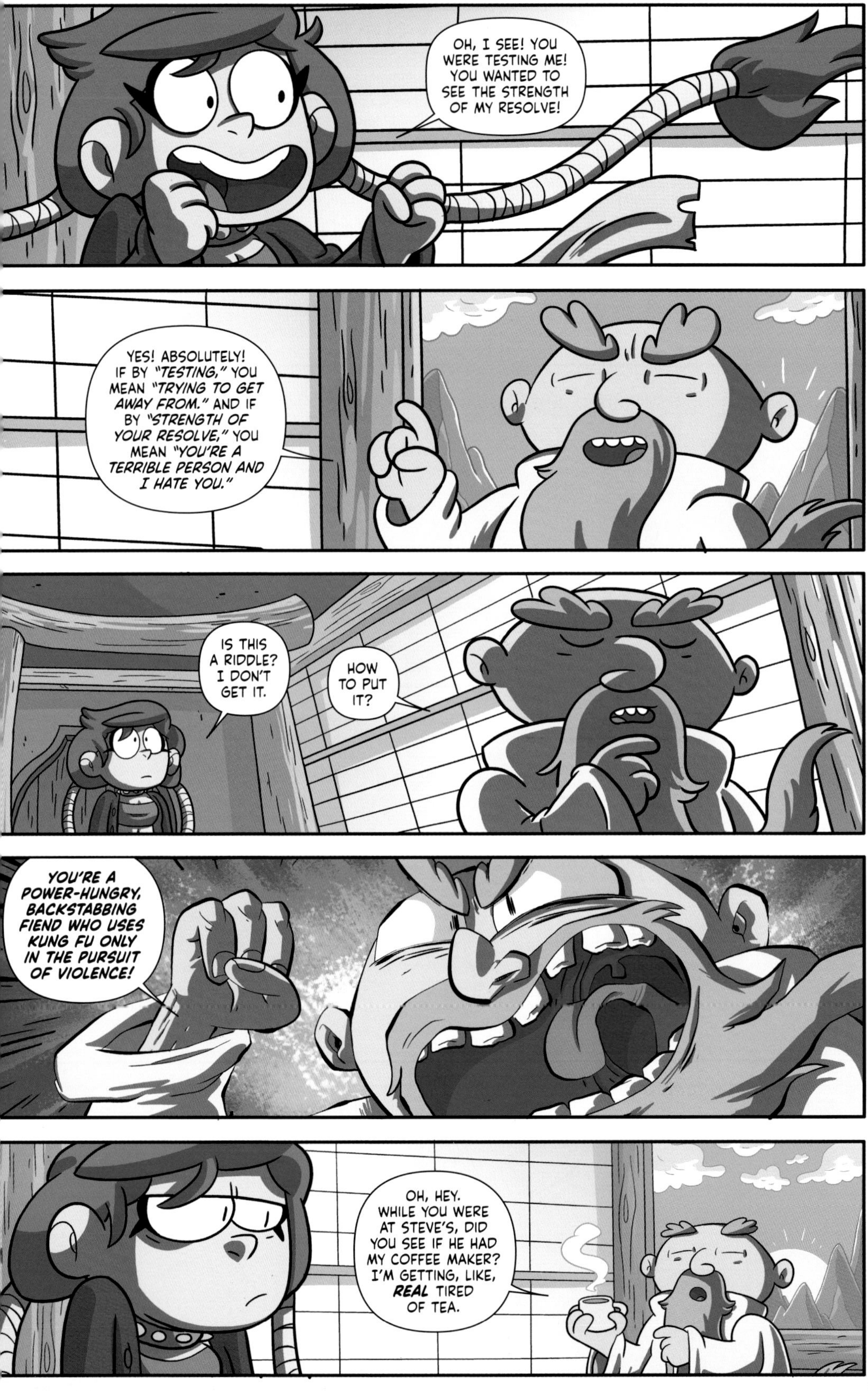
OH, I SEE! YOU WERE TESTING ME! YOU WANTED TO SEE THE STRENGTH OF MY RESOLVE!
YES! ABSOLUTELY! IF BY *"TESTING,"* YOU MEAN *"TRYING TO GET AWAY FROM."* AND IF BY *"STRENGTH OF YOUR RESOLVE,"* YOU MEAN *"YOU'RE A TERRIBLE PERSON AND I HATE YOU."*
IS THIS A RIDDLE? I DON'T GET IT.
HOW TO PUT IT?
YOU'RE A POWER-HUNGRY, BACKSTABBING FIEND WHO USES KUNG FU ONLY IN THE PURSUIT OF VIOLENCE!
OH, HEY. WHILE YOU WERE AT STEVE'S, DID YOU SEE IF HE HAD MY COFFEE MAKER? I'M GETTING, LIKE, ***REAL*** TIRED OF TEA.

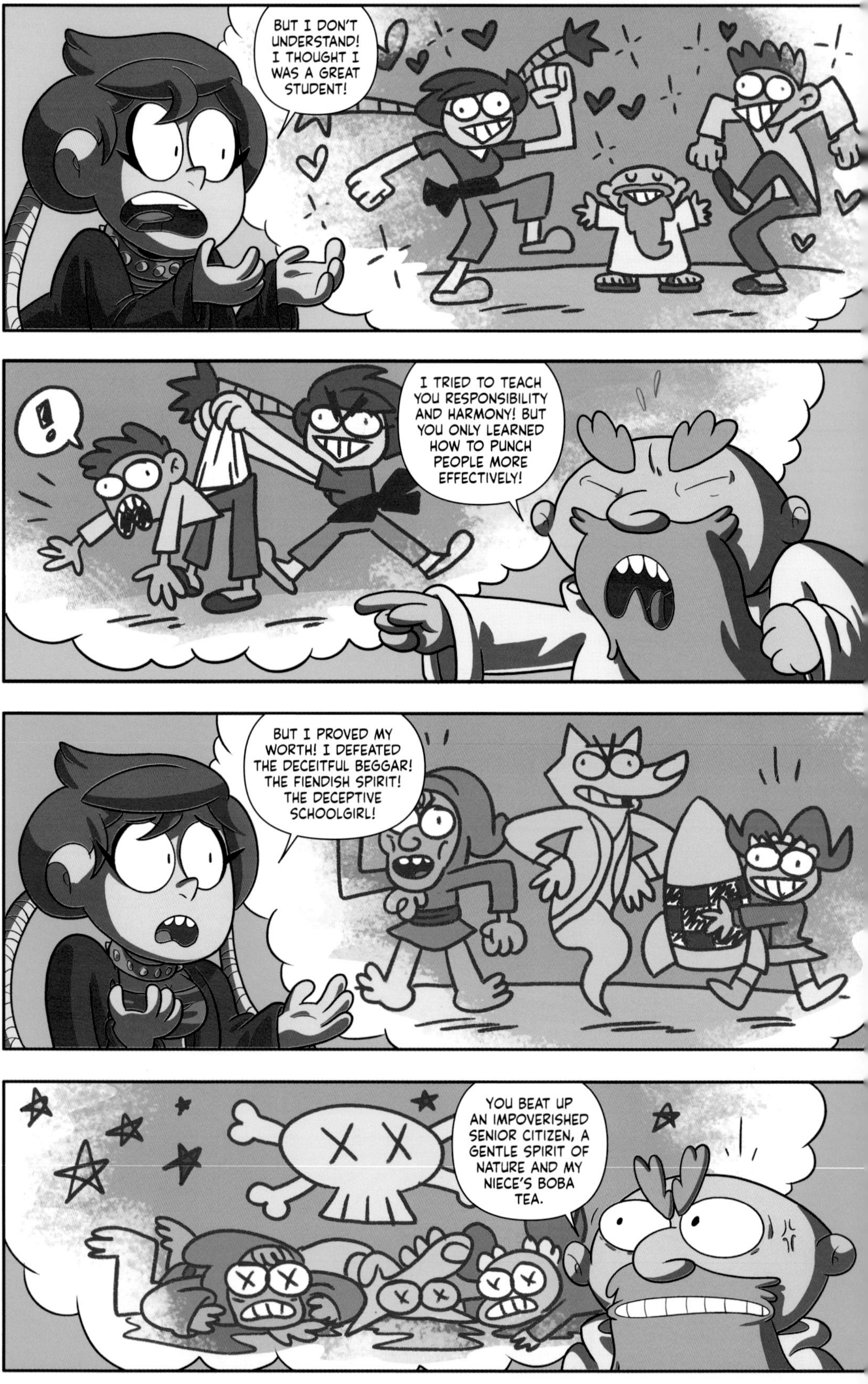

BUT I DON'T UNDERSTAND! I THOUGHT I WAS A GREAT STUDENT!
I TRIED TO TEACH YOU RESPONSIBILITY AND HARMONY! BUT YOU ONLY LEARNED HOW TO PUNCH PEOPLE MORE EFFECTIVELY!
BUT I PROVED MY WORTH! I DEFEATED THE DECEITFUL BEGGAR! THE FIENDISH SPIRIT! THE DECEPTIVE SCHOOLGIRL!
YOU BEAT UP AN IMPOVERISHED SENIOR CITIZEN, A GENTLE SPIRIT OF NATURE AND MY NIECE'S BOBA TEA.

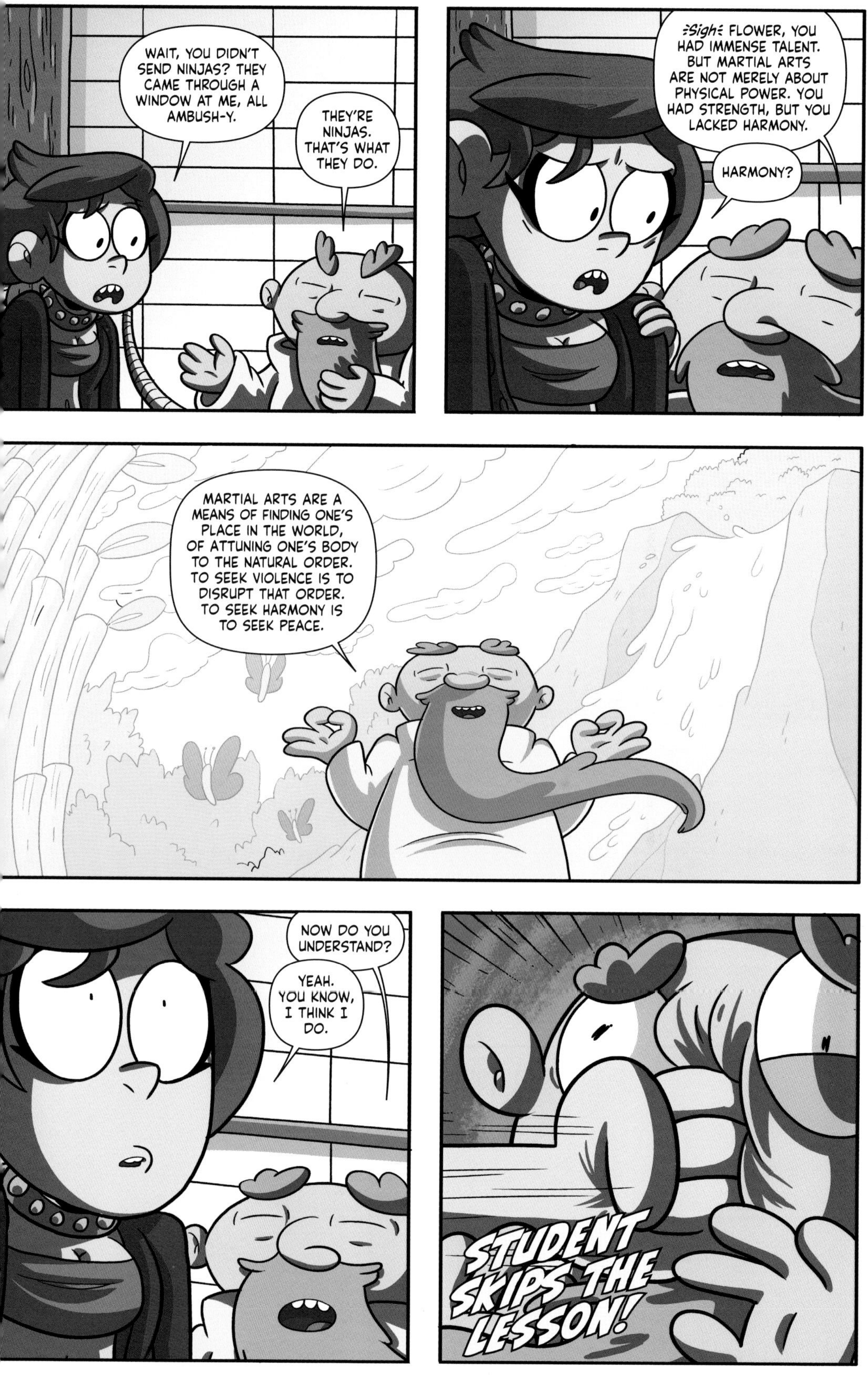
WAIT, YOU DIDN'T SEND NINJAS? THEY CAME THROUGH A WINDOW AT ME, ALL AMBUSH-Y.
THEY'RE NINJAS. THAT'S WHAT THEY DO.
Sigh FLOWER, YOU HAD IMMENSE TALENT. BUT MARTIAL ARTS ARE NOT MERELY ABOUT PHYSICAL POWER. YOU HAD STRENGTH, BUT YOU LACKED HARMONY.
HARMONY?
MARTIAL ARTS ARE A MEANS OF FINDING ONE'S PLACE IN THE WORLD, OF ATTUNING ONE'S BODY TO THE NATURAL ORDER. TO SEEK VIOLENCE IS TO DISRUPT THAT ORDER. TO SEEK HARMONY IS TO SEEK PEACE.
NOW DO YOU UNDERSTAND?
YEAH. YOU KNOW, I THINK I DO.
STUDENT SKIPS THE LESSON!

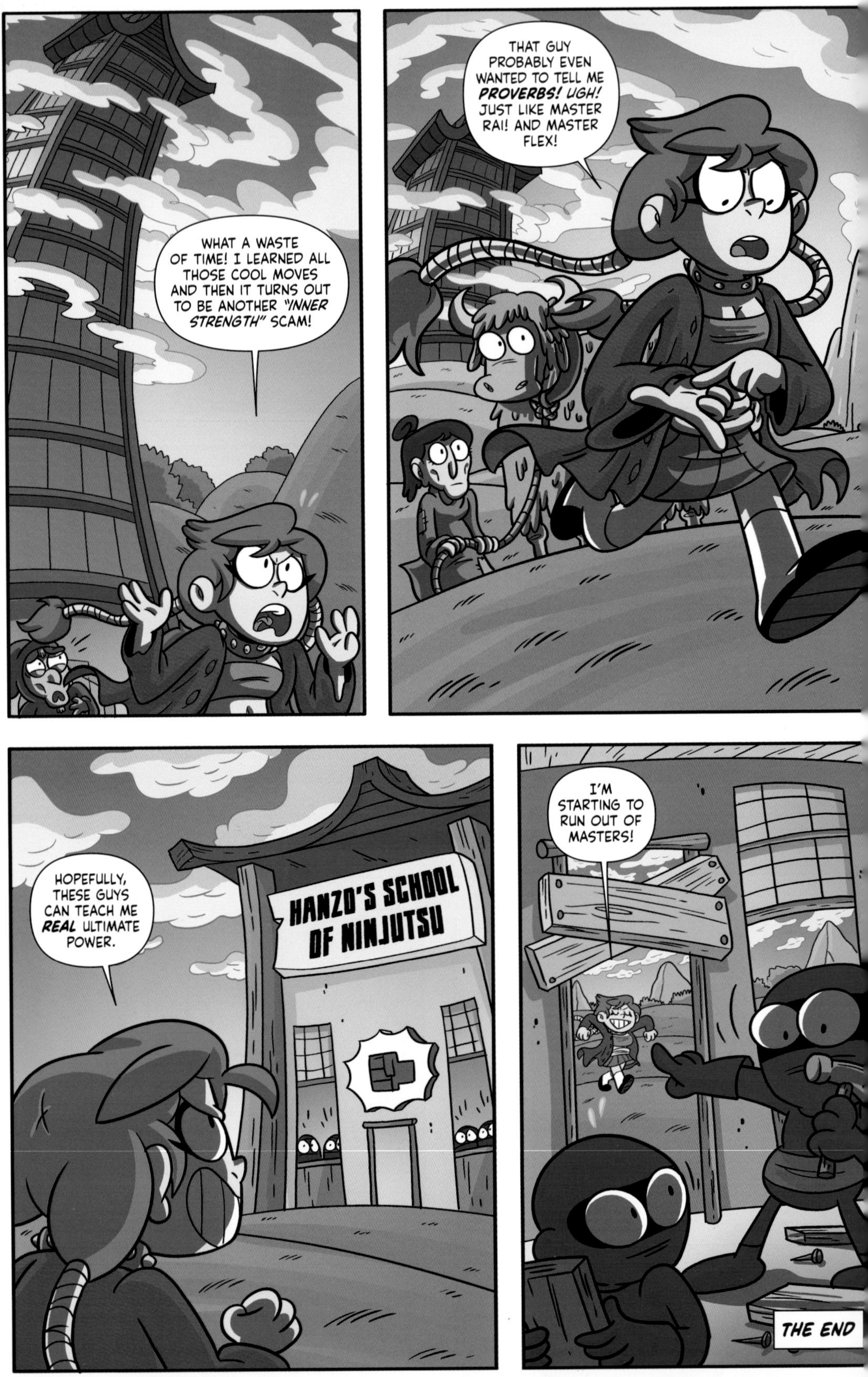
WHAT A WASTE OF TIME! I LEARNED ALL THOSE COOL MOVES AND THEN IT TURNS OUT TO BE ANOTHER "INNER STRENGTH" SCAM!
THAT GUY PROBABLY EVEN WANTED TO TELL ME PROVERBS! UGH! JUST LIKE MASTER RAI! AND MASTER FLEX!
HOPEFULLY, THESE GUYS CAN TEACH ME REAL ULTIMATE POWER.
HANZO'S SCHOOL OF NINJUTSU
I'M STARTING TO RUN OUT OF MASTERS!
THE END

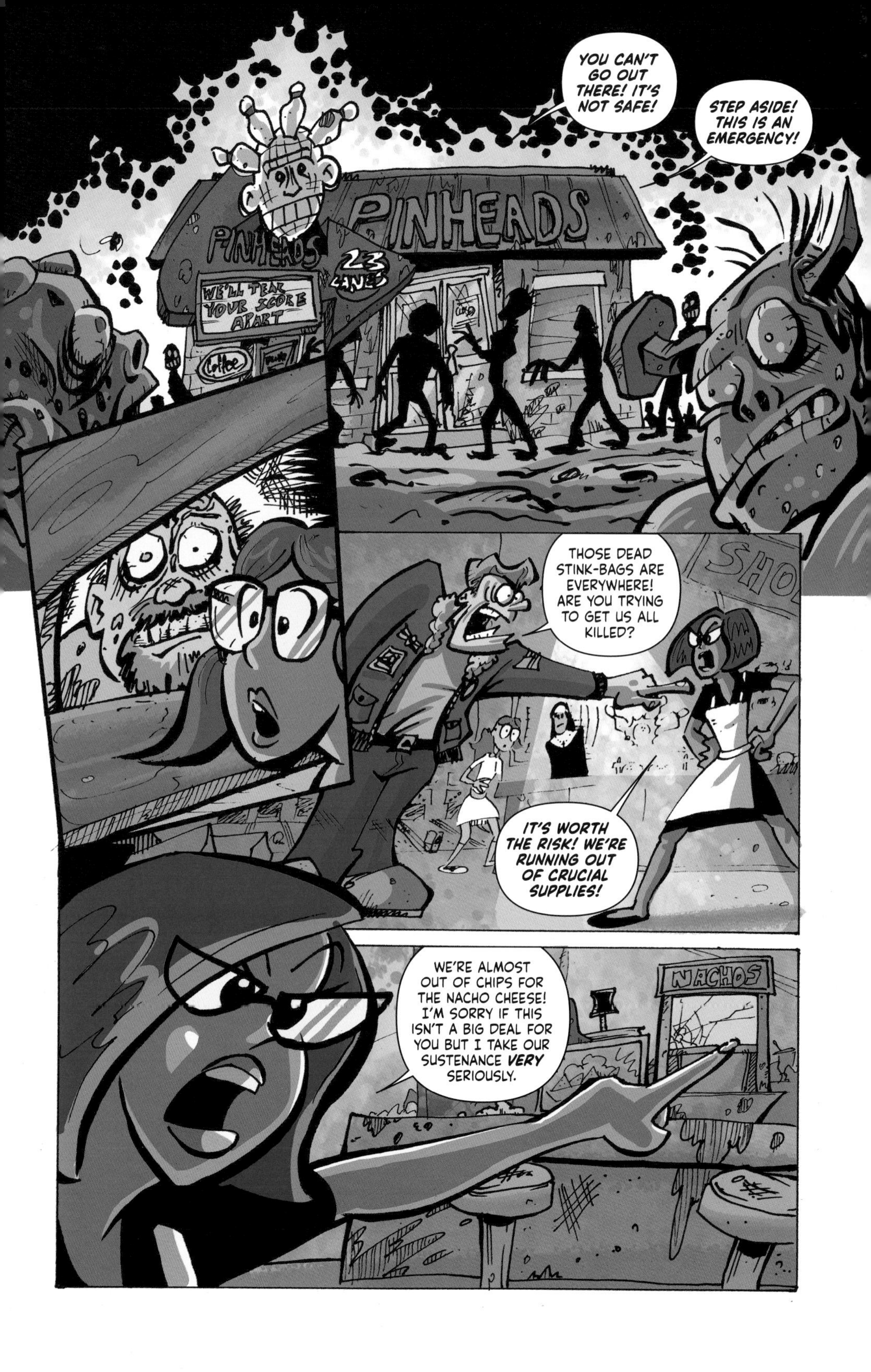
YOU CAN'T GO OUT THERE! IT'S NOT SAFE!
STEP ASIDE! THIS IS AN EMERGENCY!
PINHEADS
PINHEADS
23 LANES
WE'LL TEAR YOUR SCORE APART
THOSE DEAD STINK-BAGS ARE EVERYWHERE! ARE YOU TRYING TO GET US ALL KILLED?
IT'S WORTH THE RISK! WE'RE RUNNING OUT OF CRUCIAL SUPPLIES!
WE'RE ALMOST OUT OF CHIPS FOR THE NACHO CHEESE! I'M SORRY IF THIS ISN'T A BIG DEAL FOR YOU BUT I TAKE OUR SUSTENANCE *VERY* SERIOUSLY.
NACHOS

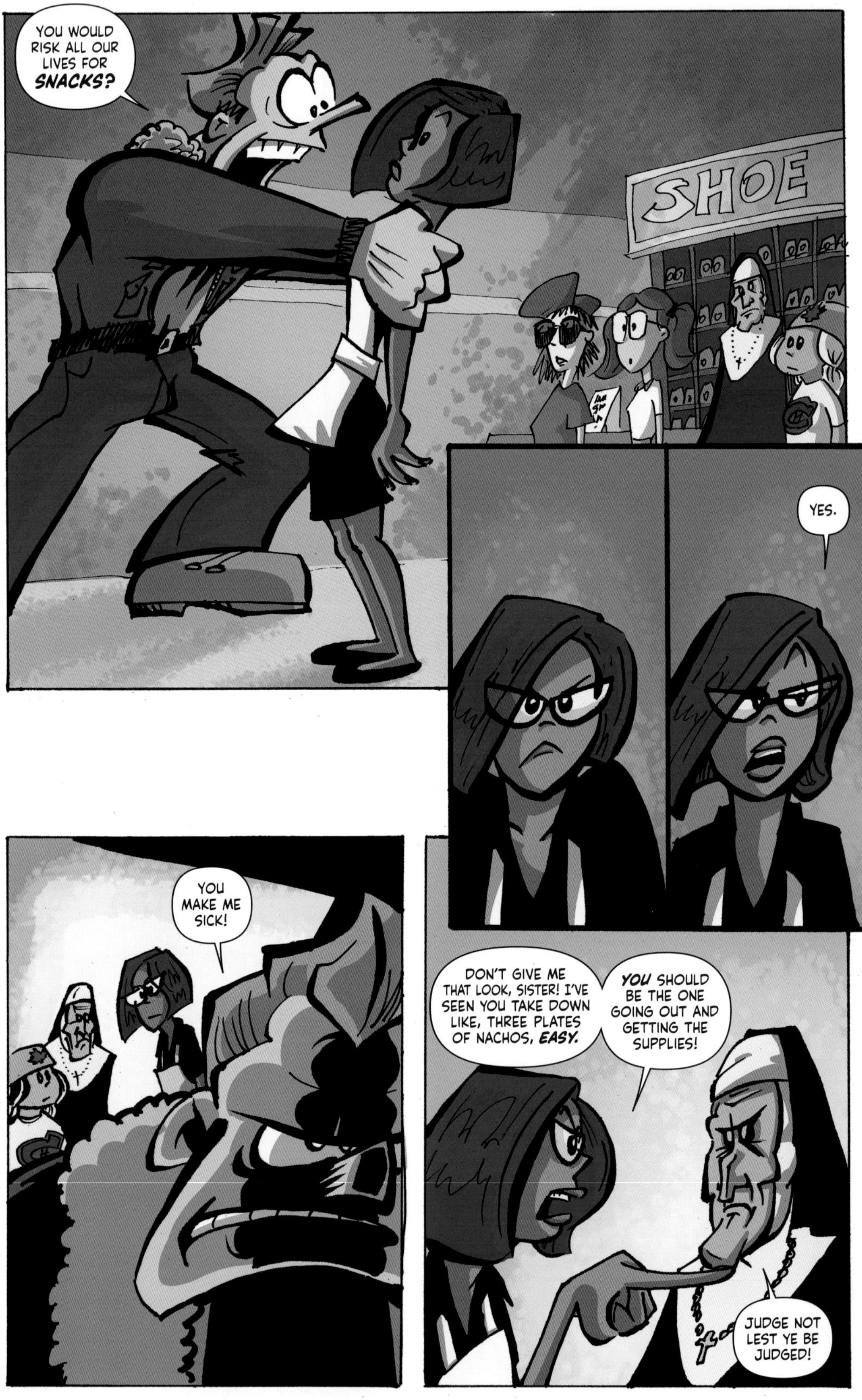
YOU WOULD RISK ALL OUR LIVES FOR SNACKS?
SHOE
YES.
YOU MAKE ME SICK!
DON'T GIVE ME THAT LOOK, SISTER! I'VE SEEN YOU TAKE DOWN LIKE, THREE PLATES OF NACHOS, EASY.
YOU SHOULD BE THE ONE GOING OUT AND GETTING THE SUPPLIES!
JUDGE NOT LEST YE BE JUDGED!

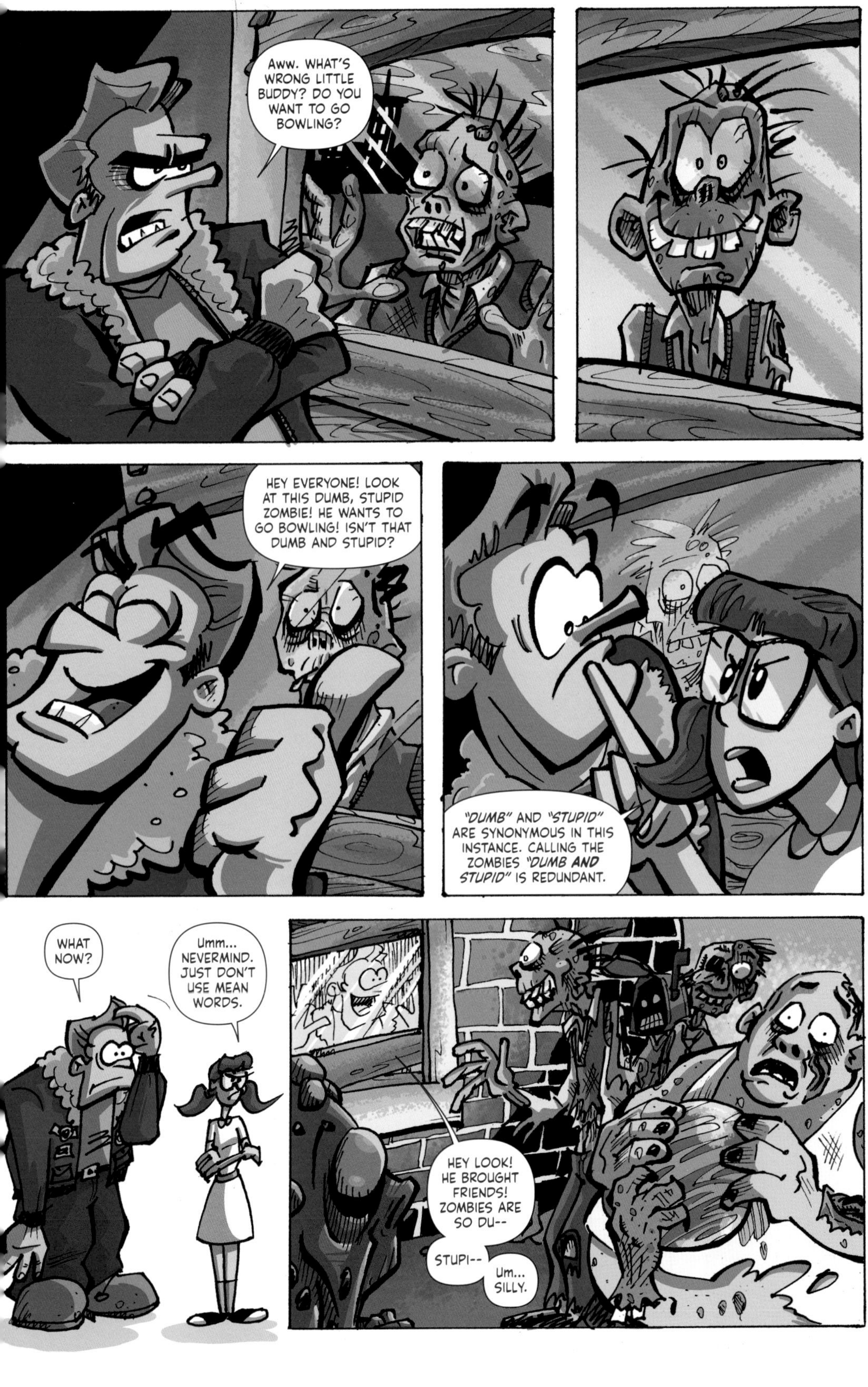

AWW. WHAT'S WRONG LITTLE BUDDY? DO YOU WANT TO GO BOWLING?
HEY EVERYONE! LOOK AT THIS DUMB, STUPID ZOMBIE! HE WANTS TO GO BOWLING! ISN'T THAT DUMB AND STUPID?
"DUMB" AND "STUPID" ARE SYNONYMOUS IN THIS INSTANCE. CALLING THE ZOMBIES "DUMB AND STUPID" IS REDUNDANT.
WHAT NOW?
Umm... NEVERMIND. JUST DON'T USE MEAN WORDS.
HEY LOOK! HE BROUGHT FRIENDS! ZOMBIES ARE SO DU--
STUPI--
Um... SILLY.

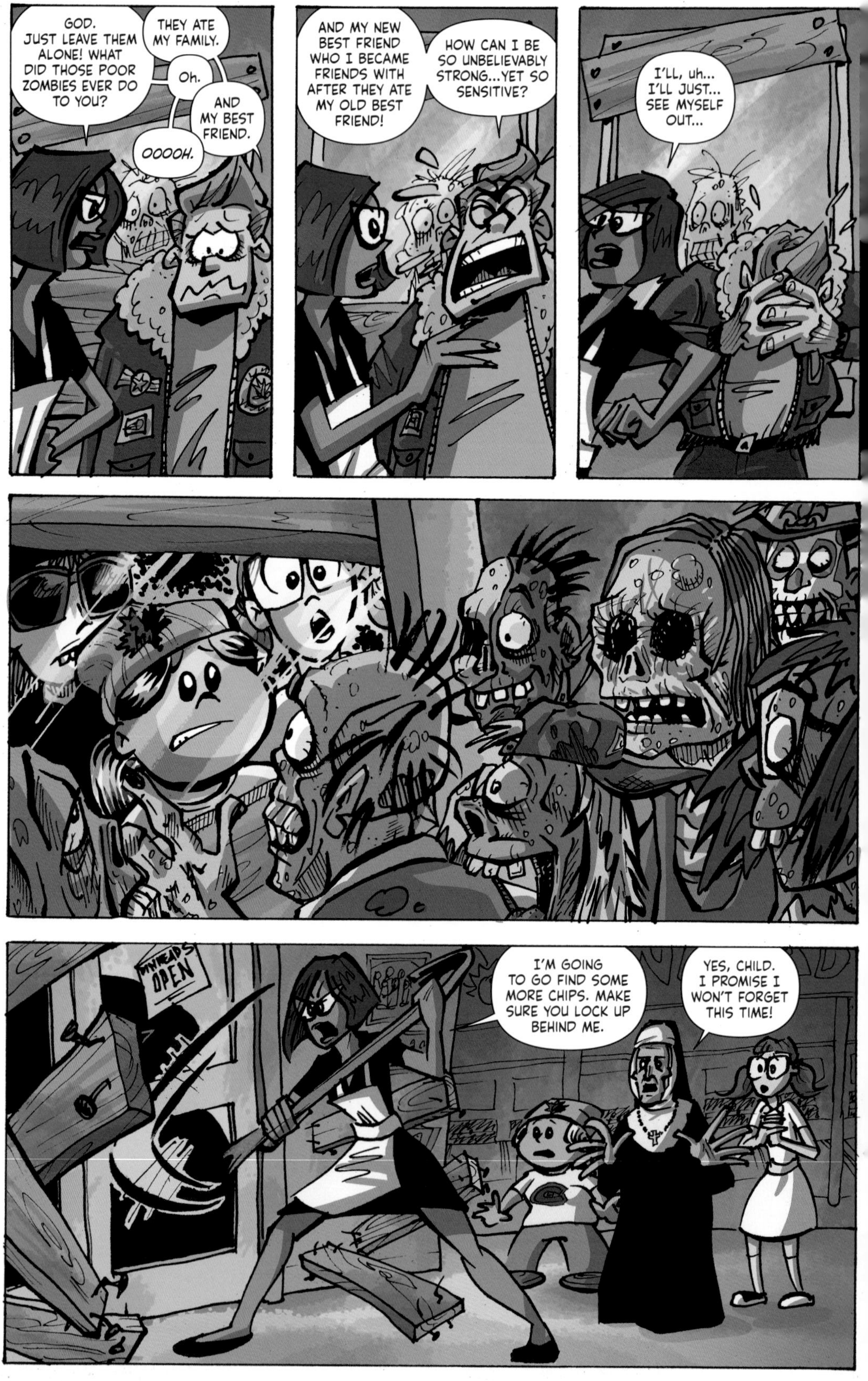
GOD. JUST LEAVE THEM ALONE! WHAT DID THOSE POOR ZOMBIES EVER DO TO YOU?
THEY ATE MY FAMILY.
Oh.
AND MY BEST FRIEND.
OOOOH.
AND MY NEW BEST FRIEND WHO I BECAME FRIENDS WITH AFTER THEY ATE MY OLD BEST FRIEND!
HOW CAN I BE SO UNBELIEVABLY STRONG...YET SO SENSITIVE?
I'LL, uh... I'LL JUST... SEE MYSELF OUT...
OPEN
I'M GOING TO GO FIND SOME MORE CHIPS. MAKE SURE YOU LOCK UP BEHIND ME.
YES, CHILD. I PROMISE I WON'T FORGET THIS TIME!

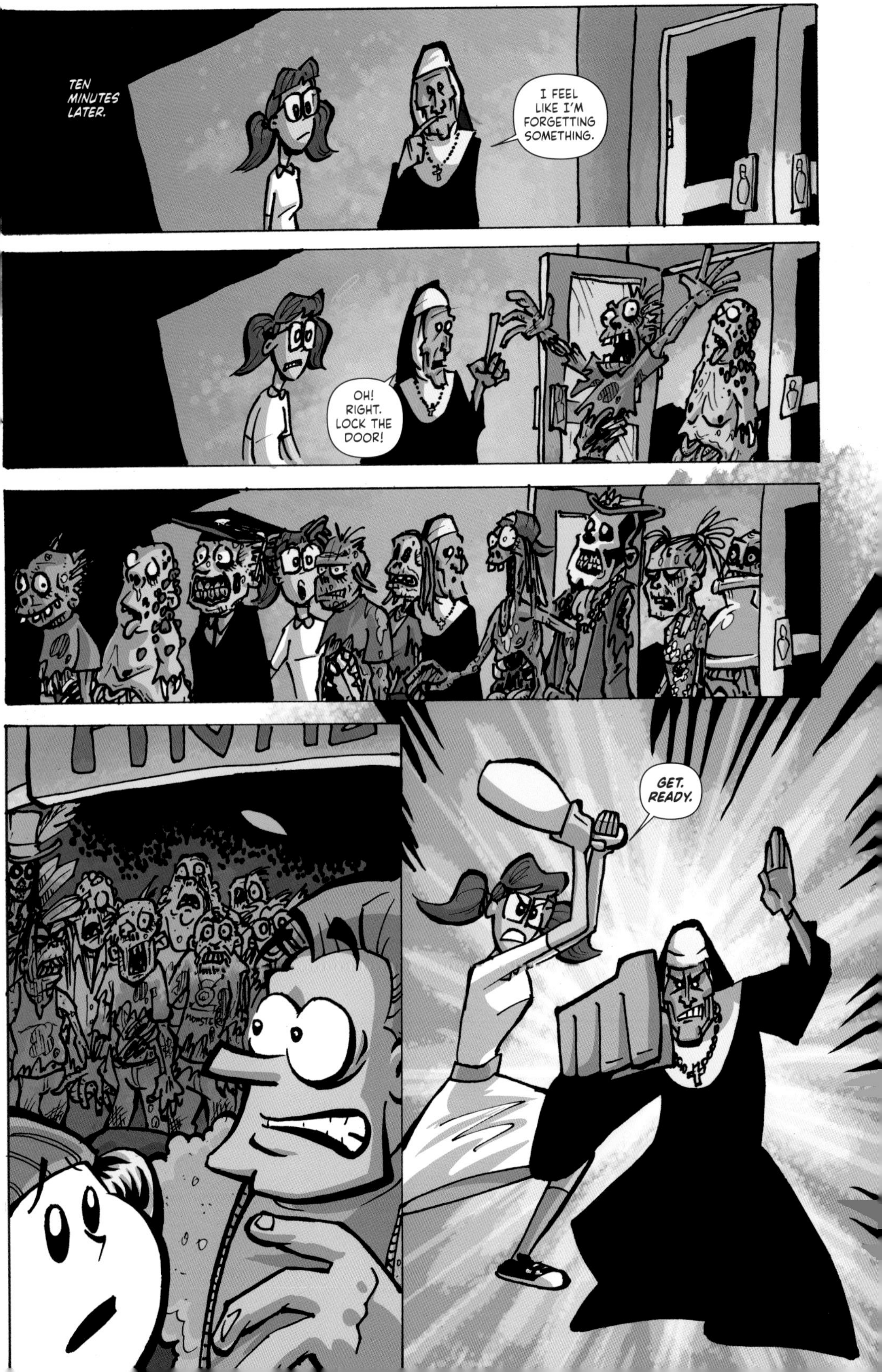

TEN MINUTES LATER.
I FEEL LIKE I'M FORGETTING SOMETHING.
OH! RIGHT. LOCK THE DOOR!
GET. READY.

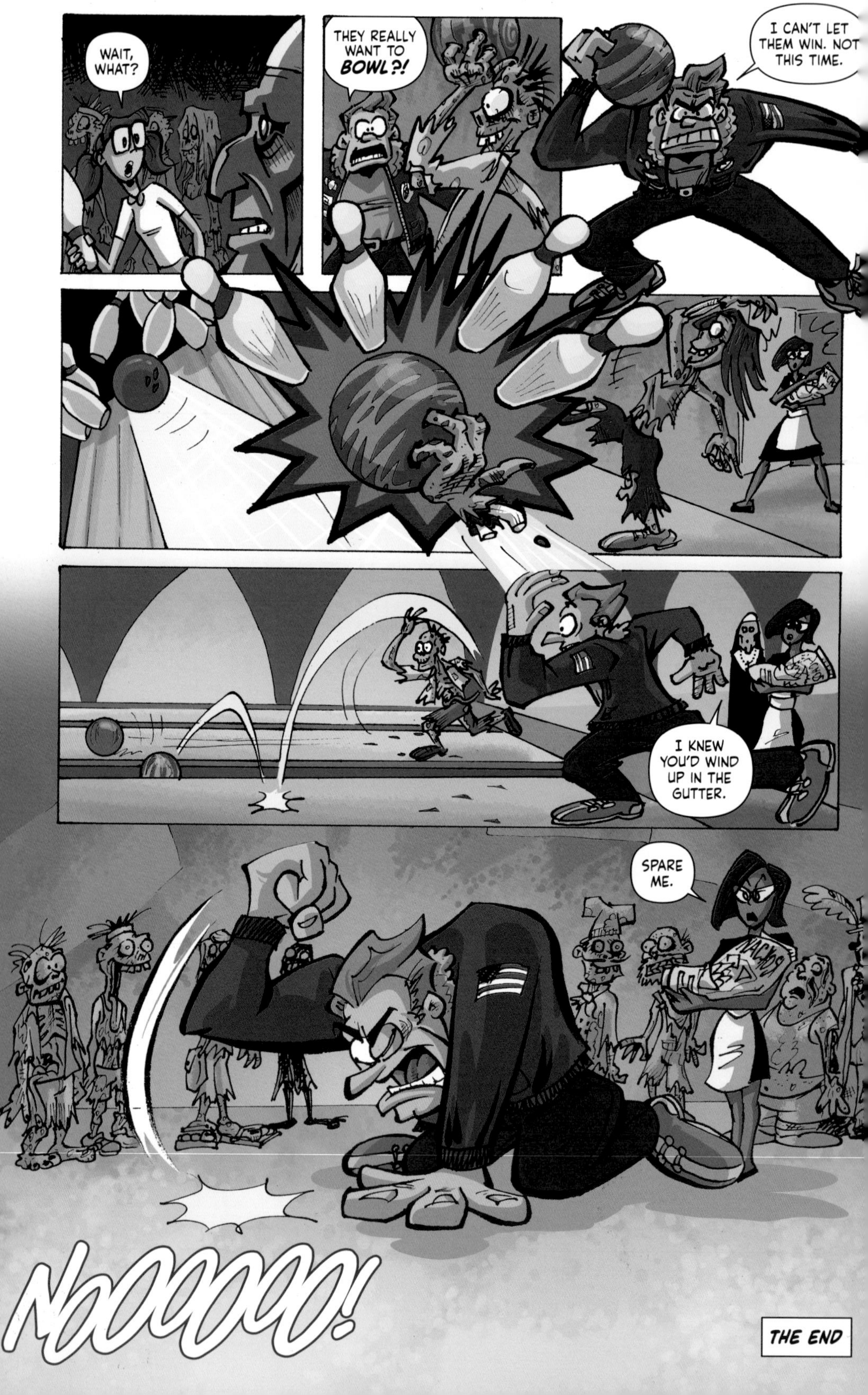
WAIT, WHAT?
THEY REALLY WANT TO BOWL?!
I CAN'T LET THEM WIN. NOT THIS TIME.
I KNEW YOU'D WIND UP IN THE GUTTER.
SPARE ME.
NOOOOO!
THE END

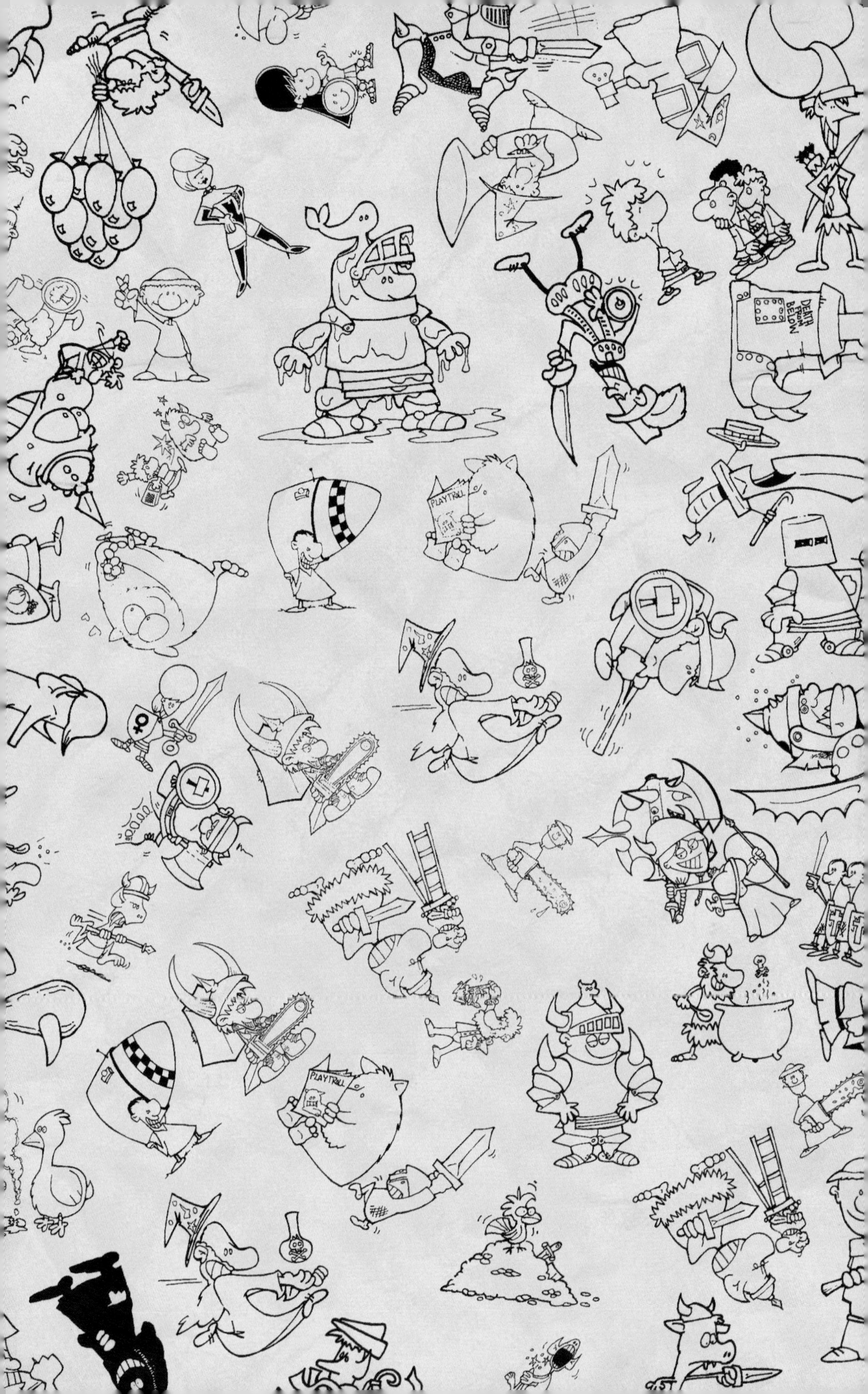
DEATH FROM BELOW
PLAYTROLL
PLAYTROLL

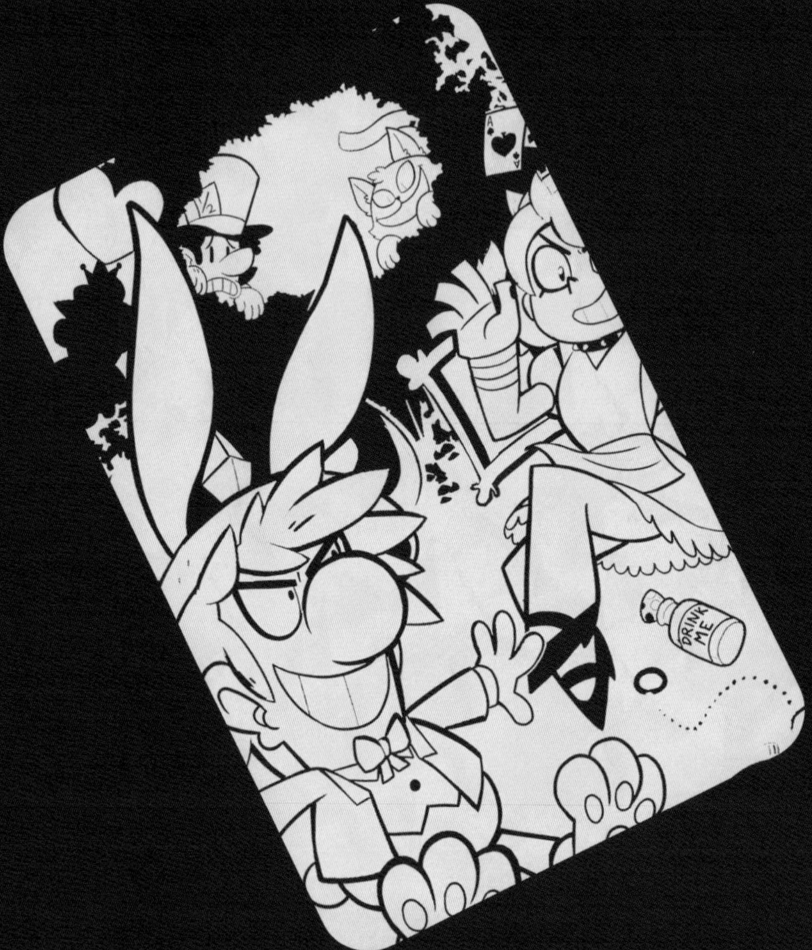
DRINK ME

CHAPTER TWENTY-TWO

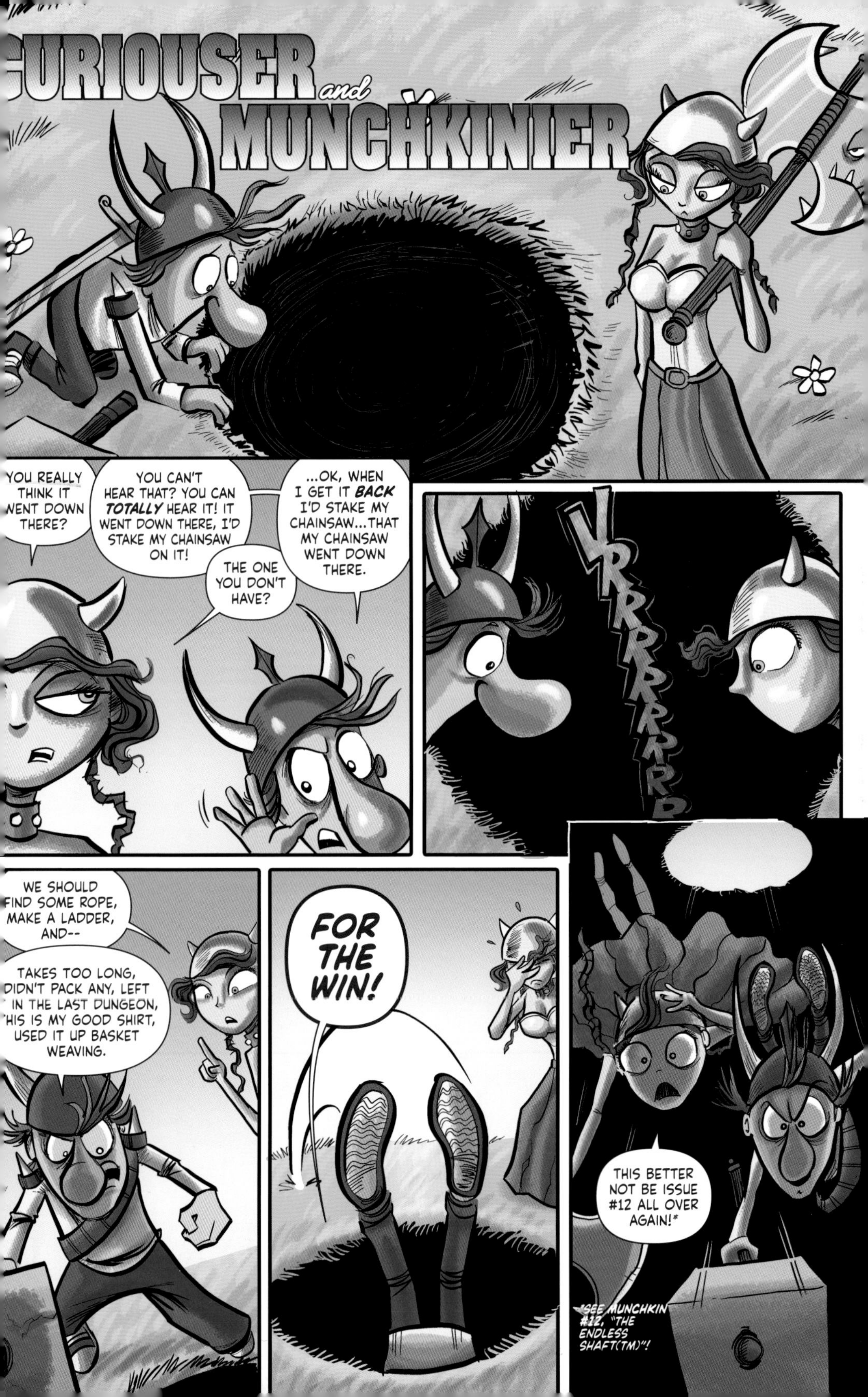
CURIOUSER and MUNCHKINIER
YOU REALLY THINK IT WENT DOWN THERE?
YOU CAN'T HEAR THAT? YOU CAN TOTALLY HEAR IT! IT WENT DOWN THERE, I'D STAKE MY CHAINSAW ON IT!
THE ONE YOU DON'T HAVE?
...OK, WHEN I GET IT BACK I'D STAKE MY CHAINSAW...THAT MY CHAINSAW WENT DOWN THERE.
VRRRRRRRRR
WE SHOULD FIND SOME ROPE, MAKE A LADDER, AND--
TAKES TOO LONG, DIDN'T PACK ANY, LEFT IT IN THE LAST DUNGEON, THIS IS MY GOOD SHIRT, USED IT UP BASKET WEAVING.
FOR THE WIN!
THIS BETTER NOT BE ISSUE #12 ALL OVER AGAIN!*
*SEE MUNCHKIN #12, "THE ENDLESS SHAFT(TM)"!

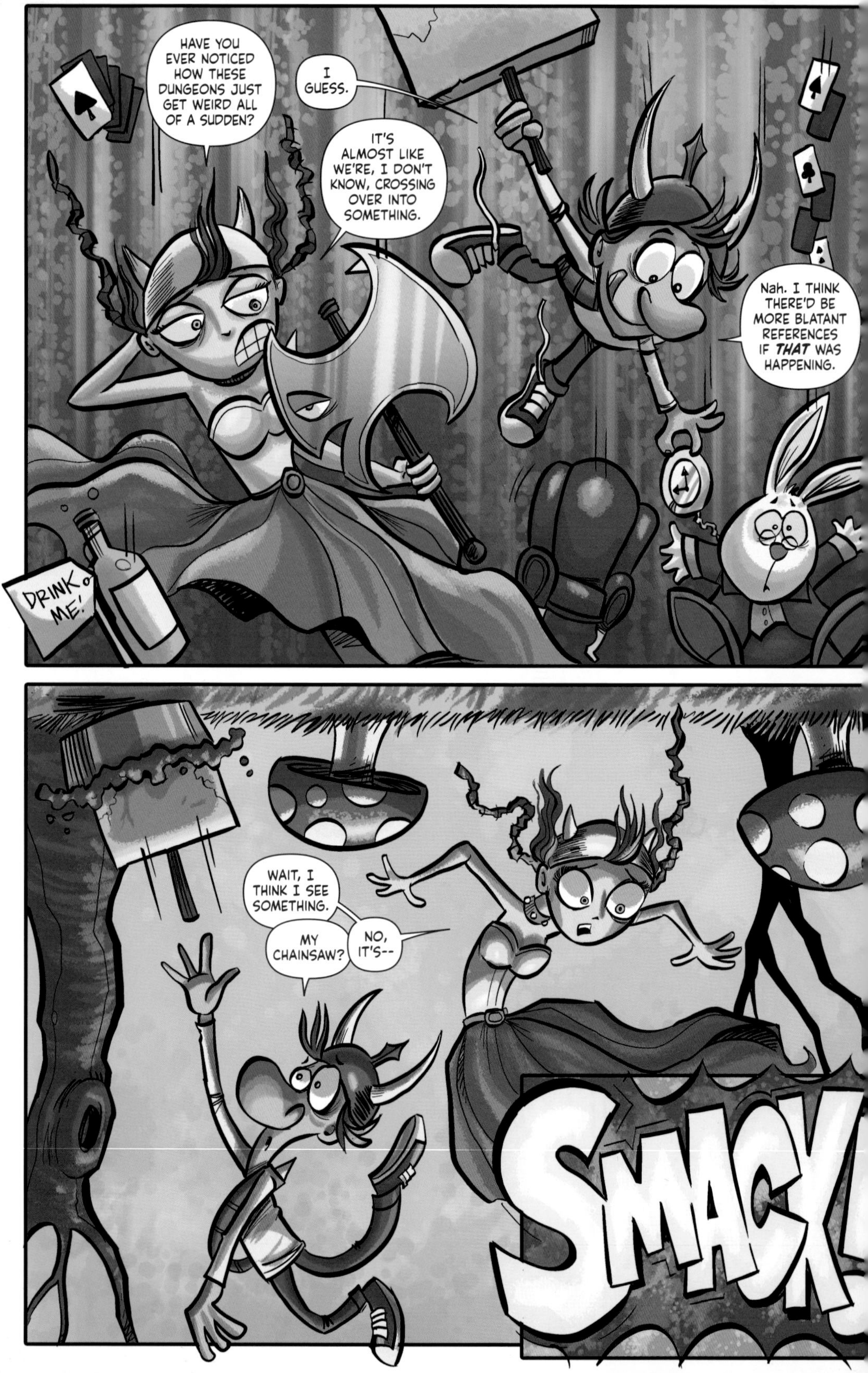
HAVE YOU EVER NOTICED HOW THESE DUNGEONS JUST GET WEIRD ALL OF A SUDDEN?
I GUESS.
IT'S ALMOST LIKE WE'RE, I DON'T KNOW, CROSSING OVER INTO SOMETHING.
Nah. I THINK THERE'D BE MORE BLATANT REFERENCES IF THAT WAS HAPPENING.
DRINK ME!
WAIT, I THINK I SEE SOMETHING.
MY CHAINSAW?
NO, IT'S--
SMACK

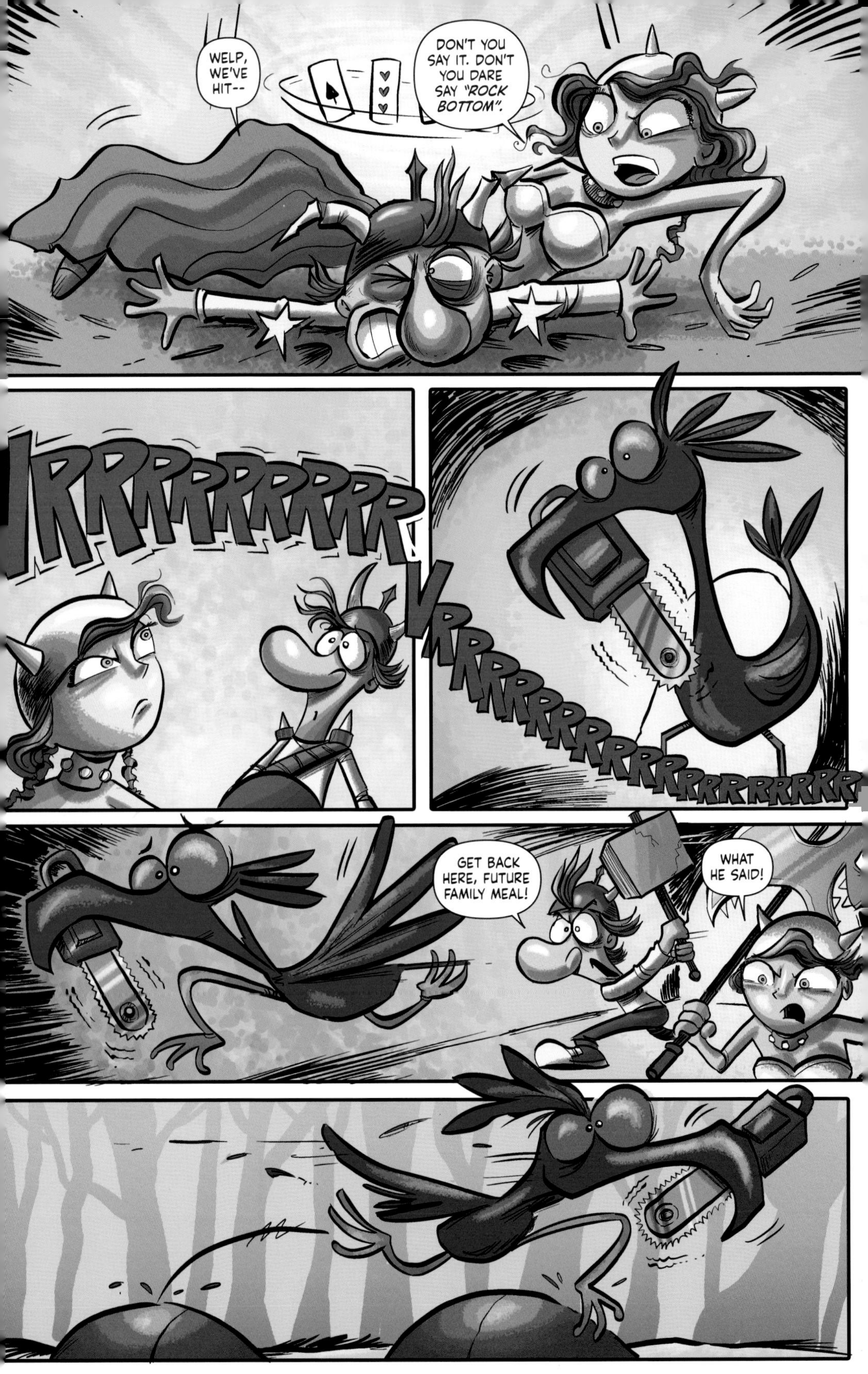
WELP, WE'VE HIT--
DON'T YOU SAY IT. DON'T YOU DARE SAY "ROCK BOTTOM".
VRRRRRRRRRRRVRRRRRRRRRRRRRRRRRRRRRRRRR
GET BACK HERE, FUTURE FAMILY MEAL!
WHAT HE SAID!

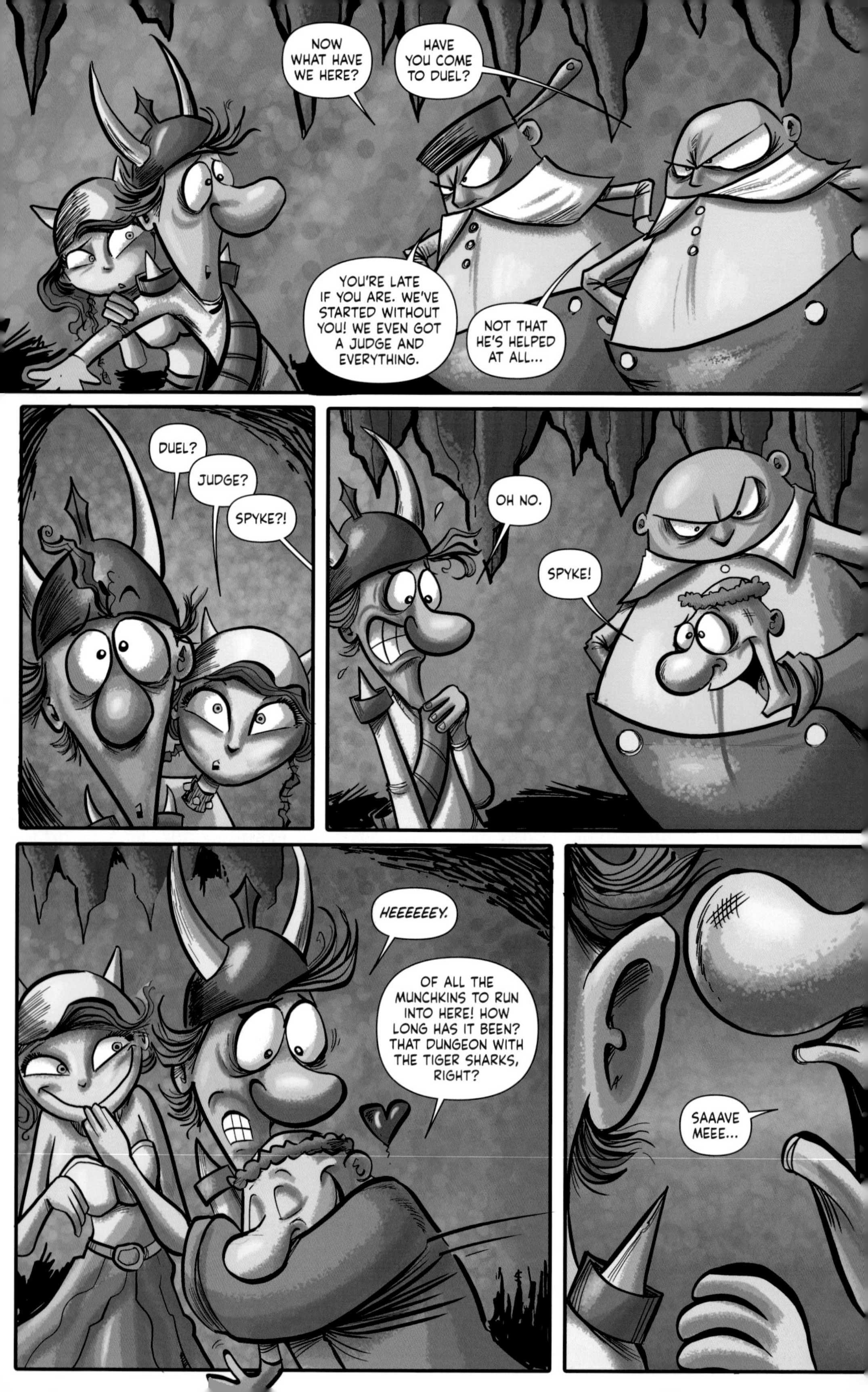
NOW WHAT HAVE WE HERE?
HAVE YOU COME TO DUEL?
YOU'RE LATE IF YOU ARE. WE'VE STARTED WITHOUT YOU! WE EVEN GOT A JUDGE AND EVERYTHING.
NOT THAT HE'S HELPED AT ALL...
DUEL?
JUDGE?
SPYKE?!
OH NO.
SPYKE!
HEEEEEEY.
OF ALL THE MUNCHKINS TO RUN INTO HERE! HOW LONG HAS IT BEEN? THAT DUNGEON WITH THE TIGER SHARKS, RIGHT?
SAAAVE MEEE...

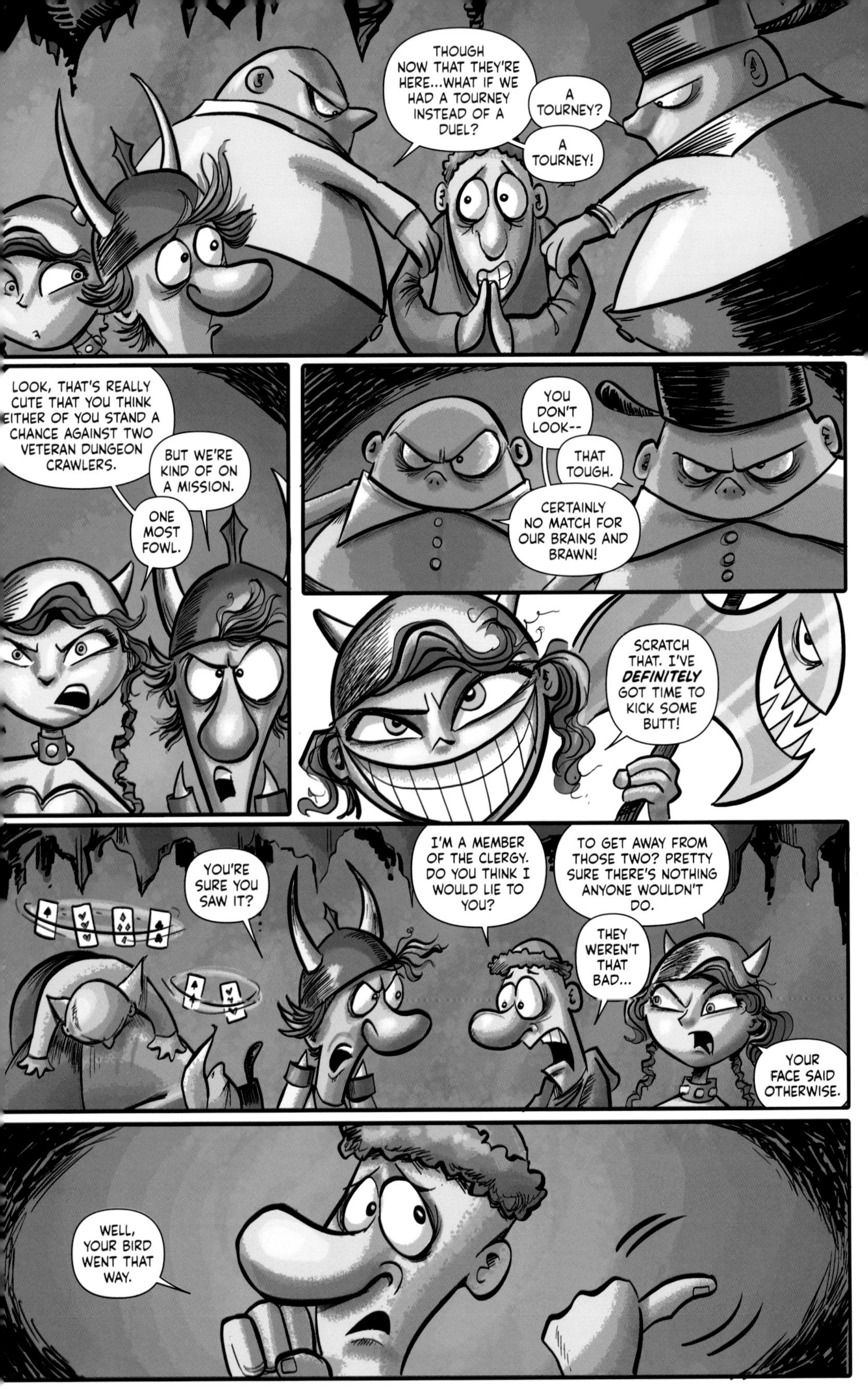
THOUGH NOW THAT THEY'RE HERE...WHAT IF WE HAD A TOURNEY INSTEAD OF A DUEL?
A TOURNEY?
A TOURNEY!
LOOK, THAT'S REALLY CUTE THAT YOU THINK EITHER OF YOU STAND A CHANCE AGAINST TWO VETERAN DUNGEON CRAWLERS.
BUT WE'RE KIND OF ON A MISSION.
ONE MOST FOWL.
YOU DON'T LOOK--
THAT TOUGH.
CERTAINLY NO MATCH FOR OUR BRAINS AND BRAWN!
SCRATCH THAT. I'VE *DEFINITELY* GOT TIME TO KICK SOME BUTT!
YOU'RE SURE YOU SAW IT?
I'M A MEMBER OF THE CLERGY. DO YOU THINK I WOULD LIE TO YOU?
TO GET AWAY FROM THOSE TWO? PRETTY SURE THERE'S NOTHING ANYONE WOULDN'T DO.
THEY WEREN'T THAT BAD...
YOUR FACE SAID OTHERWISE.
WELL, YOUR BIRD WENT THAT WAY.

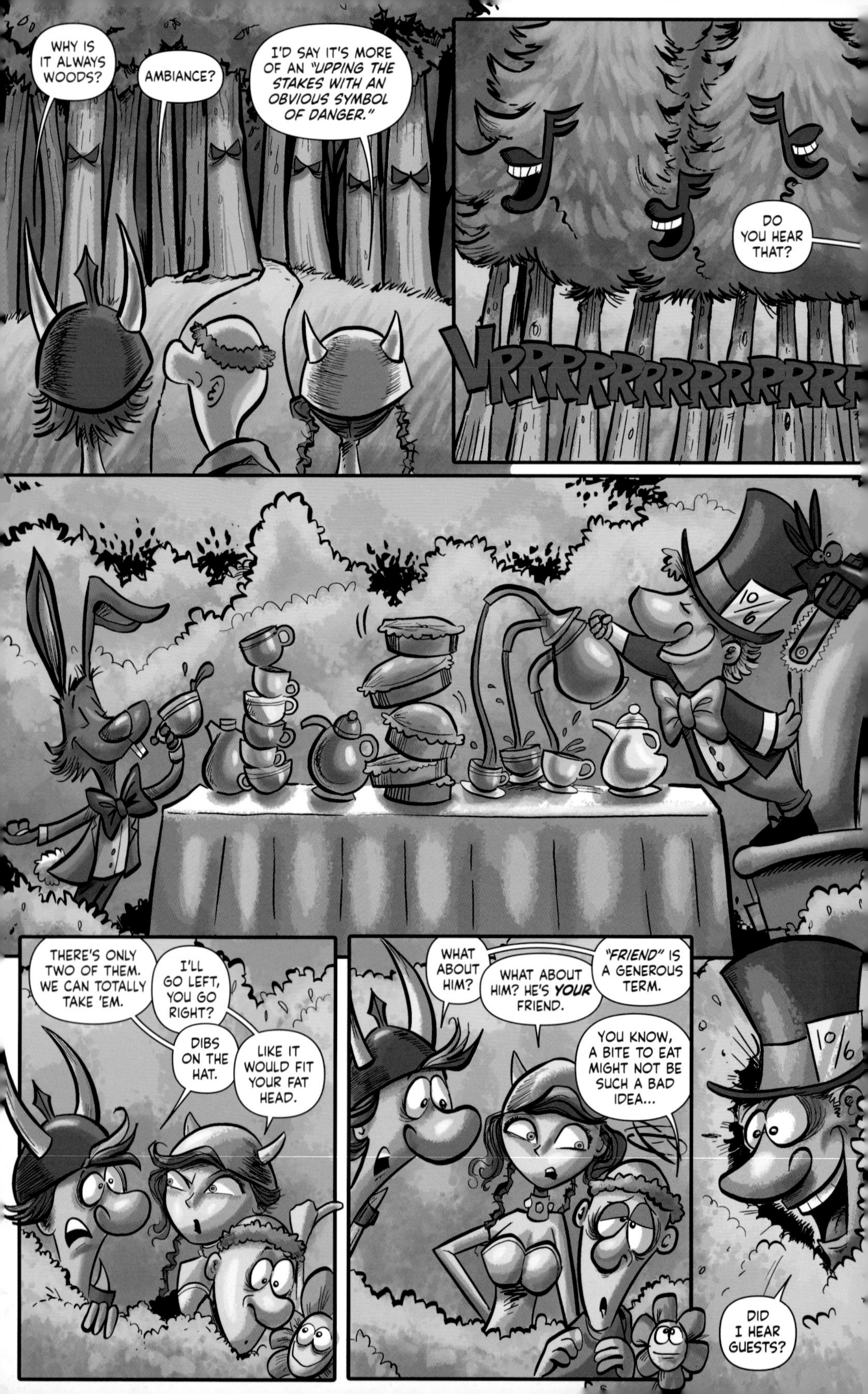

WHY IS IT ALWAYS WOODS?
AMBIANCE?
I'D SAY IT'S MORE OF AN "UPPING THE STAKES WITH AN OBVIOUS SYMBOL OF DANGER."
DO YOU HEAR THAT?
VRRRRRRRRRRRRR
THERE'S ONLY TWO OF THEM. WE CAN TOTALLY TAKE 'EM.
I'LL GO LEFT, YOU GO RIGHT?
DIBS ON THE HAT.
LIKE IT WOULD FIT YOUR FAT HEAD.
WHAT ABOUT HIM?
WHAT ABOUT HIM? HE'S YOUR FRIEND.
"FRIEND" IS A GENEROUS TERM.
YOU KNOW, A BITE TO EAT MIGHT NOT BE SUCH A BAD IDEA...
DID I HEAR GUESTS?

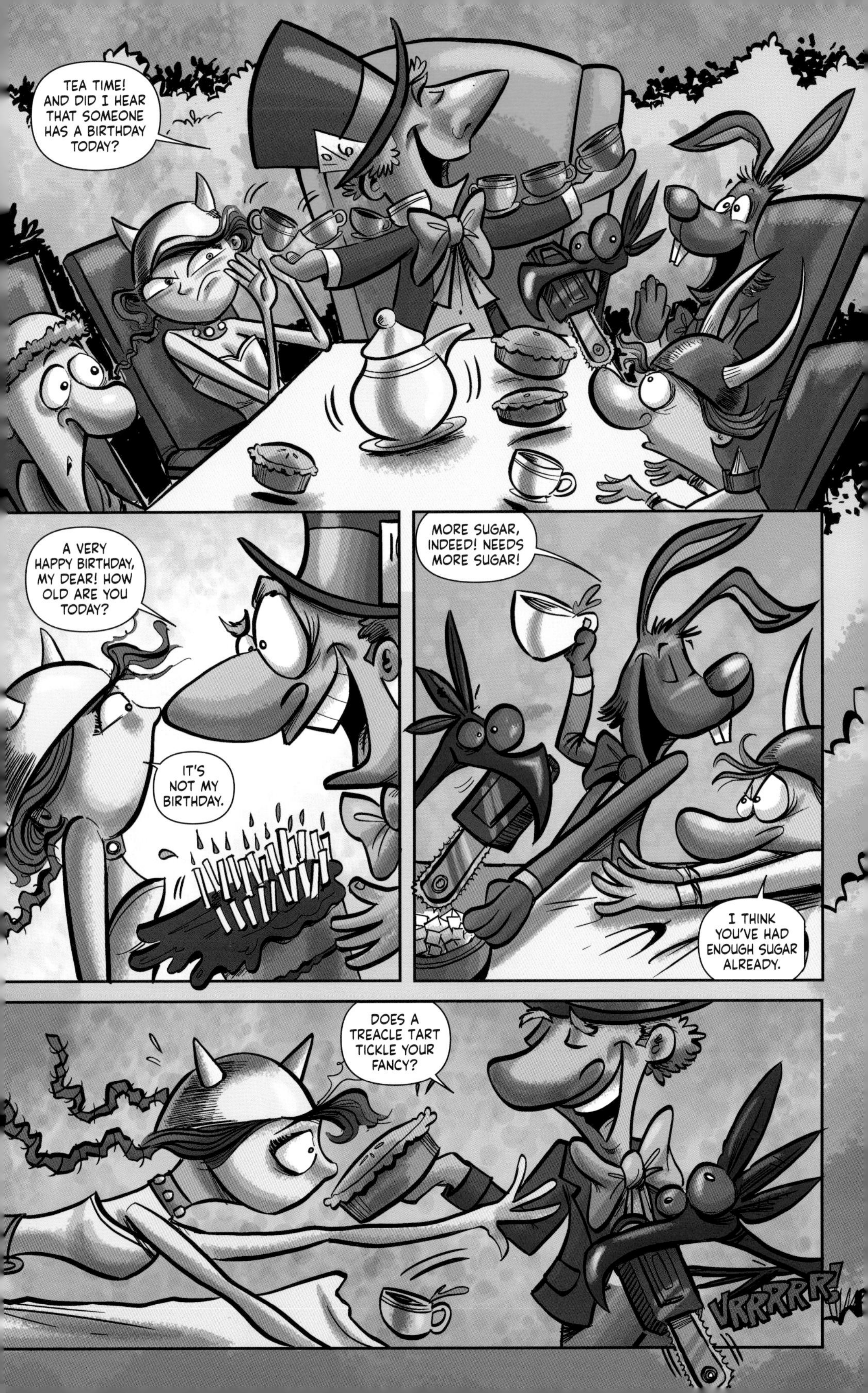
TEA TIME! AND DID I HEAR THAT SOMEONE HAS A BIRTHDAY TODAY?
A VERY HAPPY BIRTHDAY, MY DEAR! HOW OLD ARE YOU TODAY?
IT'S NOT MY BIRTHDAY.
MORE SUGAR, INDEED! NEEDS MORE SUGAR!
I THINK YOU'VE HAD ENOUGH SUGAR ALREADY.
DOES A TREACLE TART TICKLE YOUR FANCY?
VRRRRRRR!

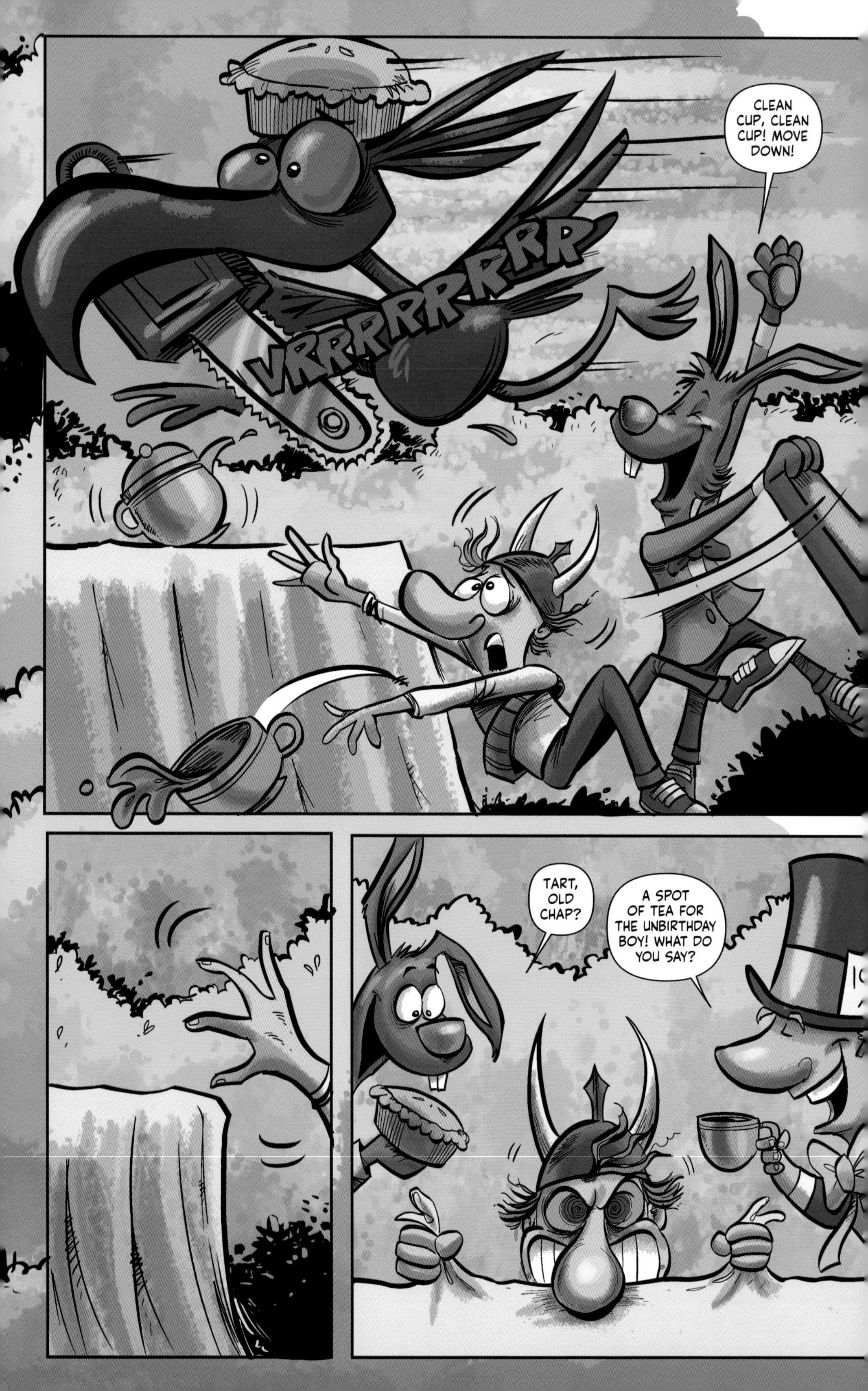
CLEAN CUP, CLEAN CUP! MOVE DOWN!
VRRRRRRRRR
TART, OLD CHAP?
A SPOT OF TEA FOR THE UNBIRTHDAY BOY! WHAT DO YOU SAY?

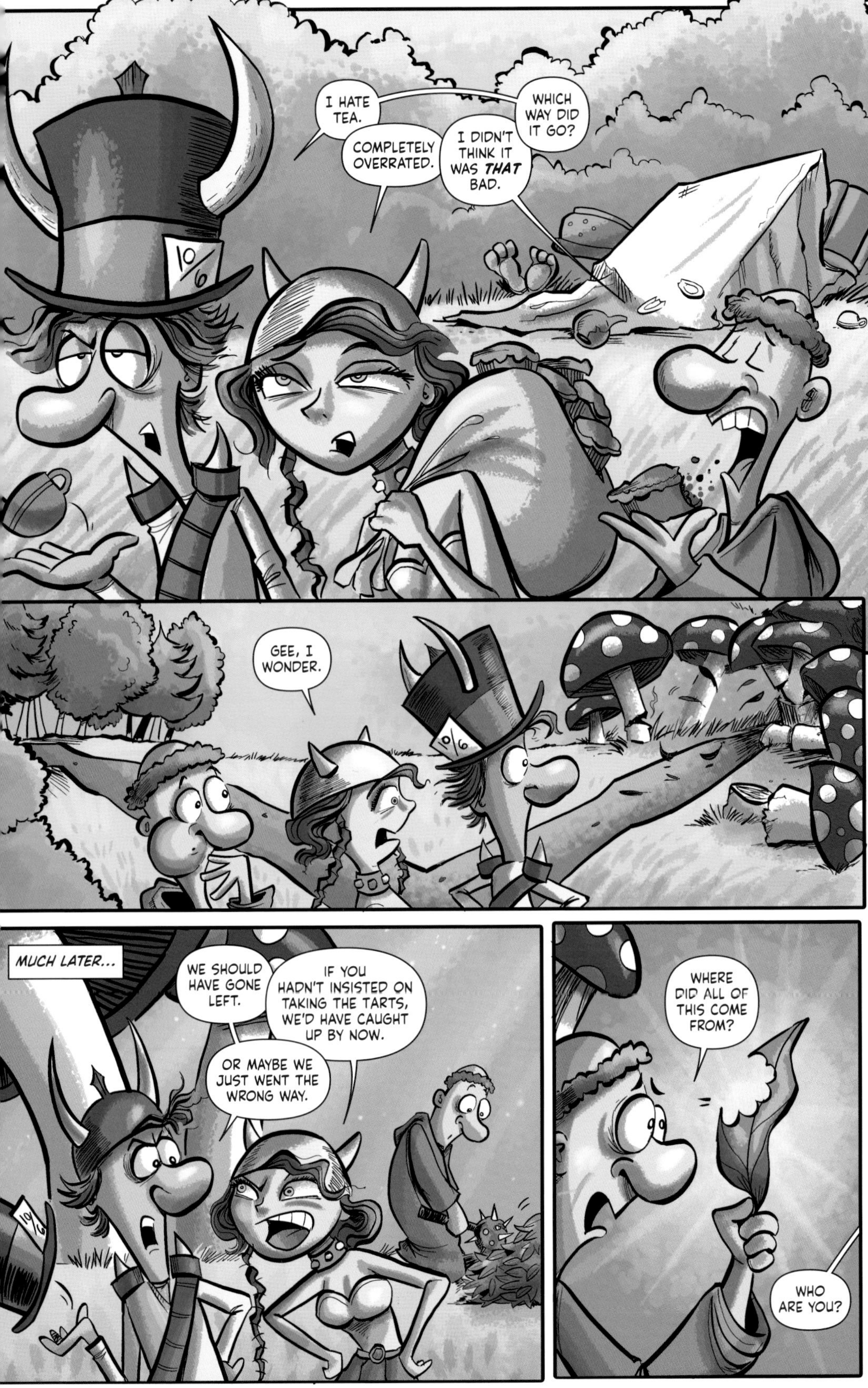
I HATE TEA.
COMPLETELY OVERRATED.
I DIDN'T THINK IT WAS *THAT* BAD.
WHICH WAY DID IT GO?
GEE, I WONDER.
MUCH LATER...
WE SHOULD HAVE GONE LEFT.
IF YOU HADN'T INSISTED ON TAKING THE TARTS, WE'D HAVE CAUGHT UP BY NOW.
OR MAYBE WE JUST WENT THE WRONG WAY.
WHERE DID ALL OF THIS COME FROM?
WHO ARE YOU?

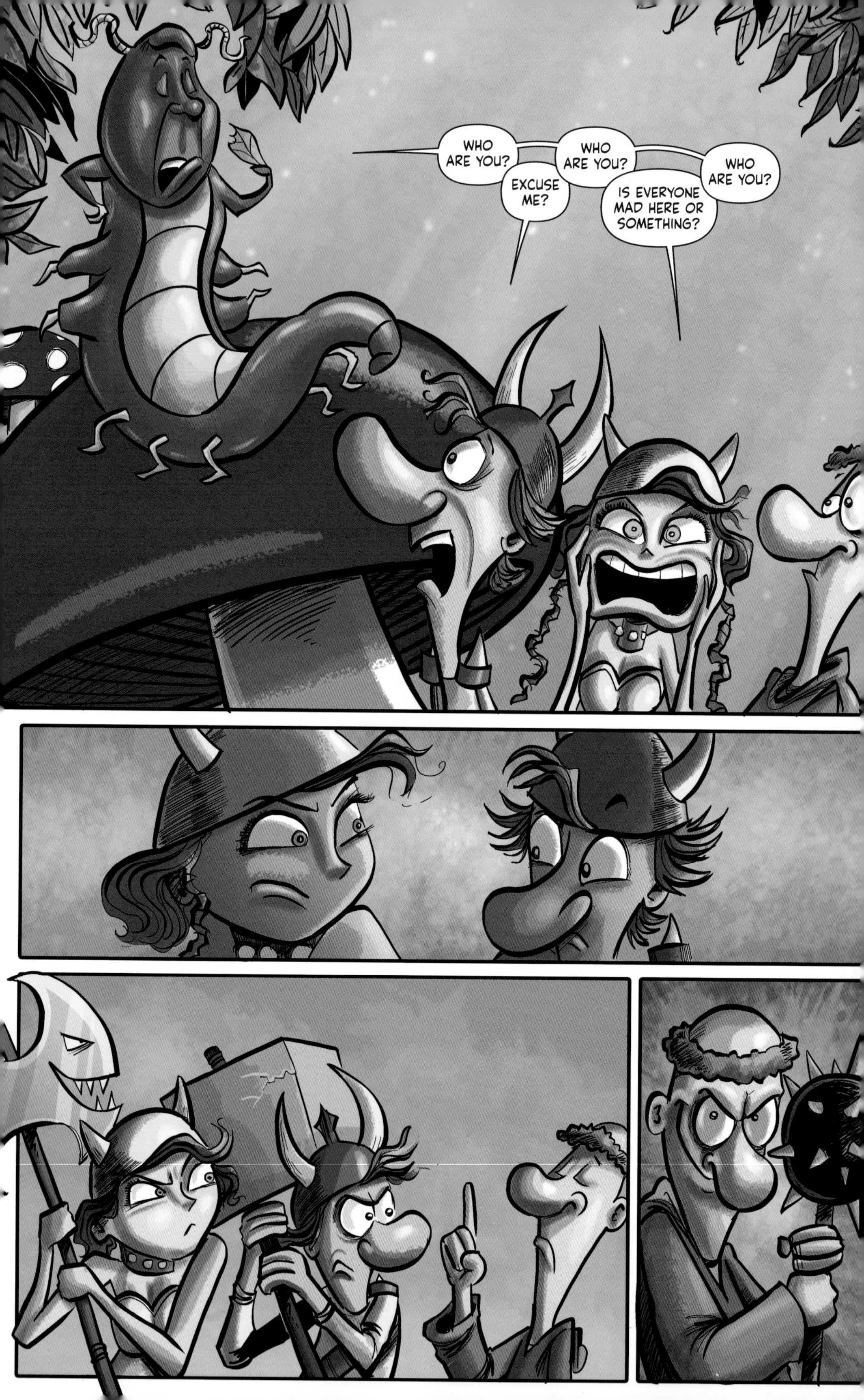
WHO ARE YOU?
EXCUSE ME?
WHO ARE YOU?
IS EVERYONE MAD HERE OR SOMETHING?
WHO ARE YOU?

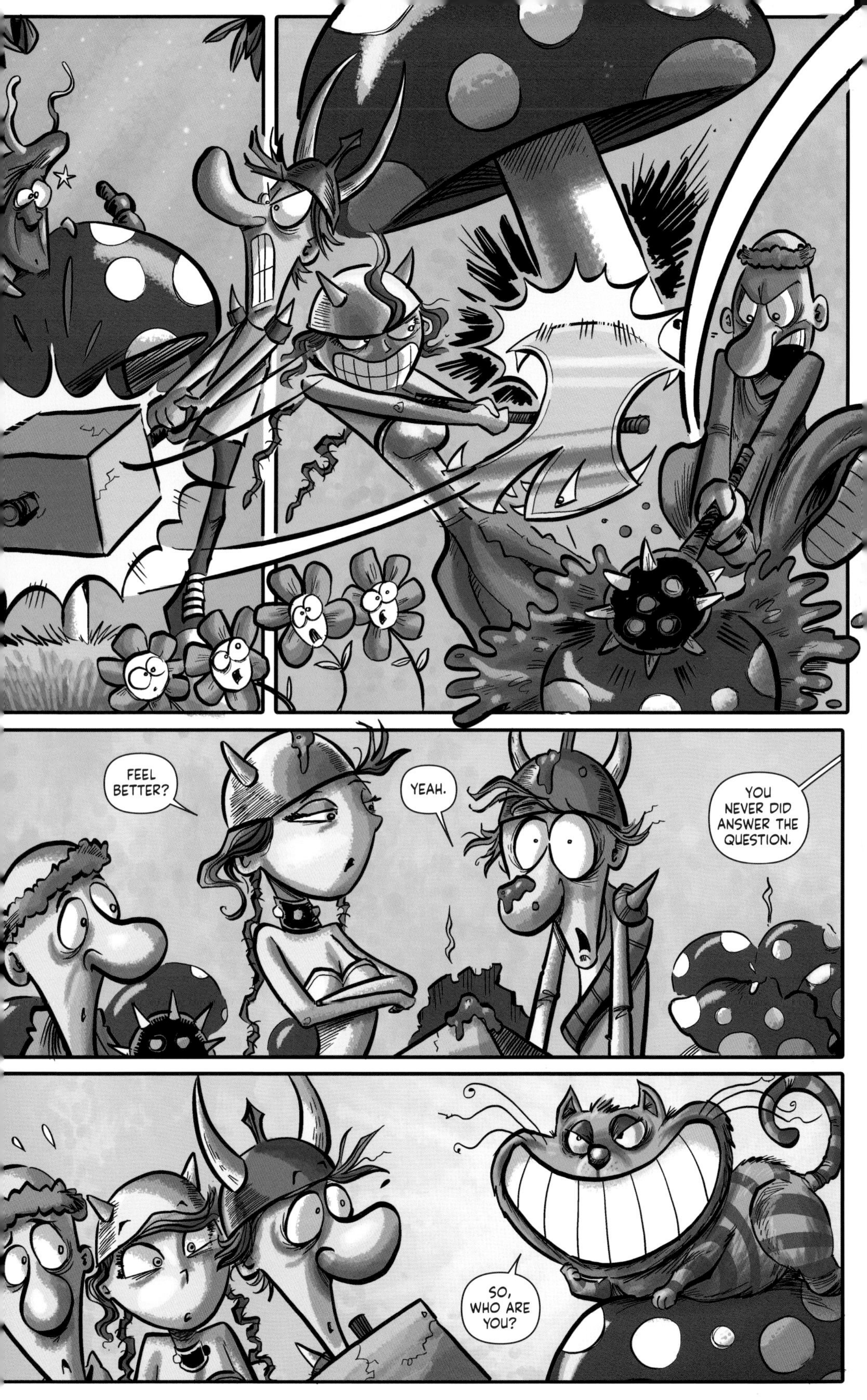
FEEL BETTER?
YEAH.
YOU NEVER DID ANSWER THE QUESTION.
SO, WHO ARE YOU?

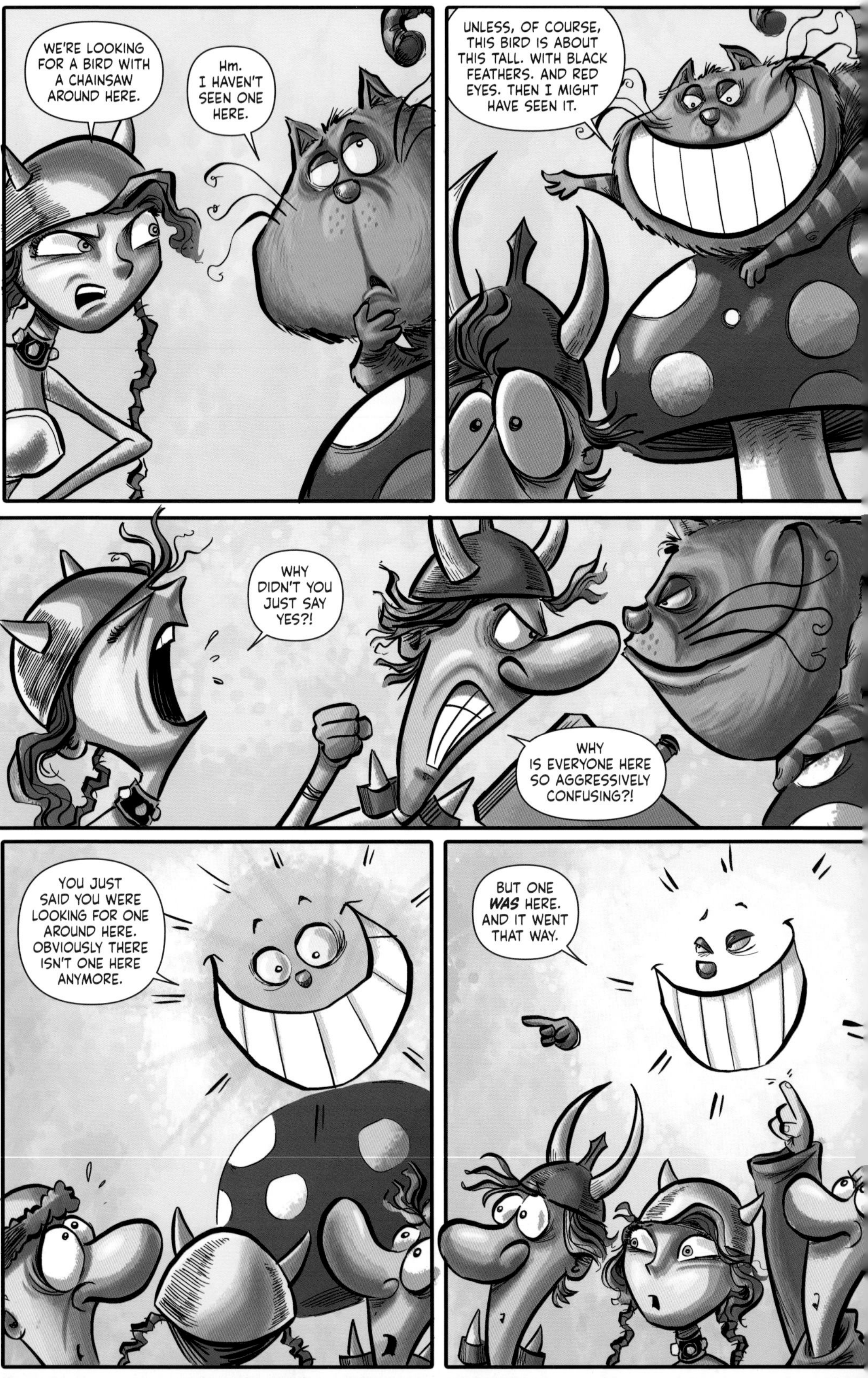
WE'RE LOOKING FOR A BIRD WITH A CHAINSAW AROUND HERE.
Hm. I HAVEN'T SEEN ONE HERE.
UNLESS, OF COURSE, THIS BIRD IS ABOUT THIS TALL. WITH BLACK FEATHERS. AND RED EYES. THEN I MIGHT HAVE SEEN IT.
WHY DIDN'T YOU JUST SAY YES?!
WHY IS EVERYONE HERE SO AGGRESSIVELY CONFUSING?!
YOU JUST SAID YOU WERE LOOKING FOR ONE AROUND HERE. OBVIOUSLY THERE ISN'T ONE HERE ANYMORE.
BUT ONE ***WAS*** HERE. AND IT WENT THAT WAY.

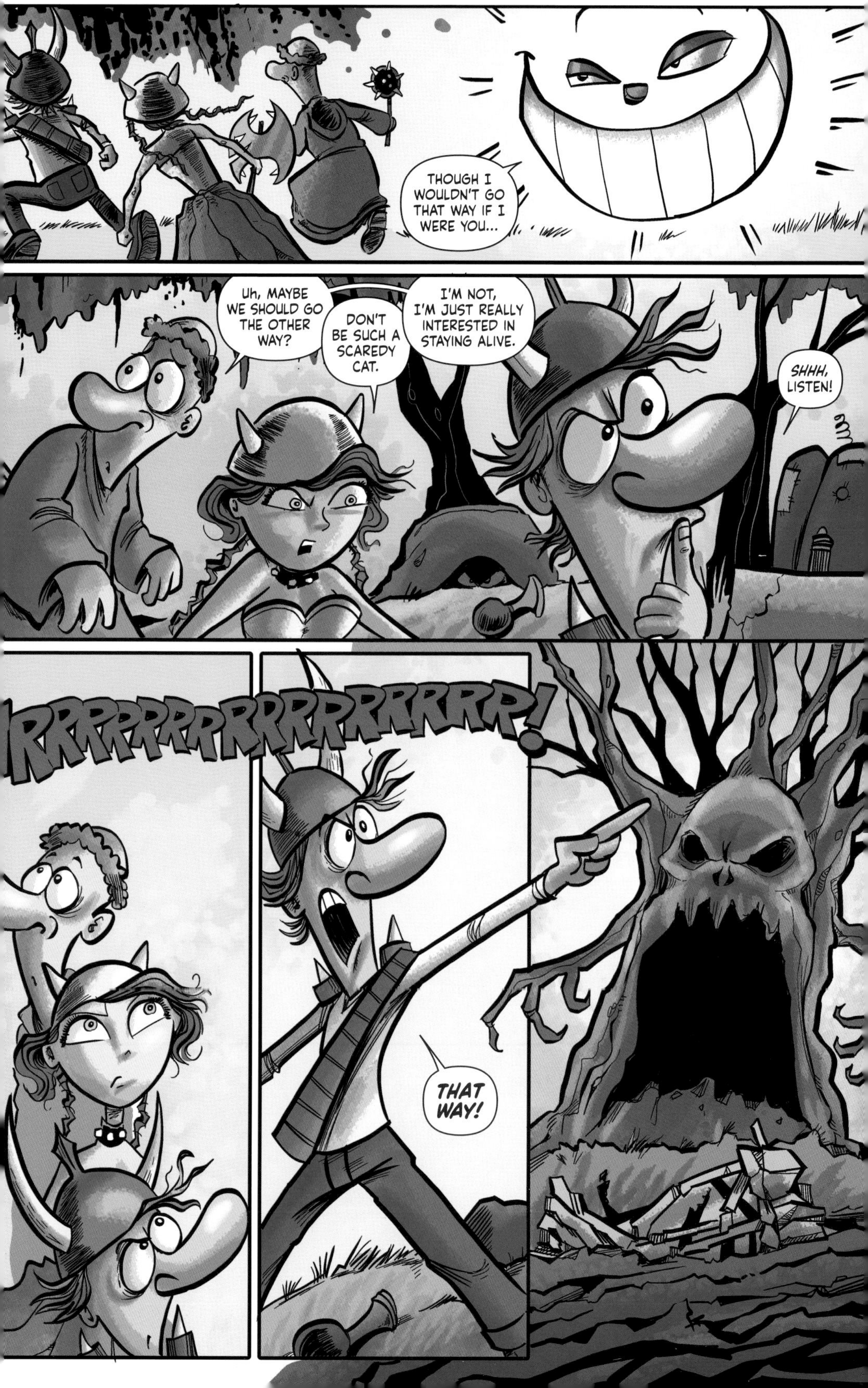
THOUGH I WOULDN'T GO THAT WAY IF I WERE YOU...
Uh, MAYBE WE SHOULD GO THE OTHER WAY?
DON'T BE SUCH A SCAREDY CAT.
I'M NOT, I'M JUST REALLY INTERESTED IN STAYING ALIVE.
SHHH, LISTEN!
RRRRRRRRRRRRRRRRRRRP!
THAT WAY!

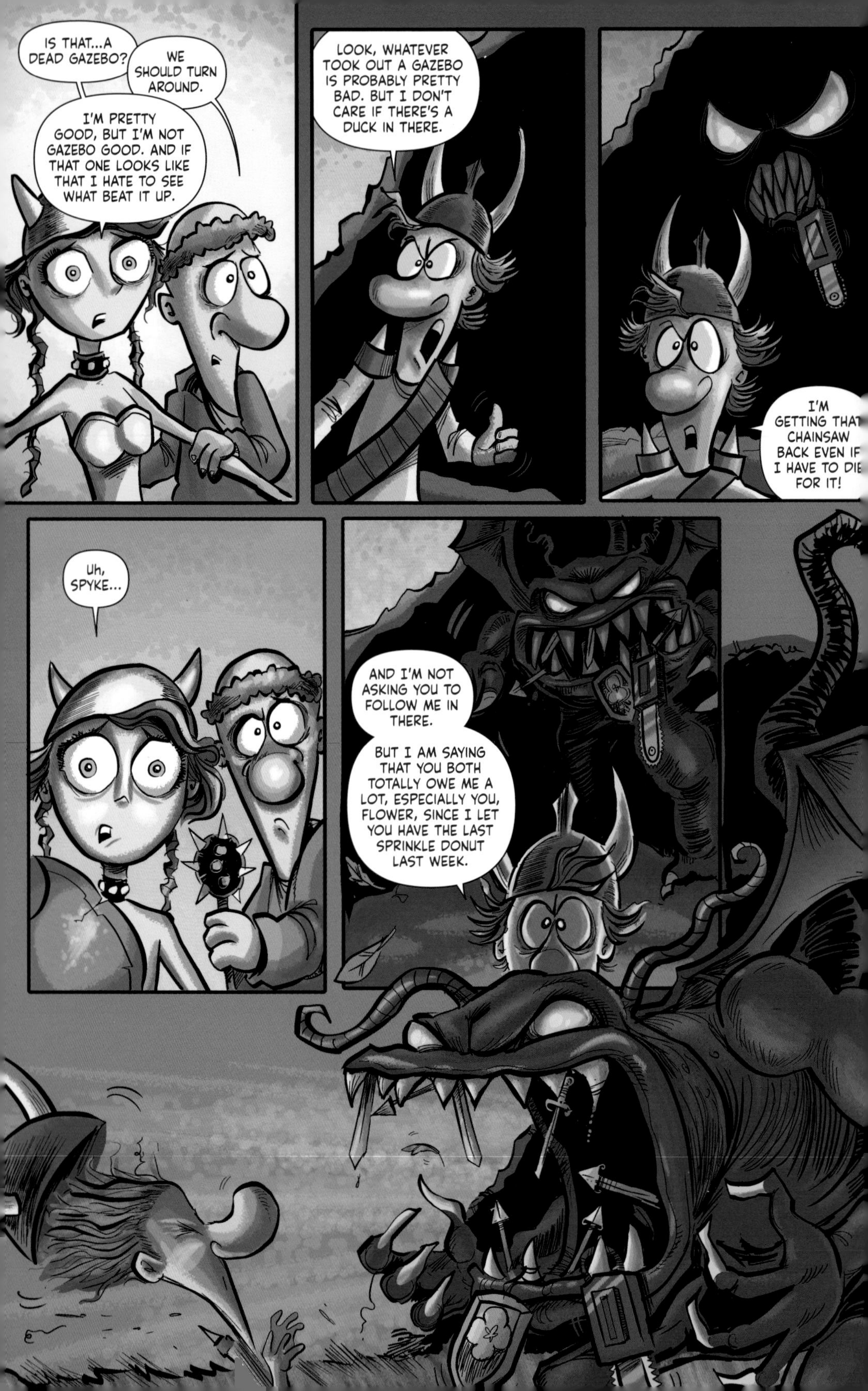
IS THAT...A DEAD GAZEBO?
WE SHOULD TURN AROUND.
I'M PRETTY GOOD, BUT I'M NOT GAZEBO GOOD. AND IF THAT ONE LOOKS LIKE THAT I HATE TO SEE WHAT BEAT IT UP.
LOOK, WHATEVER TOOK OUT A GAZEBO IS PROBABLY PRETTY BAD. BUT I DON'T CARE IF THERE'S A DUCK IN THERE.
I'M GETTING THAT CHAINSAW BACK EVEN IF I HAVE TO DIE FOR IT!
Uh, SPYKE...
AND I'M NOT ASKING YOU TO FOLLOW ME IN THERE.
BUT I AM SAYING THAT YOU BOTH TOTALLY OWE ME A LOT, ESPECIALLY YOU, FLOWER, SINCE I LET YOU HAVE THE LAST SPRINKLE DONUT LAST WEEK.

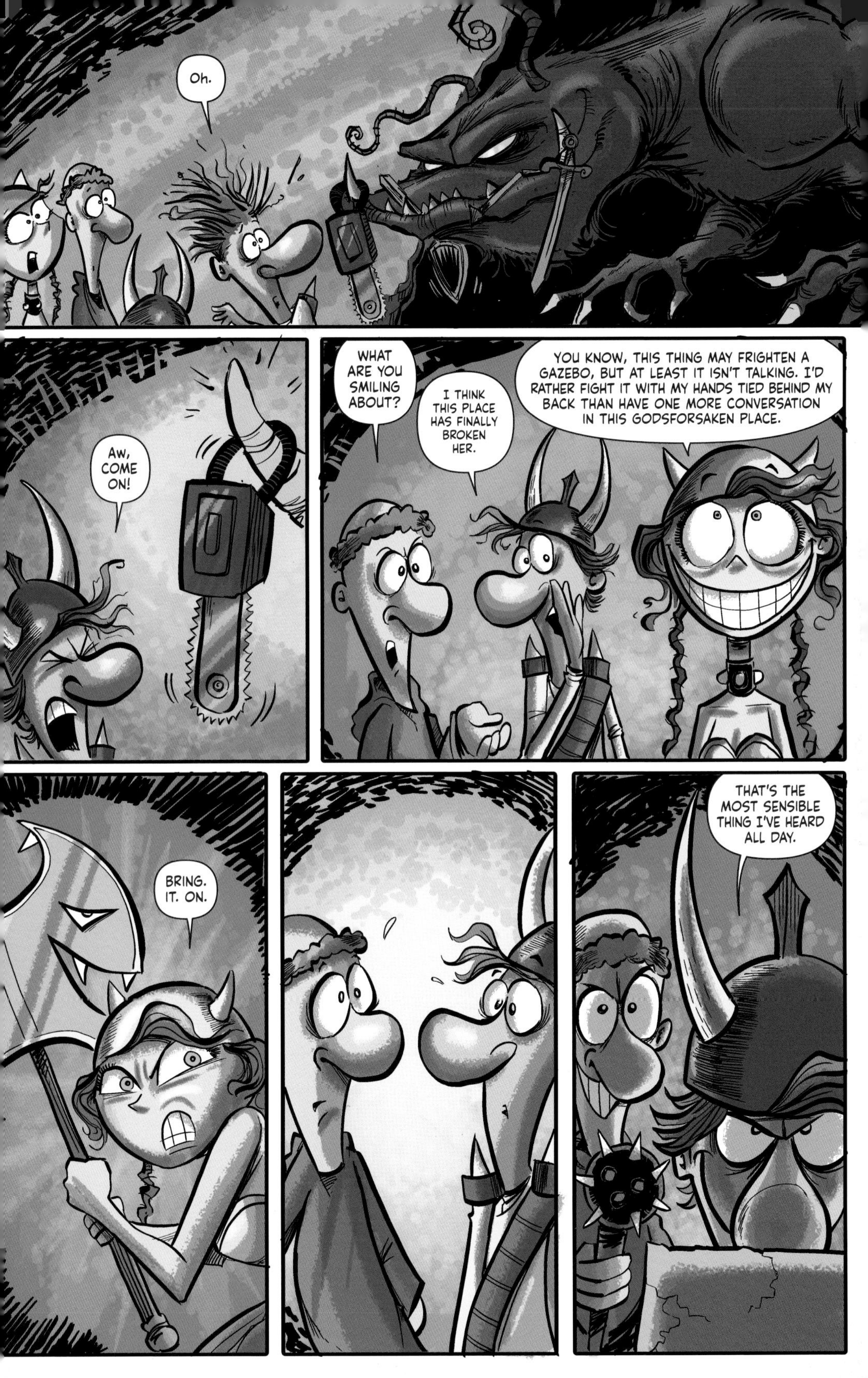
Oh.
AW, COME ON!
WHAT ARE YOU SMILING ABOUT?
I THINK THIS PLACE HAS FINALLY BROKEN HER.
YOU KNOW, THIS THING MAY FRIGHTEN A GAZEBO, BUT AT LEAST IT ISN'T TALKING. I'D RATHER FIGHT IT WITH MY HANDS TIED BEHIND MY BACK THAN HAVE ONE MORE CONVERSATION IN THIS GODSFORSAKEN PLACE.
BRING. IT. ON.
THAT'S THE MOST SENSIBLE THING I'VE HEARD ALL DAY.

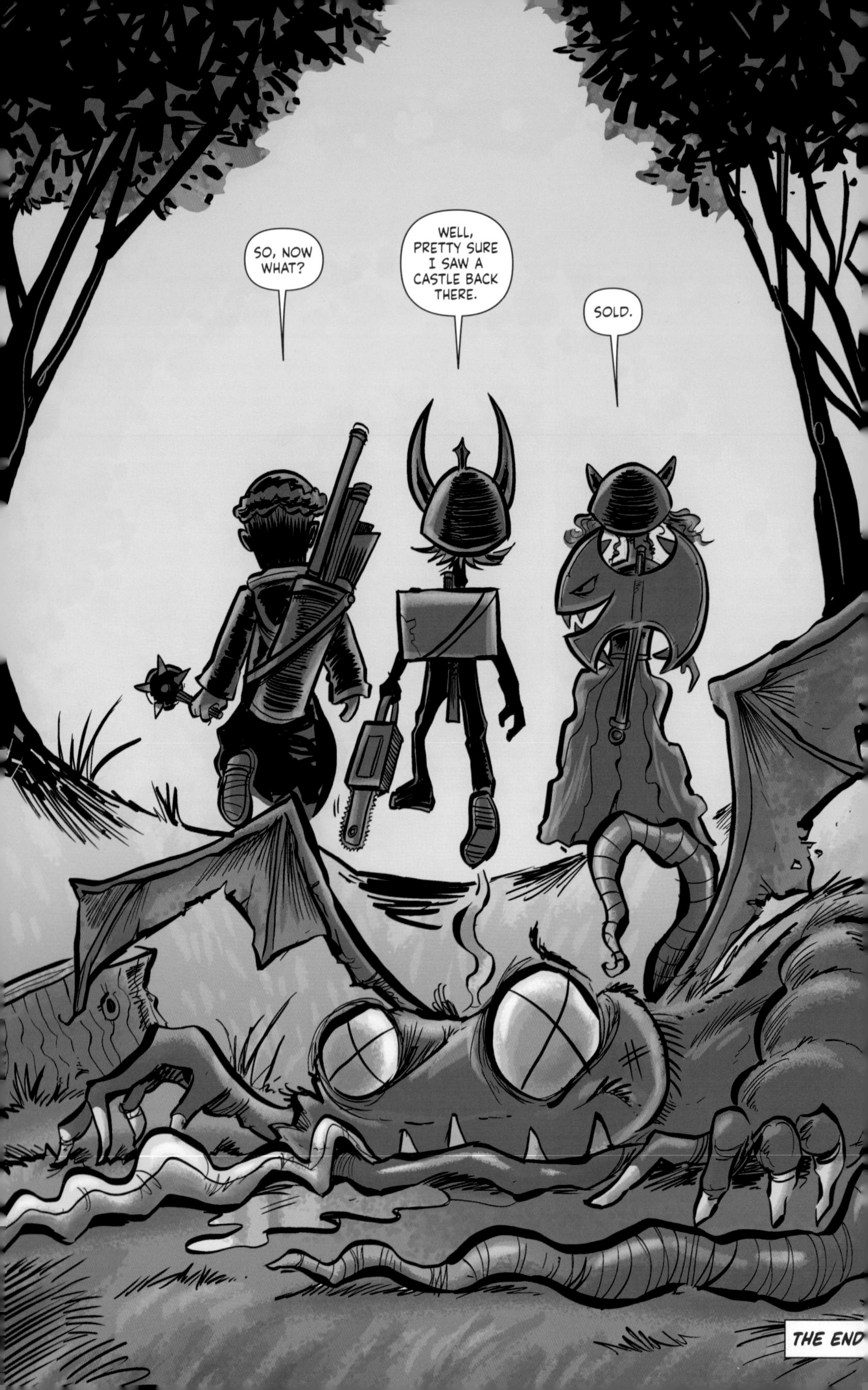
SO, NOW WHAT?
WELL, PRETTY SURE I SAW A CASTLE BACK THERE.
SOLD.
THE END

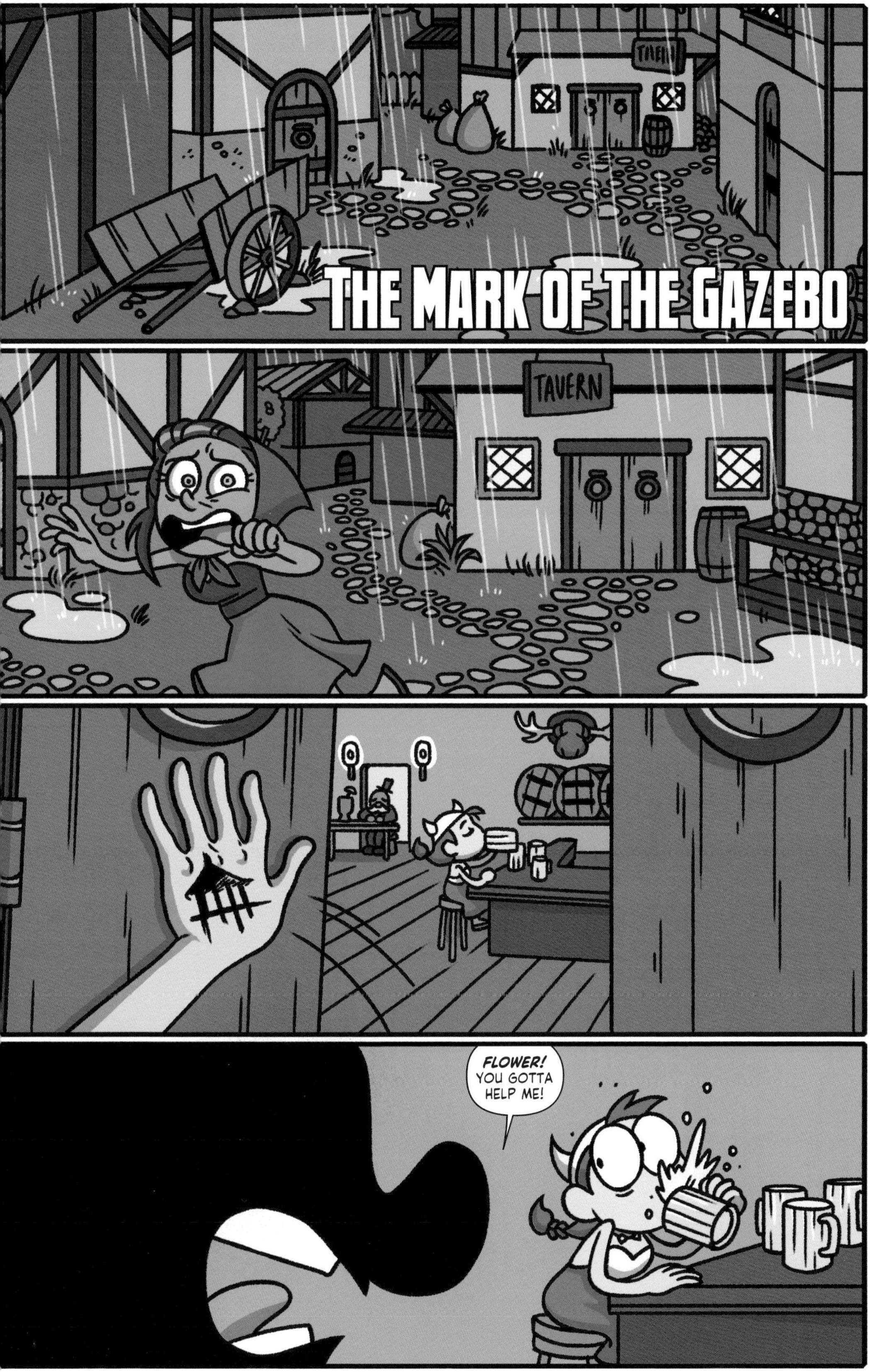
THE MARK OF THE GAZEBO
TAVERN
TAVERN
FLOWER! YOU GOTTA HELP ME!

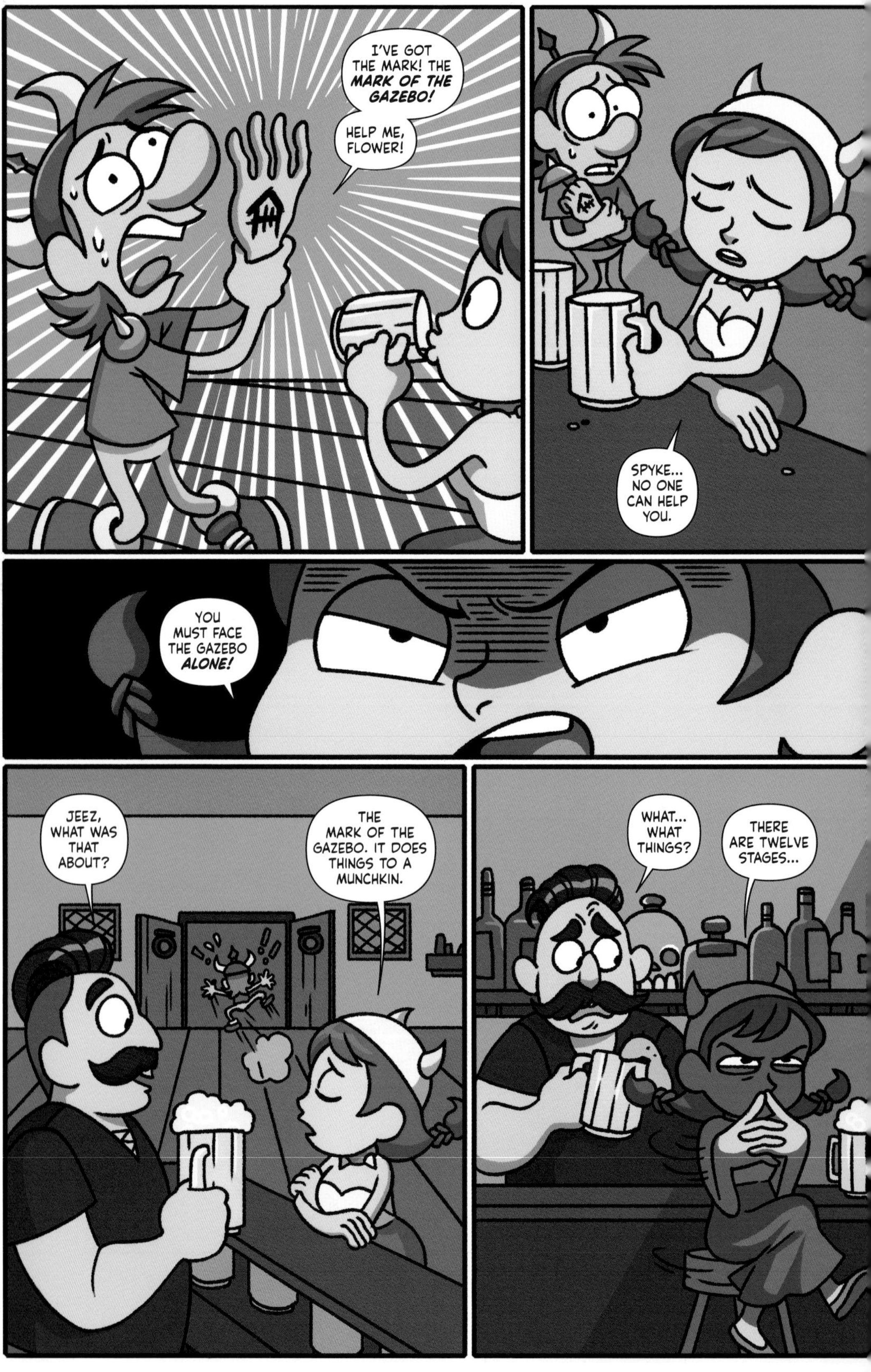
I'VE GOT THE MARK! THE ***MARK OF THE GAZEBO!***
HELP ME, FLOWER!
SPYKE... NO ONE CAN HELP YOU.
YOU MUST FACE THE GAZEBO ***ALONE!***
JEEZ, WHAT WAS THAT ABOUT?
THE MARK OF THE GAZEBO. IT DOES THINGS TO A MUNCHKIN.
WHAT... WHAT THINGS?
THERE ARE TWELVE STAGES...

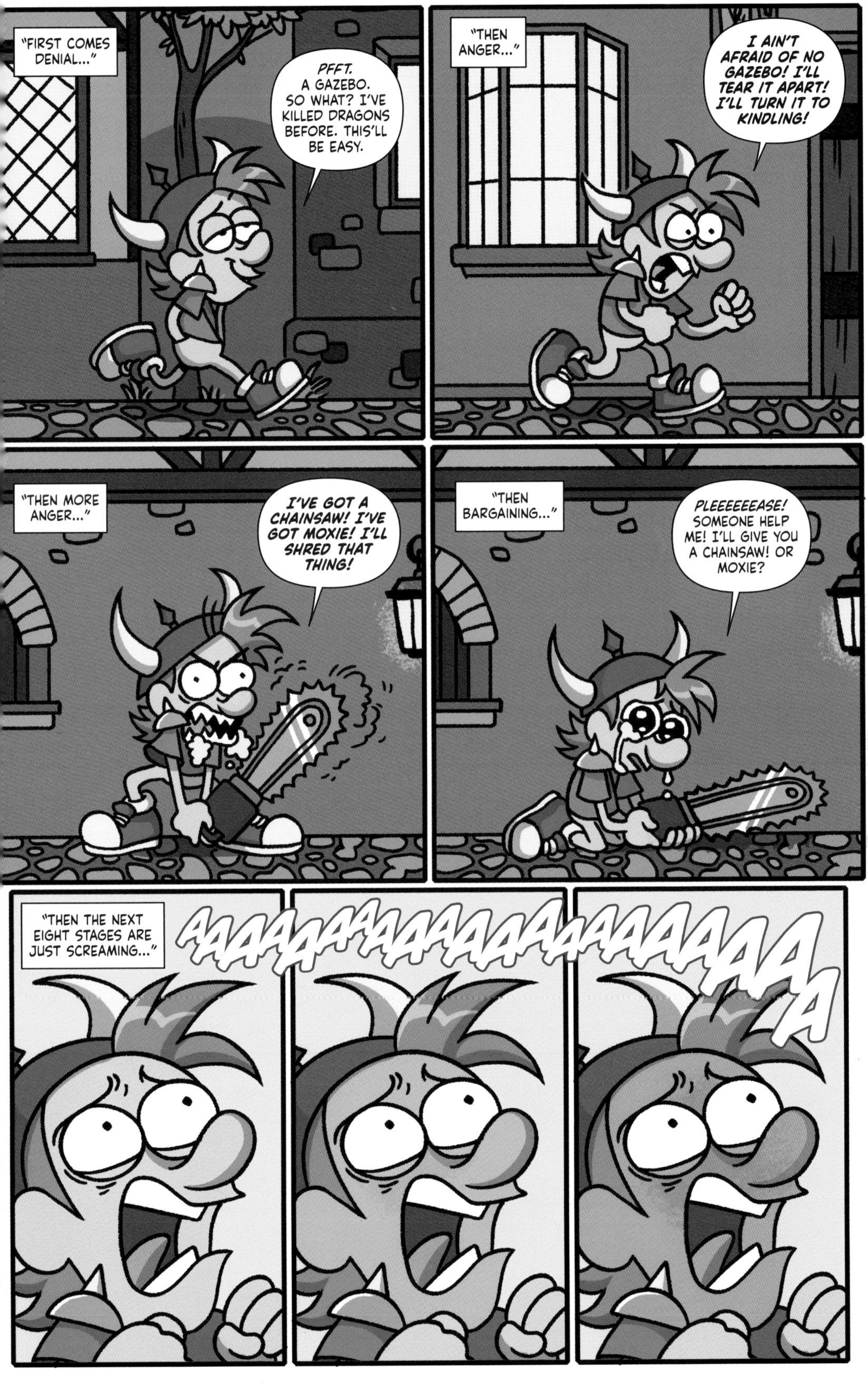
"FIRST COMES DENIAL..."
PFFT. A GAZEBO. SO WHAT? I'VE KILLED DRAGONS BEFORE. THIS'LL BE EASY.
"THEN ANGER..."
I AIN'T AFRAID OF NO GAZEBO! I'LL TEAR IT APART! I'LL TURN IT TO KINDLING!
"THEN MORE ANGER..."
I'VE GOT A CHAINSAW! I'VE GOT MOXIE! I'LL SHRED THAT THING!
"THEN BARGAINING..."
PLEEEEEEASE! SOMEONE HELP ME! I'LL GIVE YOU A CHAINSAW! OR MOXIE?
"THEN THE NEXT EIGHT STAGES ARE JUST SCREAMING..."
AAAAAAAAAAAAAAAAAAAAAAAAA

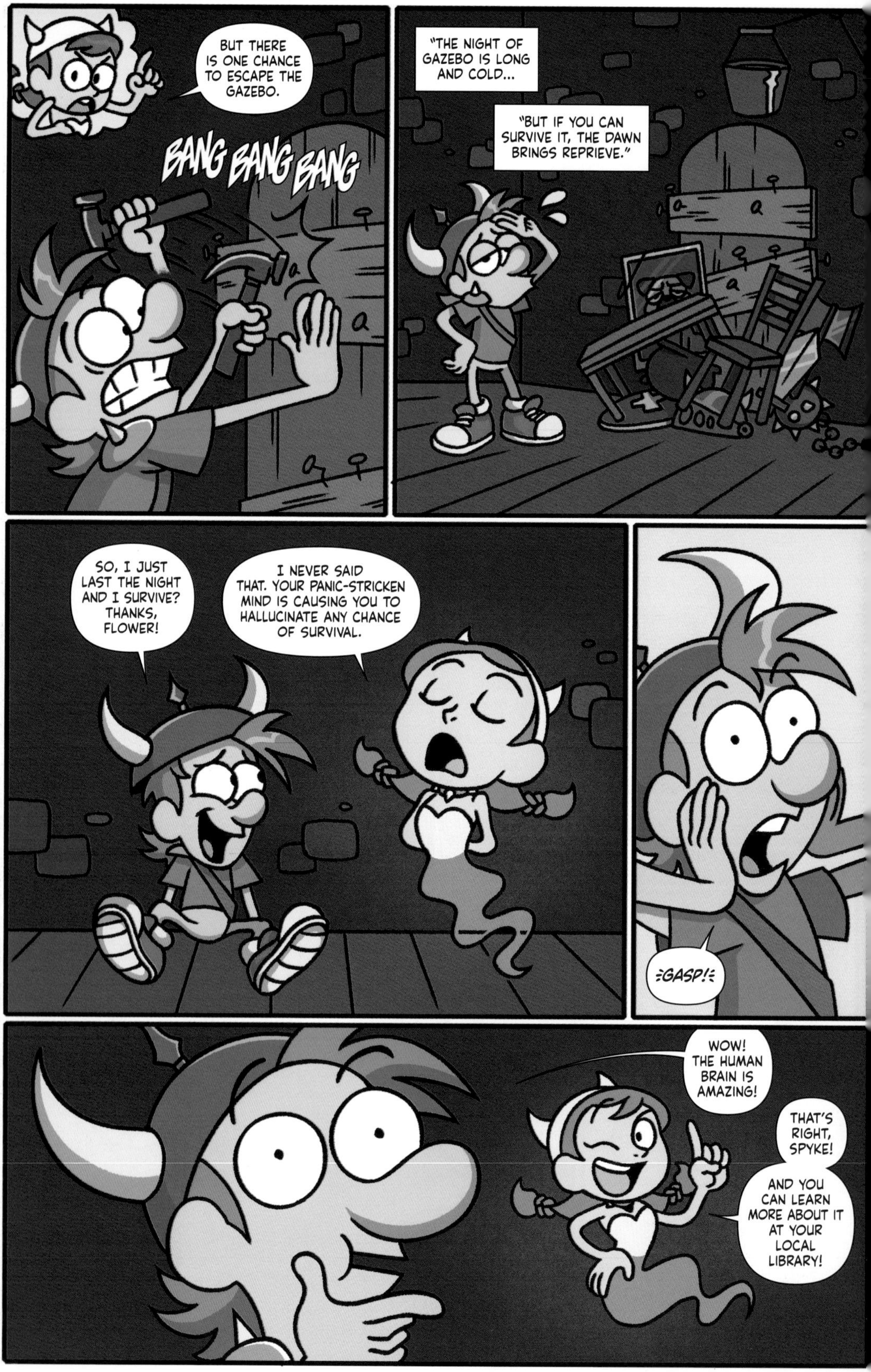
BUT THERE IS ONE CHANCE TO ESCAPE THE GAZEBO.
BANG BANG BANG
"THE NIGHT OF GAZEBO IS LONG AND COLD...
"BUT IF YOU CAN SURVIVE IT, THE DAWN BRINGS REPRIEVE."
SO, I JUST LAST THE NIGHT AND I SURVIVE? THANKS, FLOWER!
I NEVER SAID THAT. YOUR PANIC-STRICKEN MIND IS CAUSING YOU TO HALLUCINATE ANY CHANCE OF SURVIVAL.
GASP!
WOW! THE HUMAN BRAIN IS AMAZING!
THAT'S RIGHT, SPYKE!
AND YOU CAN LEARN MORE ABOUT IT AT YOUR LOCAL LIBRARY!

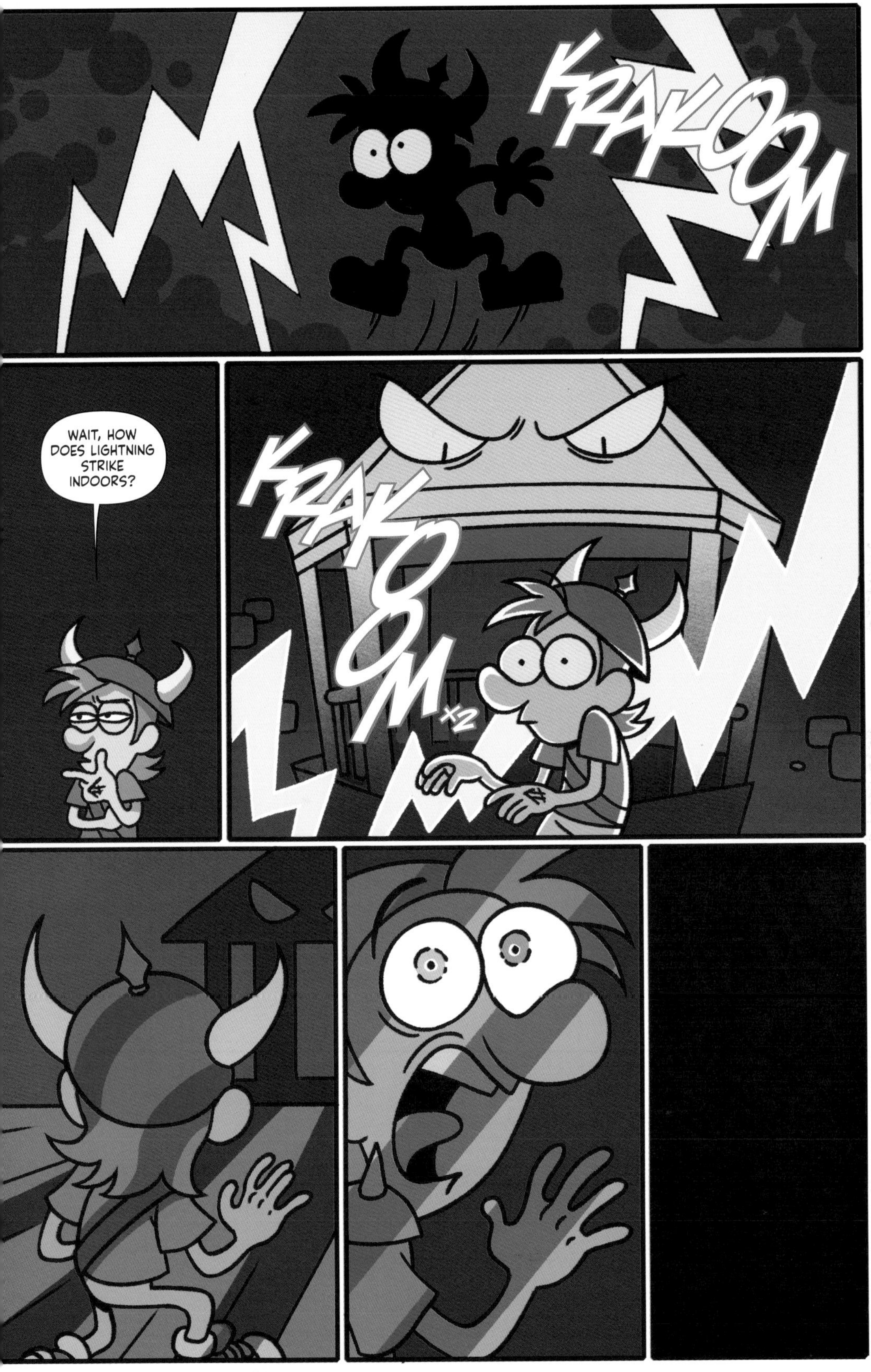
KRAKOOM
WAIT, HOW DOES LIGHTNING STRIKE INDOORS?
KRAKOOM ×2

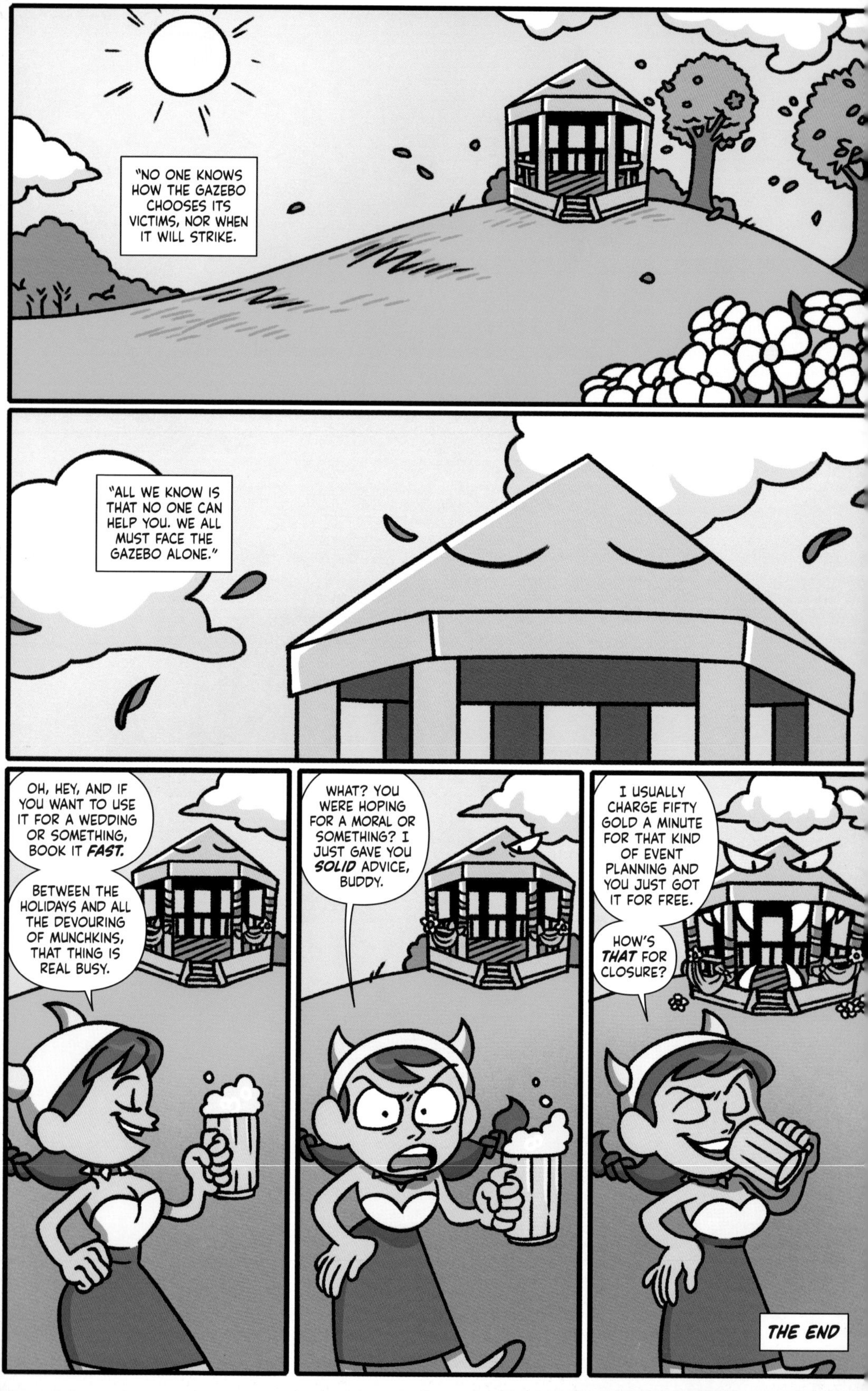
"NO ONE KNOWS HOW THE GAZEBO CHOOSES ITS VICTIMS, NOR WHEN IT WILL STRIKE.
"ALL WE KNOW IS THAT NO ONE CAN HELP YOU. WE ALL MUST FACE THE GAZEBO ALONE."
OH, HEY, AND IF YOU WANT TO USE IT FOR A WEDDING OR SOMETHING, BOOK IT *FAST.*
BETWEEN THE HOLIDAYS AND ALL THE DEVOURING OF MUNCHKINS, THAT THING IS REAL BUSY.
WHAT? YOU WERE HOPING FOR A MORAL OR SOMETHING? I JUST GAVE YOU *SOLID* ADVICE, BUDDY.
I USUALLY CHARGE FIFTY GOLD A MINUTE FOR THAT KIND OF EVENT PLANNING AND YOU JUST GOT IT FOR FREE.
HOW'S *THAT* FOR CLOSURE?
THE END

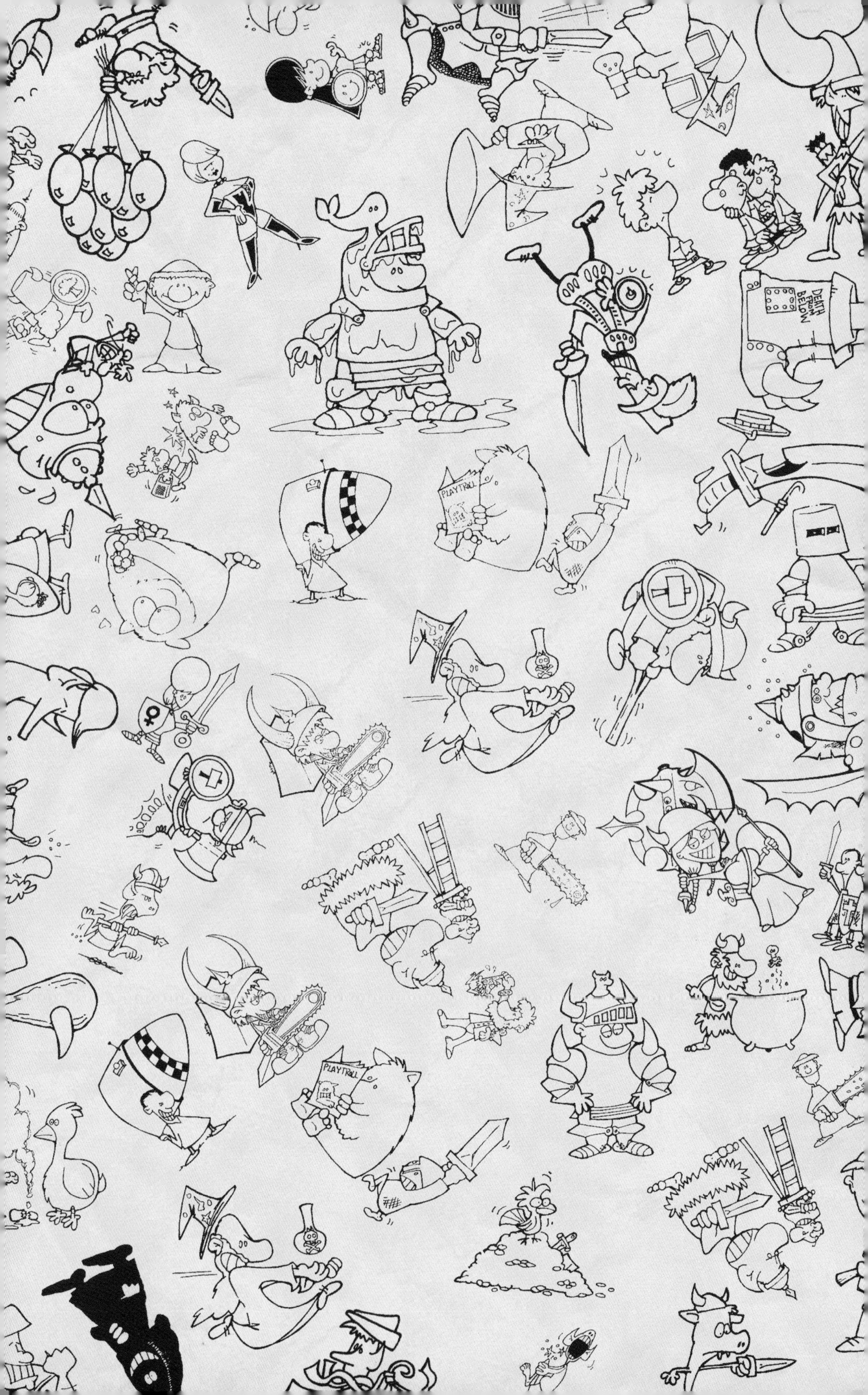
DEATH FROM BELOW
PLAYTROLL
PLAYTROLL

CHAPTER
TWENTY-THREE

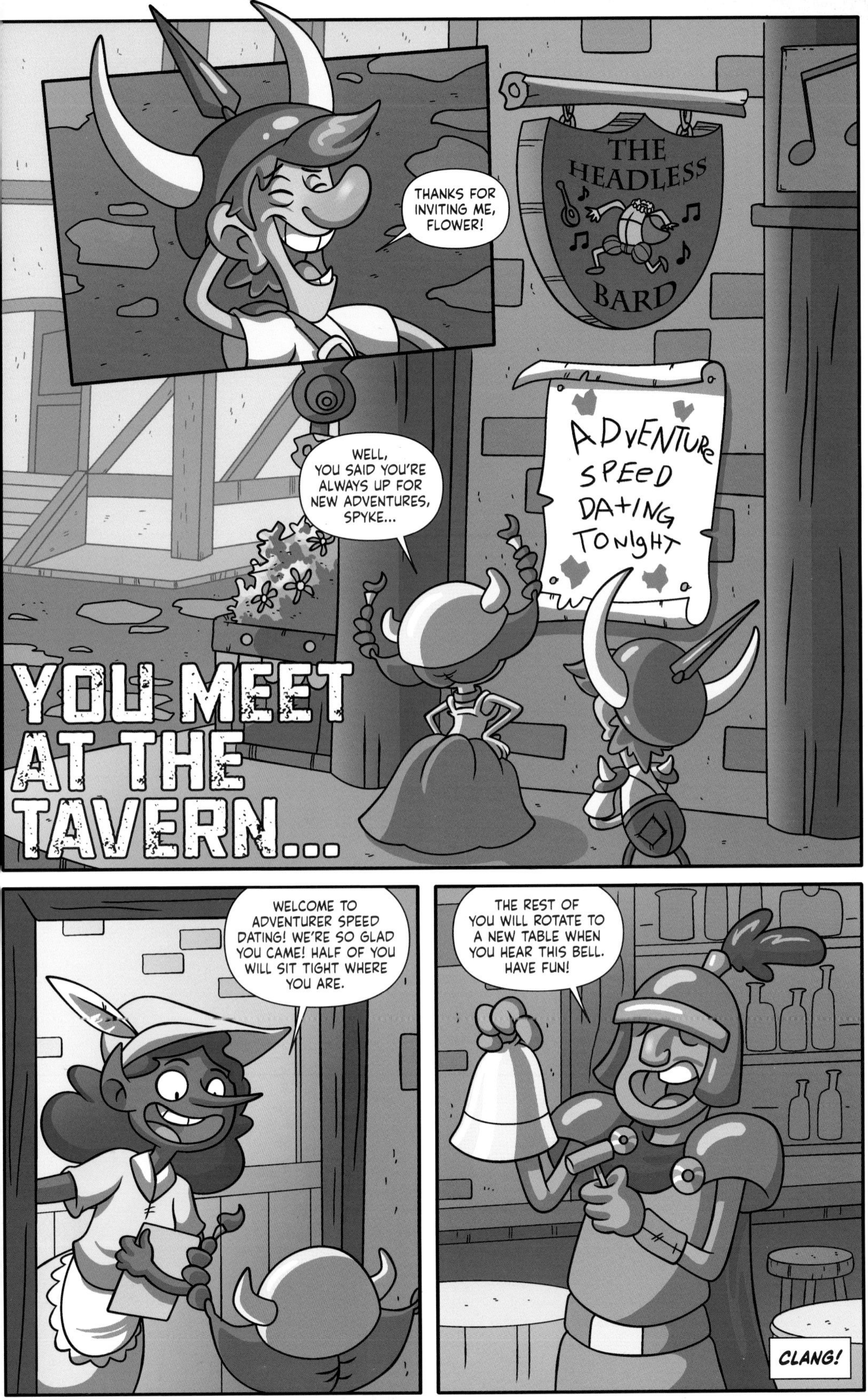
THANKS FOR INVITING ME, FLOWER!
THE HEADLESS BARD
WELL, YOU SAID YOU'RE ALWAYS UP FOR NEW ADVENTURES, SPYKE...
ADVENTURE SPEED DATING TONIGHT
YOU MEET AT THE TAVERN...
WELCOME TO ADVENTURER SPEED DATING! WE'RE SO GLAD YOU CAME! HALF OF YOU WILL SIT TIGHT WHERE YOU ARE.
THE REST OF YOU WILL ROTATE TO A NEW TABLE WHEN YOU HEAR THIS BELL. HAVE FUN!
CLANG!

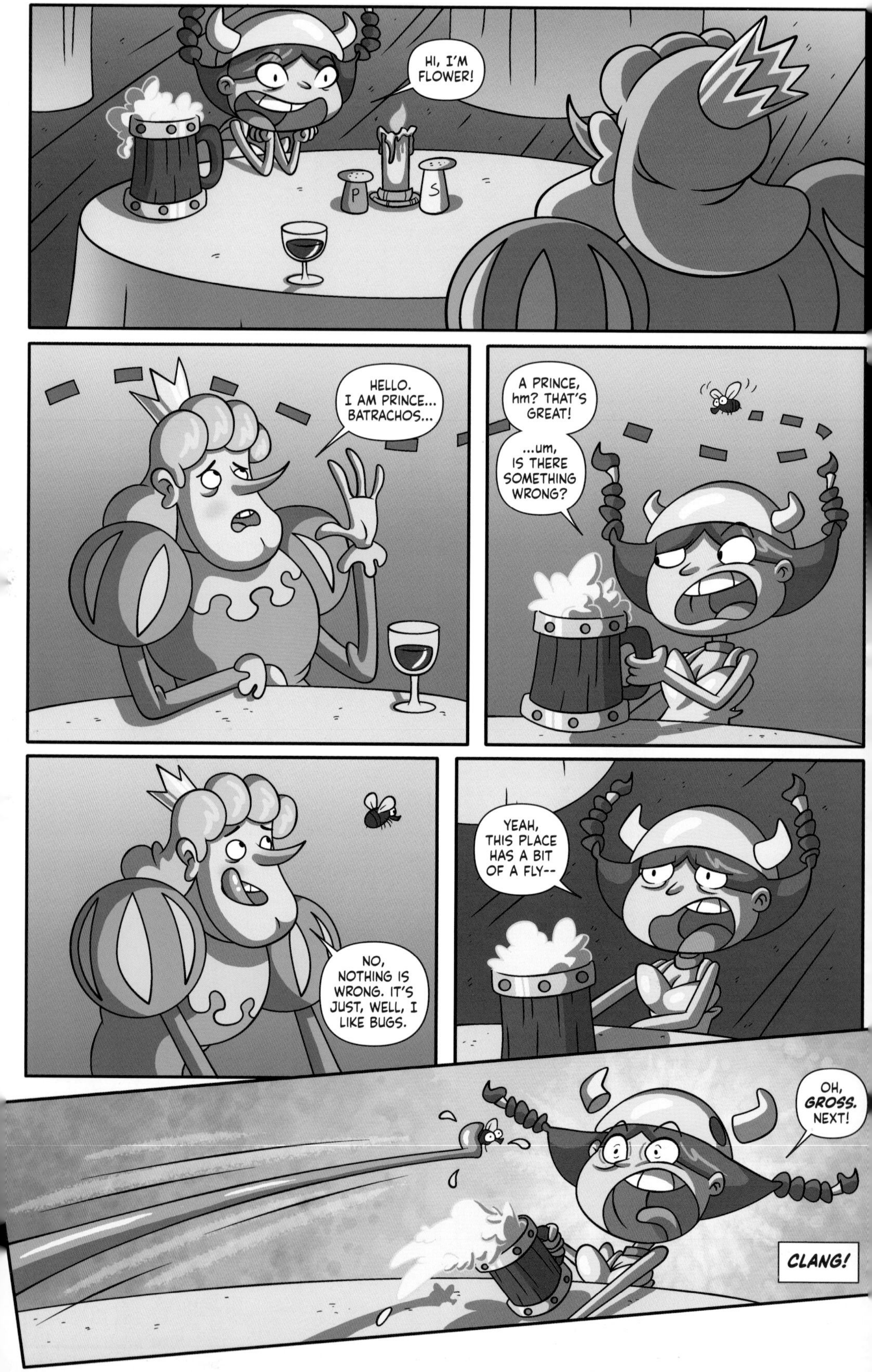
HI, I'M FLOWER!
HELLO. I AM PRINCE... BATRACHOS...
A PRINCE, hm? THAT'S GREAT!
...um, IS THERE SOMETHING WRONG?
NO, NOTHING IS WRONG. IT'S JUST, WELL, I LIKE BUGS.
YEAH, THIS PLACE HAS A BIT OF A FLY--
OH, GROSS. NEXT!
CLANG!

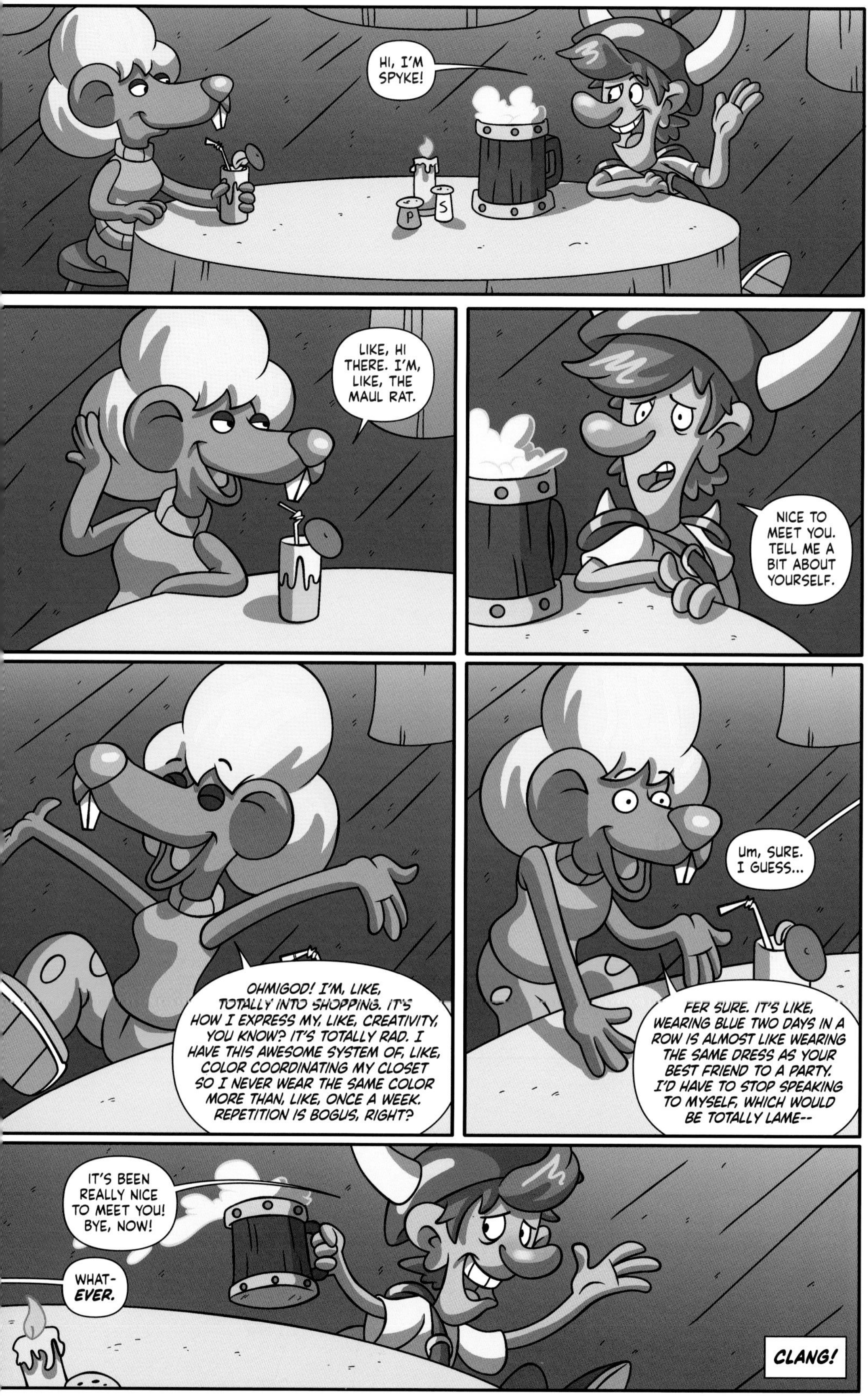
HI, I'M SPYKE!
LIKE, HI THERE. I'M, LIKE, THE MAUL RAT.
NICE TO MEET YOU. TELL ME A BIT ABOUT YOURSELF.
OHMIGOD! I'M, LIKE, TOTALLY INTO SHOPPING. IT'S HOW I EXPRESS MY, LIKE, CREATIVITY, YOU KNOW? IT'S TOTALLY RAD. I HAVE THIS AWESOME SYSTEM OF, LIKE, COLOR COORDINATING MY CLOSET SO I NEVER WEAR THE SAME COLOR MORE THAN, LIKE, ONCE A WEEK. REPETITION IS BOGUS, RIGHT?
UM, SURE. I GUESS...
FER SURE. IT'S LIKE, WEARING BLUE TWO DAYS IN A ROW IS ALMOST LIKE WEARING THE SAME DRESS AS YOUR BEST FRIEND TO A PARTY. I'D HAVE TO STOP SPEAKING TO MYSELF, WHICH WOULD BE TOTALLY LAME--
IT'S BEEN REALLY NICE TO MEET YOU! BYE, NOW!
WHAT-EVER.
CLANG!

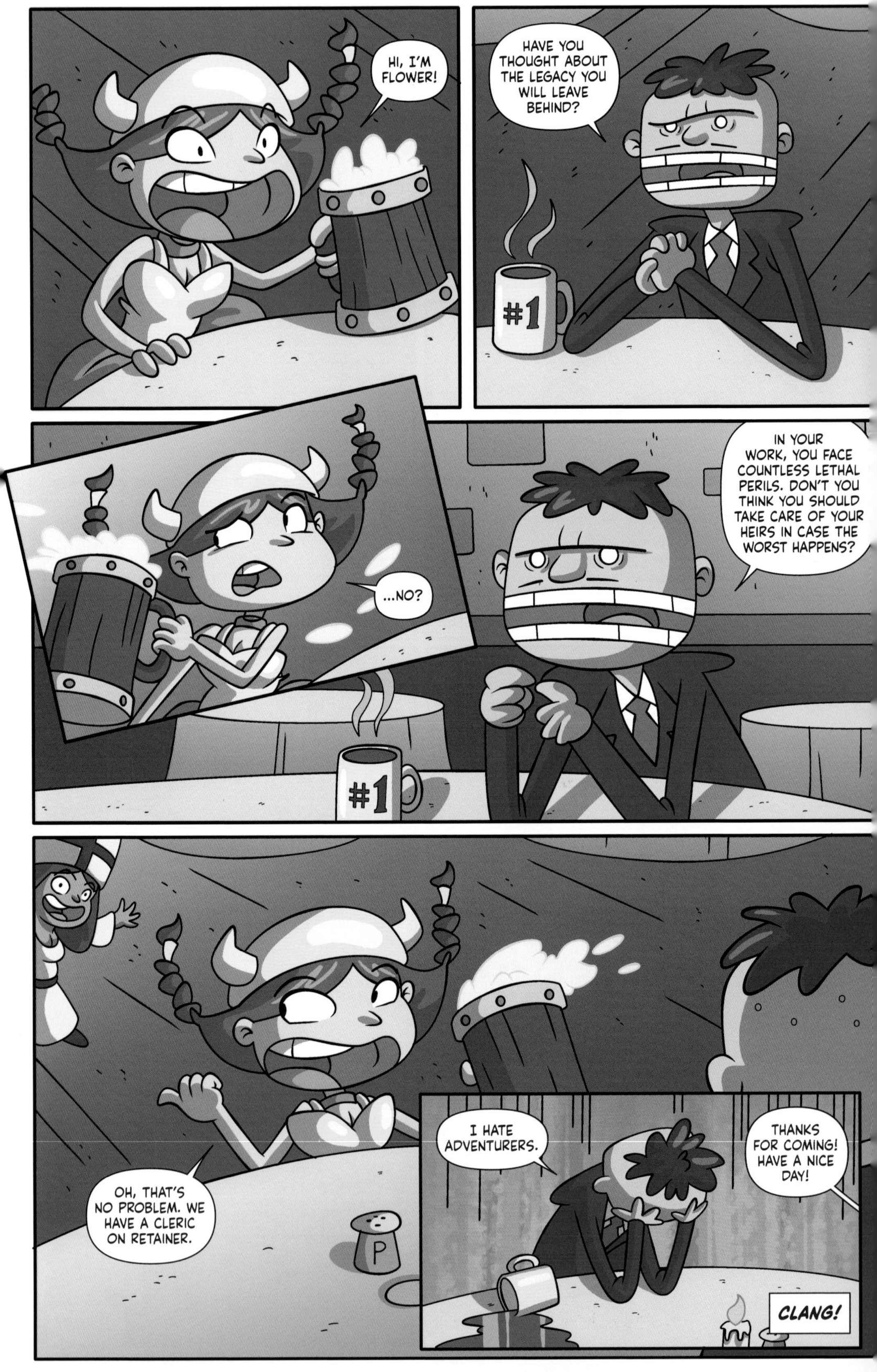
HI, I'M FLOWER!
HAVE YOU THOUGHT ABOUT THE LEGACY YOU WILL LEAVE BEHIND?
#1
...NO?
IN YOUR WORK, YOU FACE COUNTLESS LETHAL PERILS. DON'T YOU THINK YOU SHOULD TAKE CARE OF YOUR HEIRS IN CASE THE WORST HAPPENS?
#1
OH, THAT'S NO PROBLEM. WE HAVE A CLERIC ON RETAINER.
P
I HATE ADVENTURERS.
THANKS FOR COMING! HAVE A NICE DAY!
CLANG!

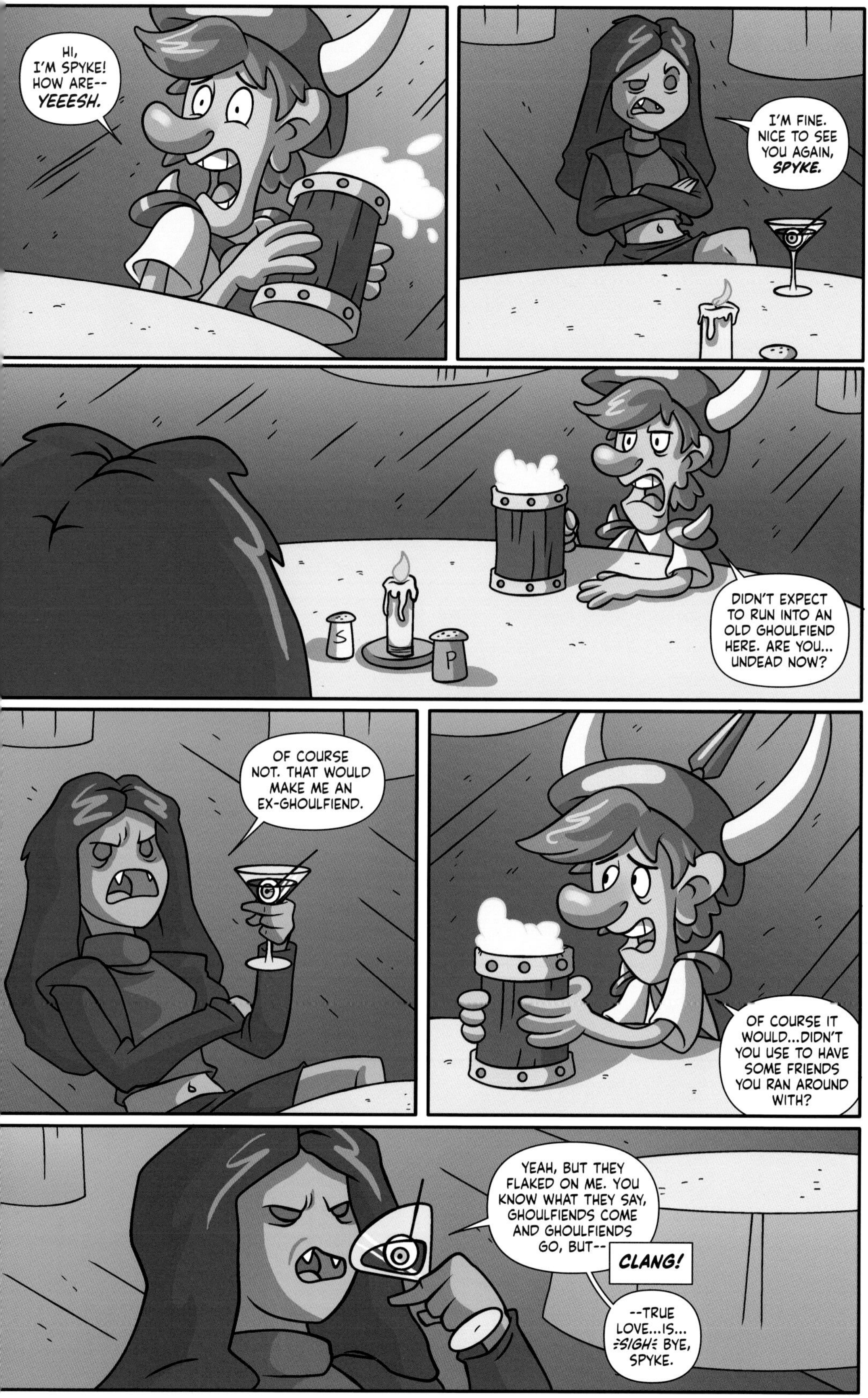
HI, I'M SPYKE! HOW ARE-- YEEESH.
I'M FINE. NICE TO SEE YOU AGAIN, SPYKE.
DIDN'T EXPECT TO RUN INTO AN OLD GHOULFIEND HERE. ARE YOU... UNDEAD NOW?
S
P
OF COURSE NOT. THAT WOULD MAKE ME AN EX-GHOULFIEND.
OF COURSE IT WOULD...DIDN'T YOU USE TO HAVE SOME FRIENDS YOU RAN AROUND WITH?
YEAH, BUT THEY FLAKED ON ME. YOU KNOW WHAT THEY SAY, GHOULFIENDS COME AND GHOULFIENDS GO, BUT--
CLANG!
--TRUE LOVE...IS... SIGH BYE, SPYKE.

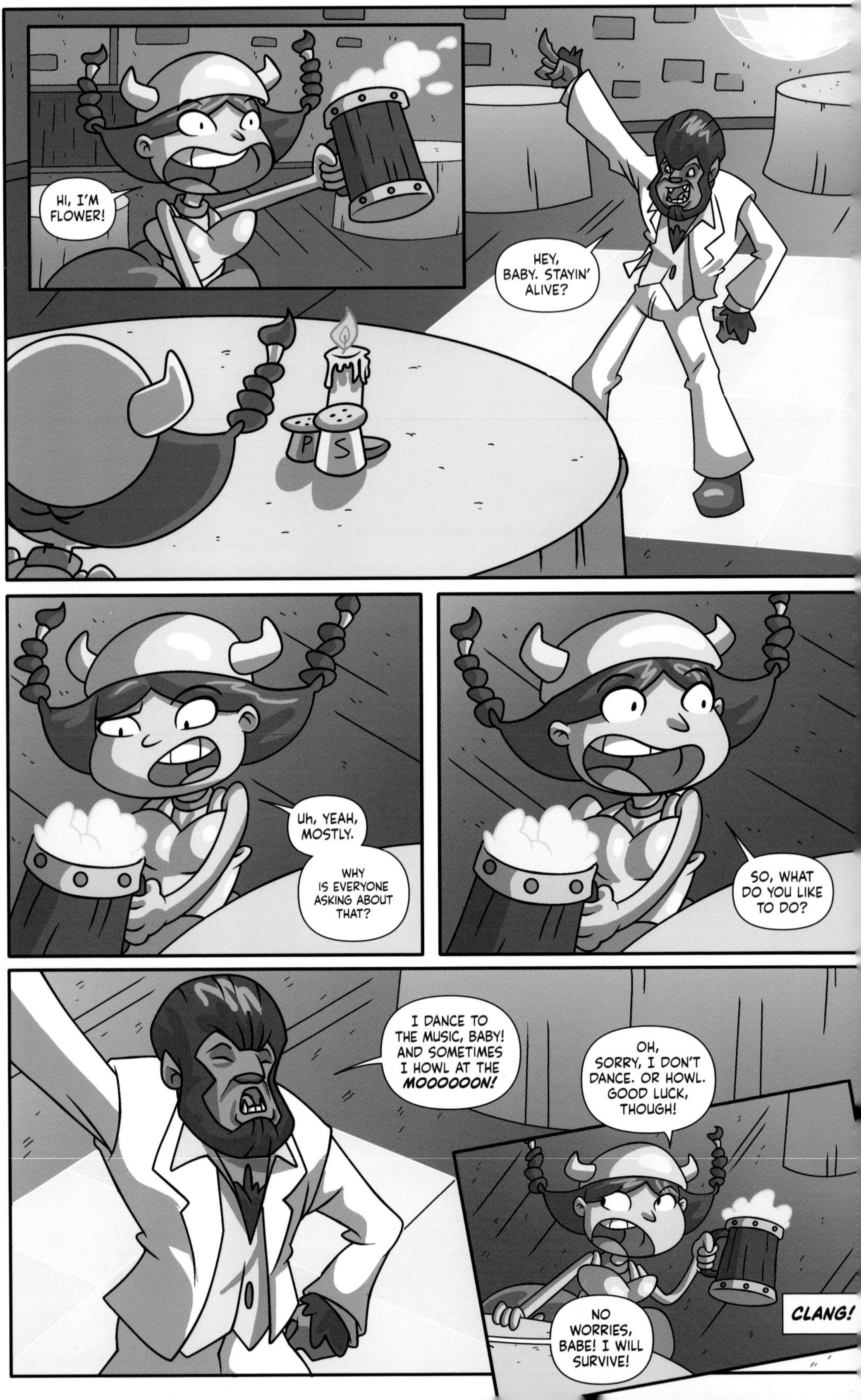

HI, I'M FLOWER!
HEY, BABY. STAYIN' ALIVE?
Uh, YEAH, MOSTLY.
WHY IS EVERYONE ASKING ABOUT THAT?
SO, WHAT DO YOU LIKE TO DO?
I DANCE TO THE MUSIC, BABY! AND SOMETIMES I HOWL AT THE MOOOOOON!
OH, SORRY, I DON'T DANCE. OR HOWL. GOOD LUCK, THOUGH!
NO WORRIES, BABE! I WILL SURVIVE!
CLANG!

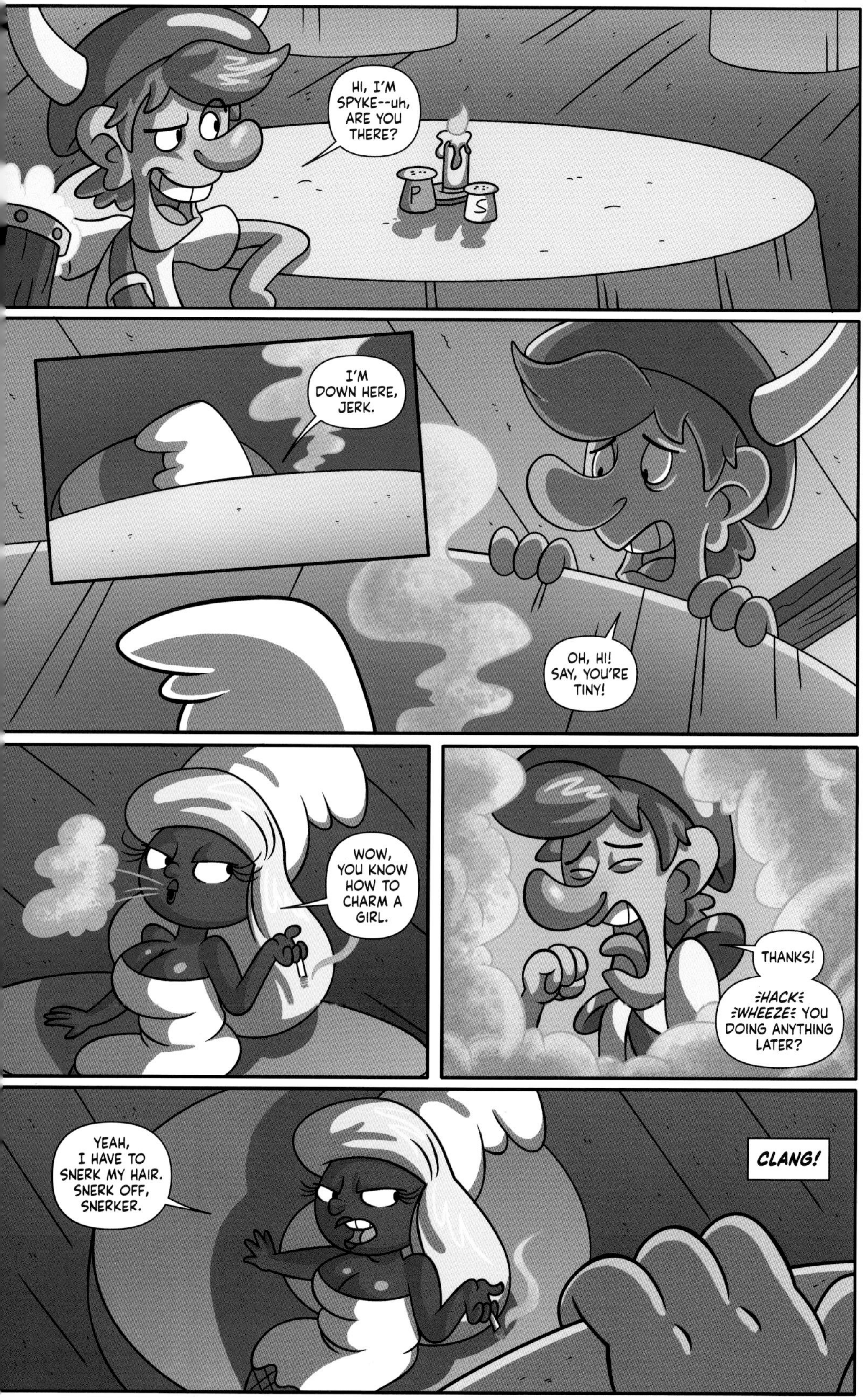
HI, I'M SPYKE--uh, ARE YOU THERE?
I'M DOWN HERE, JERK.
OH, HI! SAY, YOU'RE TINY!
WOW, YOU KNOW HOW TO CHARM A GIRL.
THANKS!
HACK WHEEZE YOU DOING ANYTHING LATER?
YEAH, I HAVE TO SNERK MY HAIR. SNERK OFF, SNERKER.
CLANG!

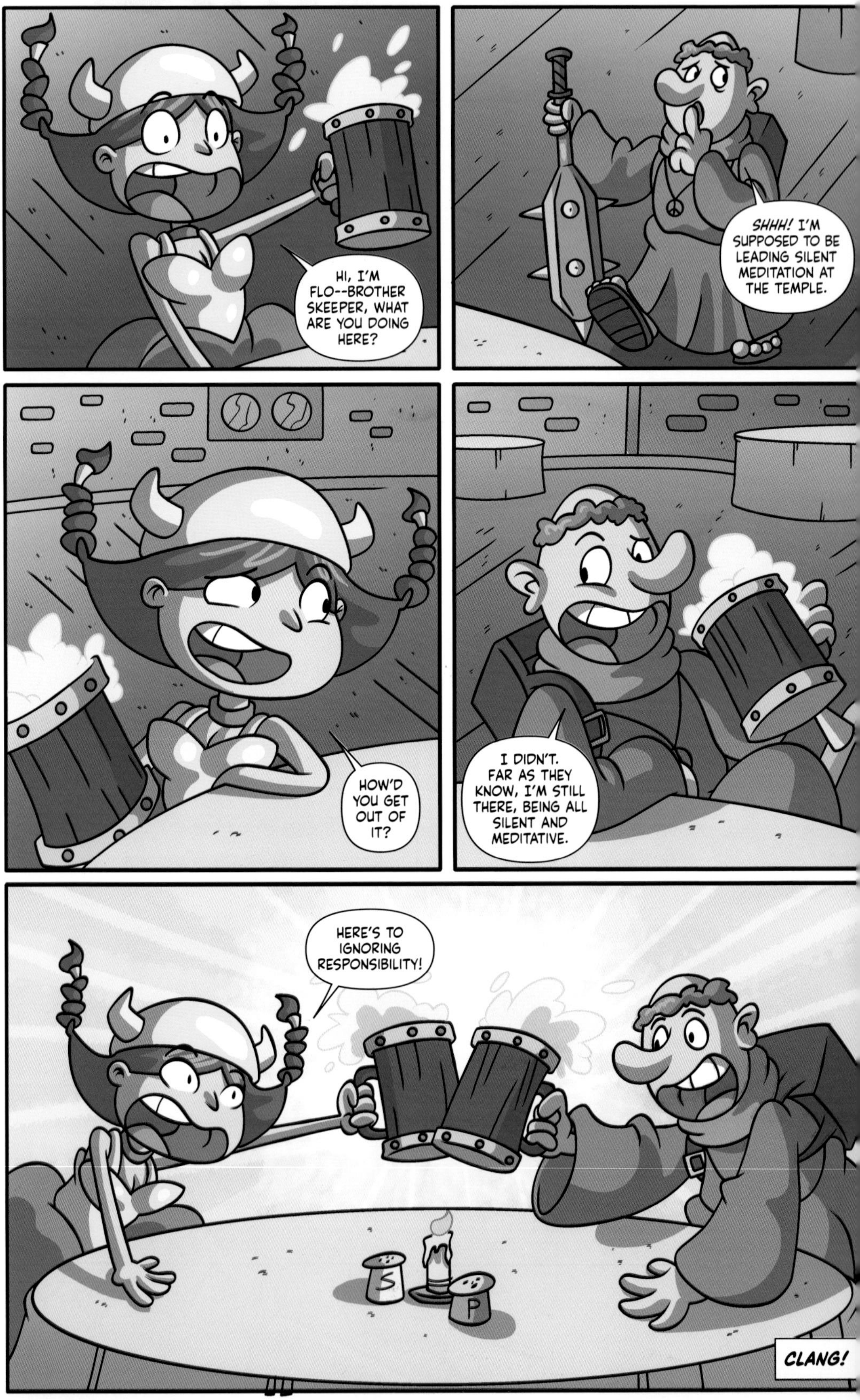
HI, I'M FLO--BROTHER SKEEPER, WHAT ARE YOU DOING HERE?
SHHH! I'M SUPPOSED TO BE LEADING SILENT MEDITATION AT THE TEMPLE.
HOW'D YOU GET OUT OF IT?
I DIDN'T. FAR AS THEY KNOW, I'M STILL THERE, BEING ALL SILENT AND MEDITATIVE.
HERE'S TO IGNORING RESPONSIBILITY!
CLANG!

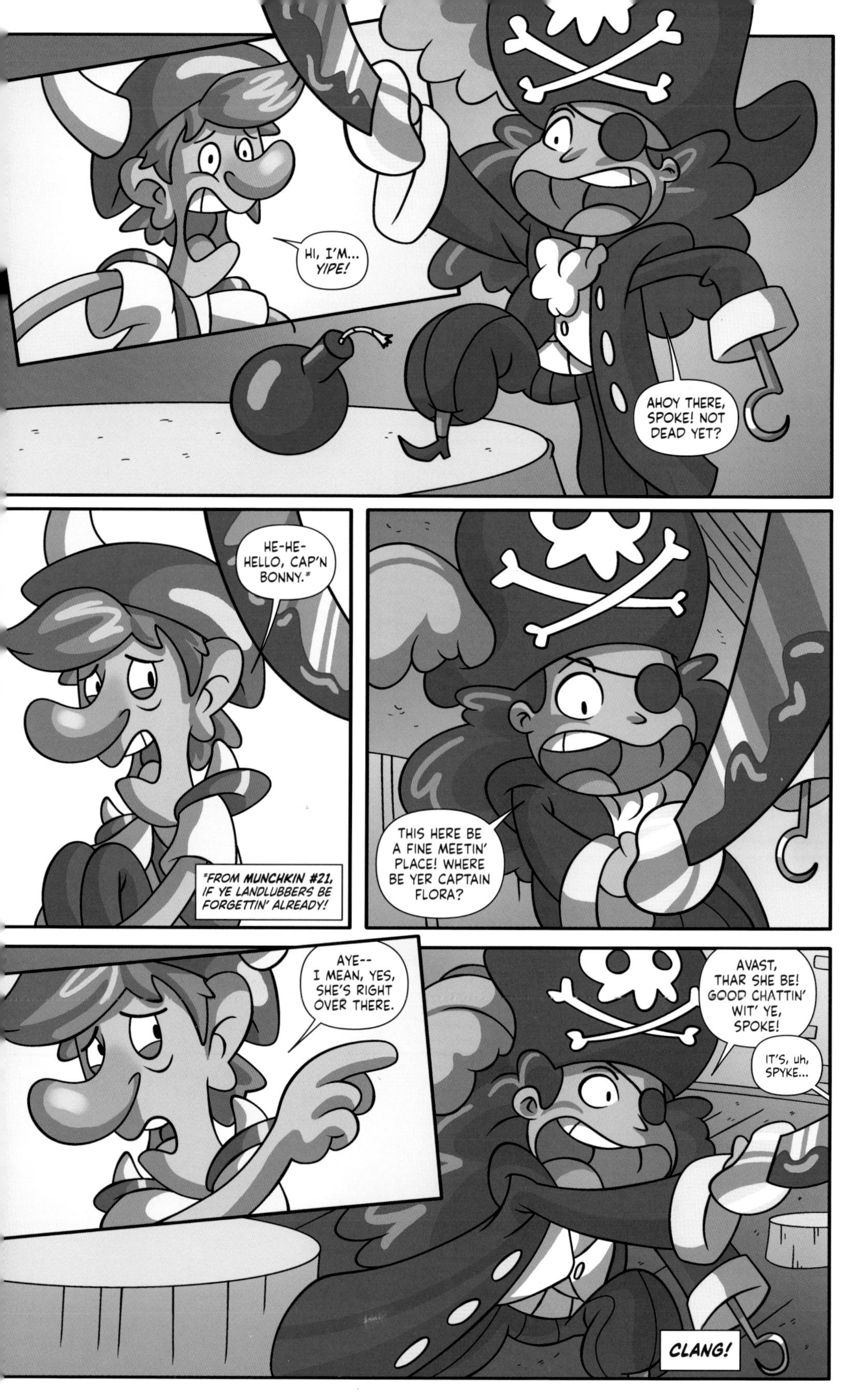
HI, I'M... YIPE!
AHOY THERE, SPOKE! NOT DEAD YET?
HE-HE-HELLO, CAP'N BONNY.*
*FROM MUNCHKIN #21, IF YE LANDLUBBERS BE FORGETTIN' ALREADY!
THIS HERE BE A FINE MEETIN' PLACE! WHERE BE YER CAPTAIN FLORA?
AYE-- I MEAN, YES, SHE'S RIGHT OVER THERE.
AVAST, THAR SHE BE! GOOD CHATTIN' WIT' YE, SPOKE!
IT'S, uh, SPYKE...
CLANG!

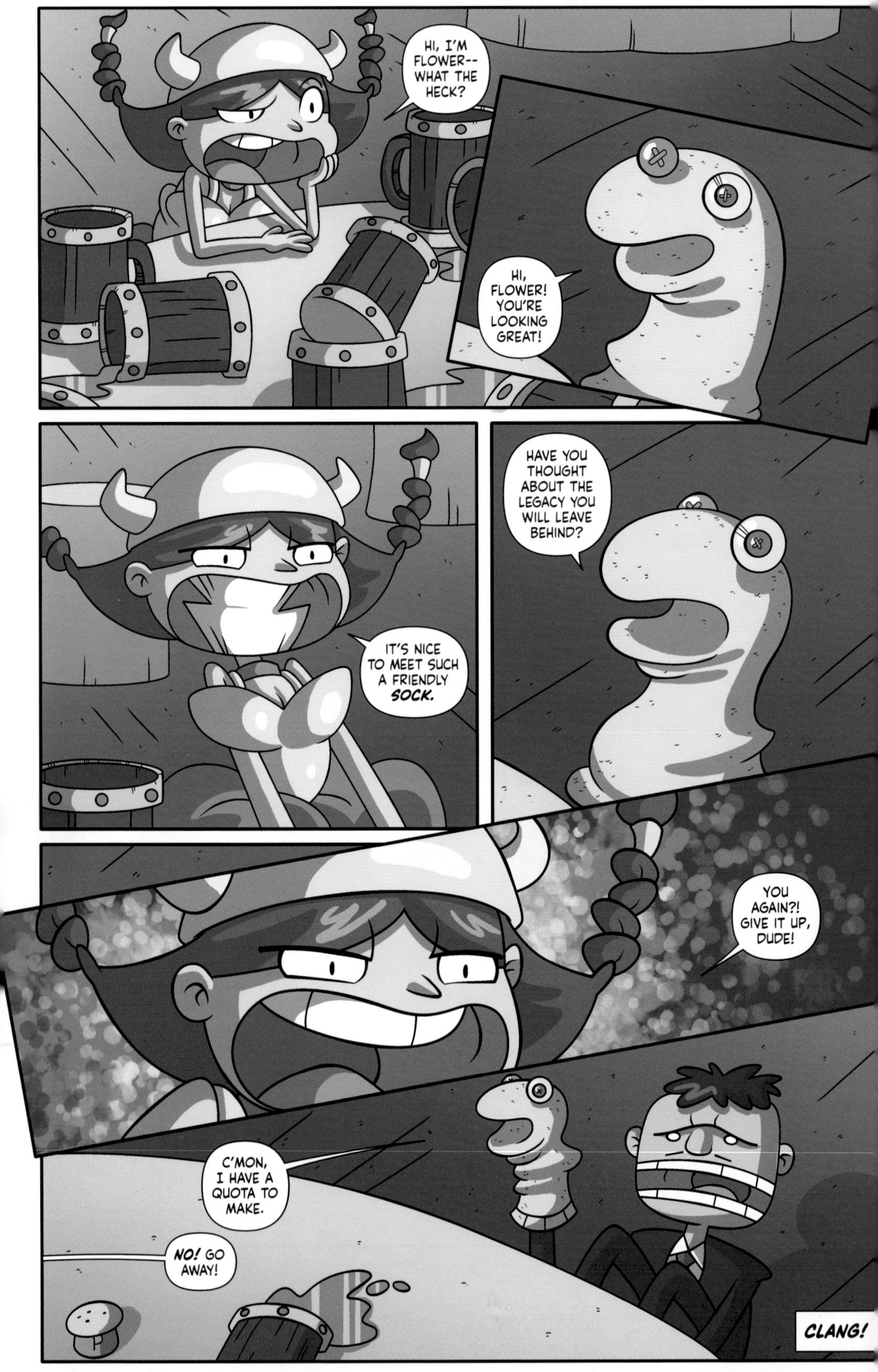
HI, I'M FLOWER-- WHAT THE HECK?
HI, FLOWER! YOU'RE LOOKING GREAT!
IT'S NICE TO MEET SUCH A FRIENDLY **SOCK.**
HAVE YOU THOUGHT ABOUT THE LEGACY YOU WILL LEAVE BEHIND?
YOU AGAIN?! GIVE IT UP, DUDE!
C'MON, I HAVE A QUOTA TO MAKE.
NO! GO AWAY!
CLANG!

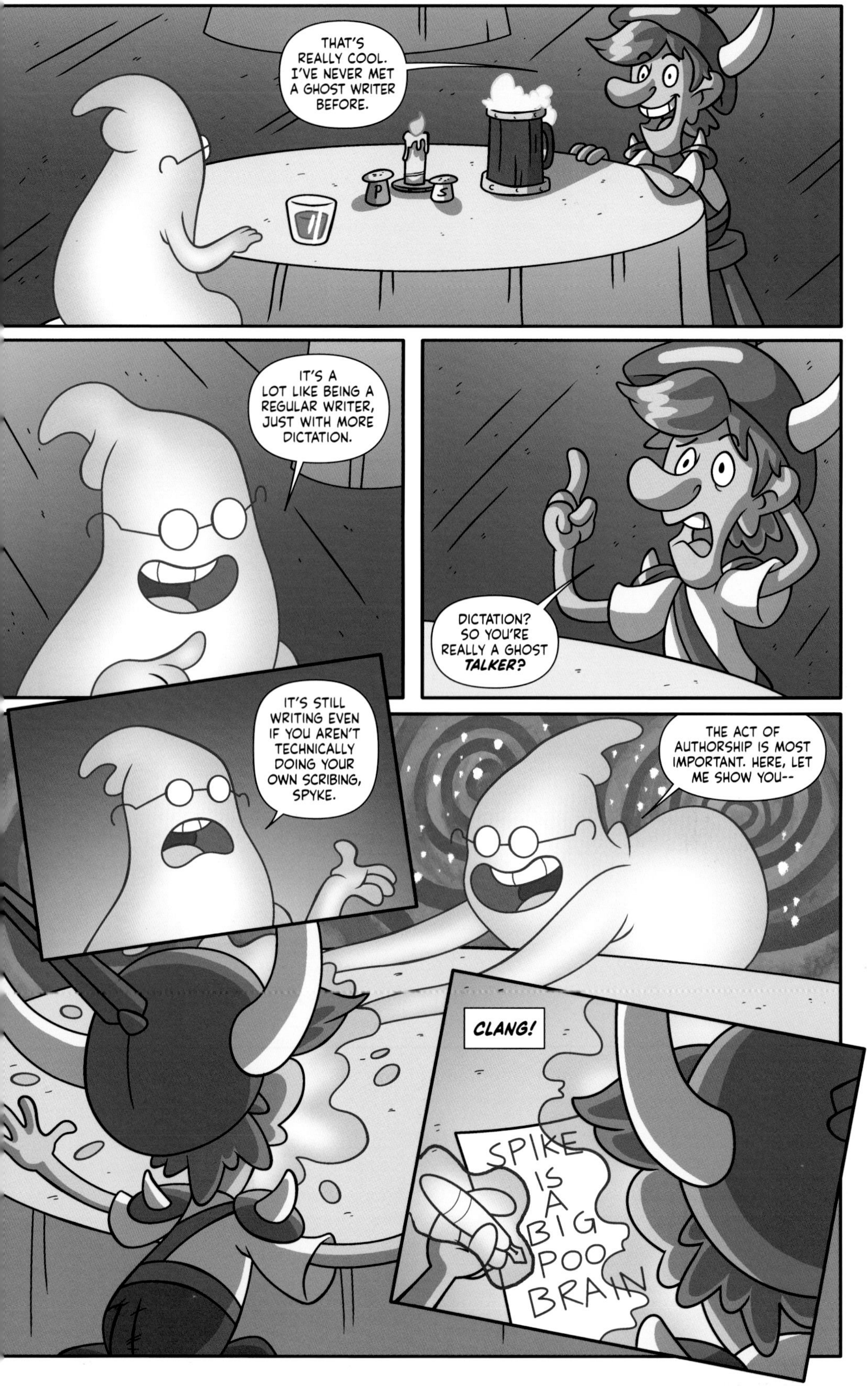
THAT'S REALLY COOL. I'VE NEVER MET A GHOST WRITER BEFORE.
IT'S A LOT LIKE BEING A REGULAR WRITER, JUST WITH MORE DICTATION.
DICTATION? SO YOU'RE REALLY A GHOST *TALKER?*
IT'S STILL WRITING EVEN IF YOU AREN'T TECHNICALLY DOING YOUR OWN SCRIBING, SPYKE.
THE ACT OF AUTHORSHIP IS MOST IMPORTANT. HERE, LET ME SHOW YOU--
CLANG!
SPIKE IS A BIG POO BRAIN

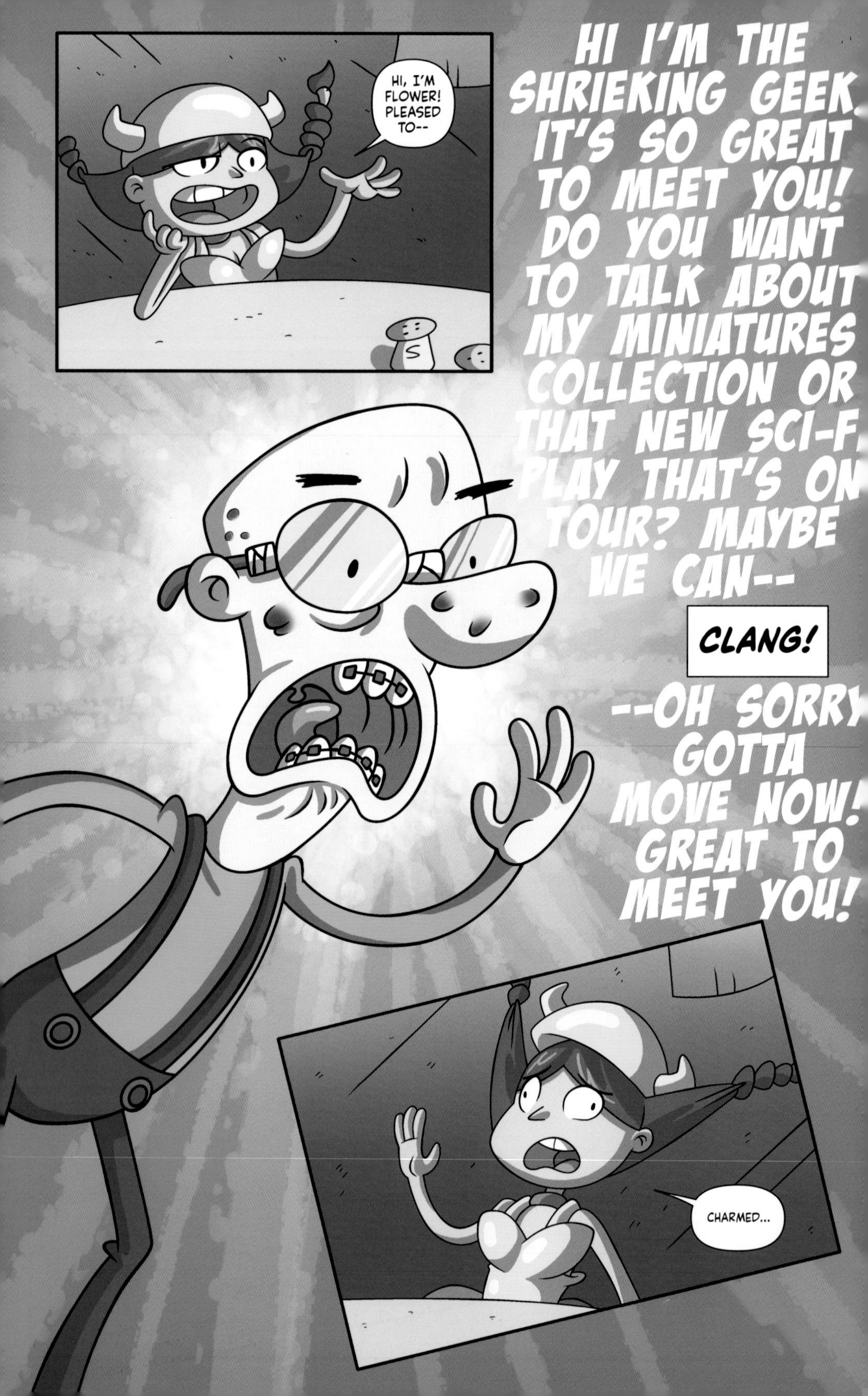
HI, I'M FLOWER! PLEASED TO--
HI I'M THE SHRIEKING GEEK. IT'S SO GREAT TO MEET YOU! DO YOU WANT TO TALK ABOUT MY MINIATURES COLLECTION OR THAT NEW SCI-FI PLAY THAT'S ON TOUR? MAYBE WE CAN--
CLANG!
--OH SORRY GOTTA MOVE NOW! GREAT TO MEET YOU!
CHARMED...

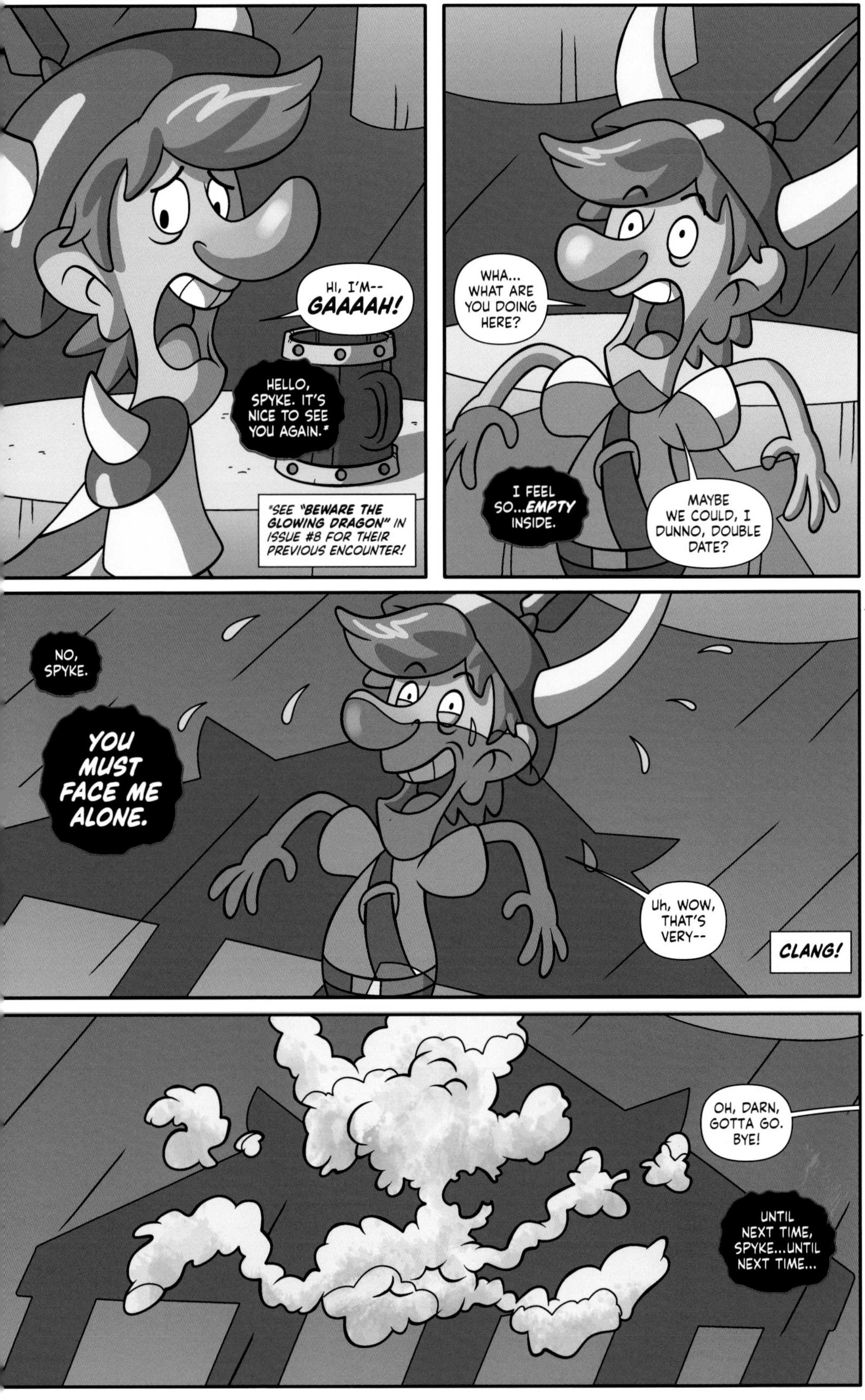
HI, I'M--
GAAAAH!
HELLO, SPYKE. IT'S NICE TO SEE YOU AGAIN.*
*SEE "BEWARE THE GLOWING DRAGON" IN ISSUE #8 FOR THEIR PREVIOUS ENCOUNTER!
WHA... WHAT ARE YOU DOING HERE?
I FEEL SO...EMPTY INSIDE.
MAYBE WE COULD, I DUNNO, DOUBLE DATE?
NO, SPYKE.
YOU MUST FACE ME ALONE.
UH, WOW, THAT'S VERY--
CLANG!
OH, DARN, GOTTA GO. BYE!
UNTIL NEXT TIME, SPYKE...UNTIL NEXT TIME...

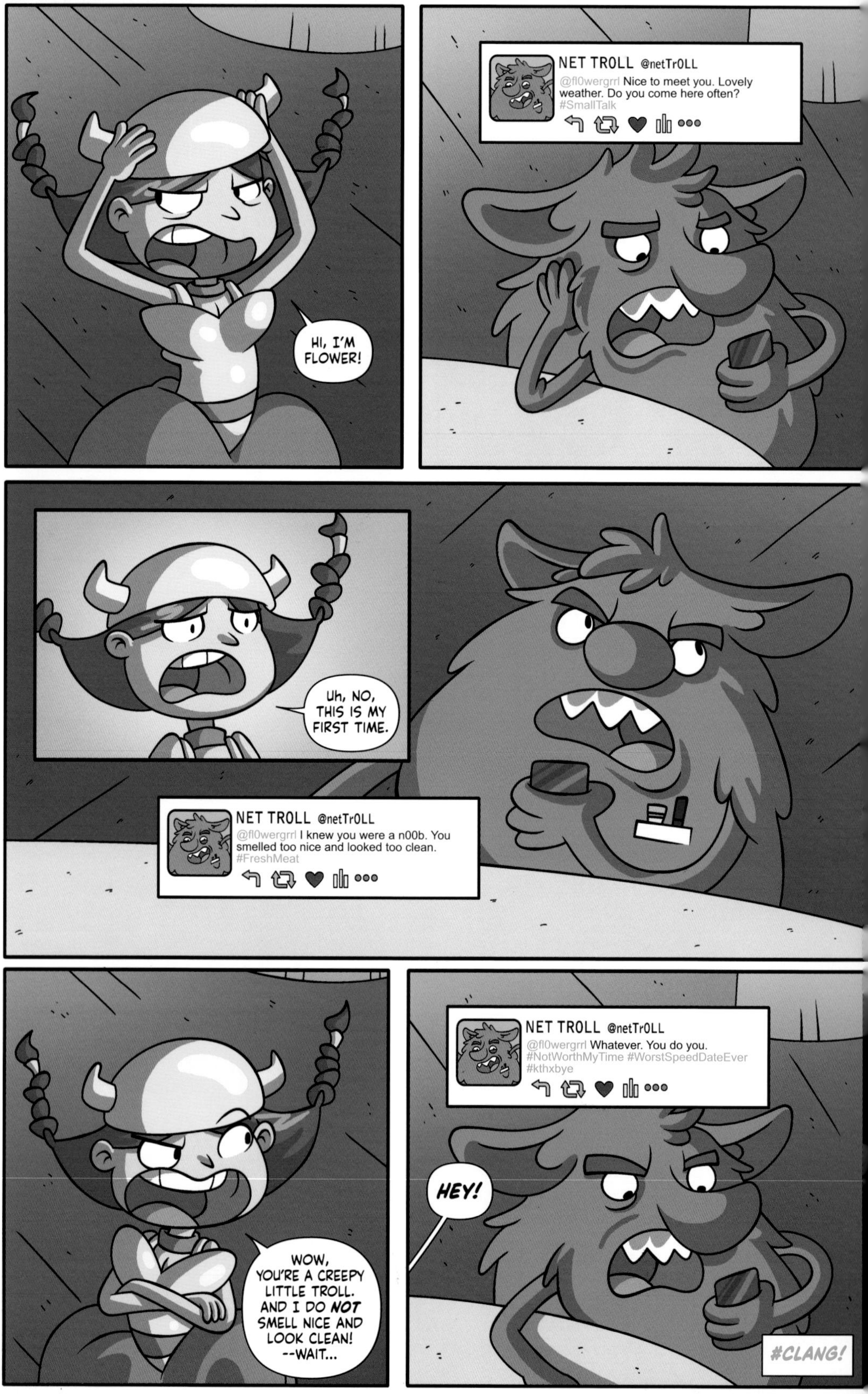

HI, I'M FLOWER!
NET TROLL @netTr0LL
@fl0wergrrl Nice to meet you. Lovely weather. Do you come here often? #SmallTalk
UH, NO, THIS IS MY FIRST TIME.
NET TROLL @netTr0LL
@fl0wergrrl I knew you were a n00b. You smelled too nice and looked too clean. #FreshMeat
WOW, YOU'RE A CREEPY LITTLE TROLL. AND I DO NOT SMELL NICE AND LOOK CLEAN! --WAIT...
NET TROLL @netTr0LL
@fl0wergrrl Whatever. You do you. #NotWorthMyTime #WorstSpeedDateEver #kthxbye
HEY!
#CLANG!

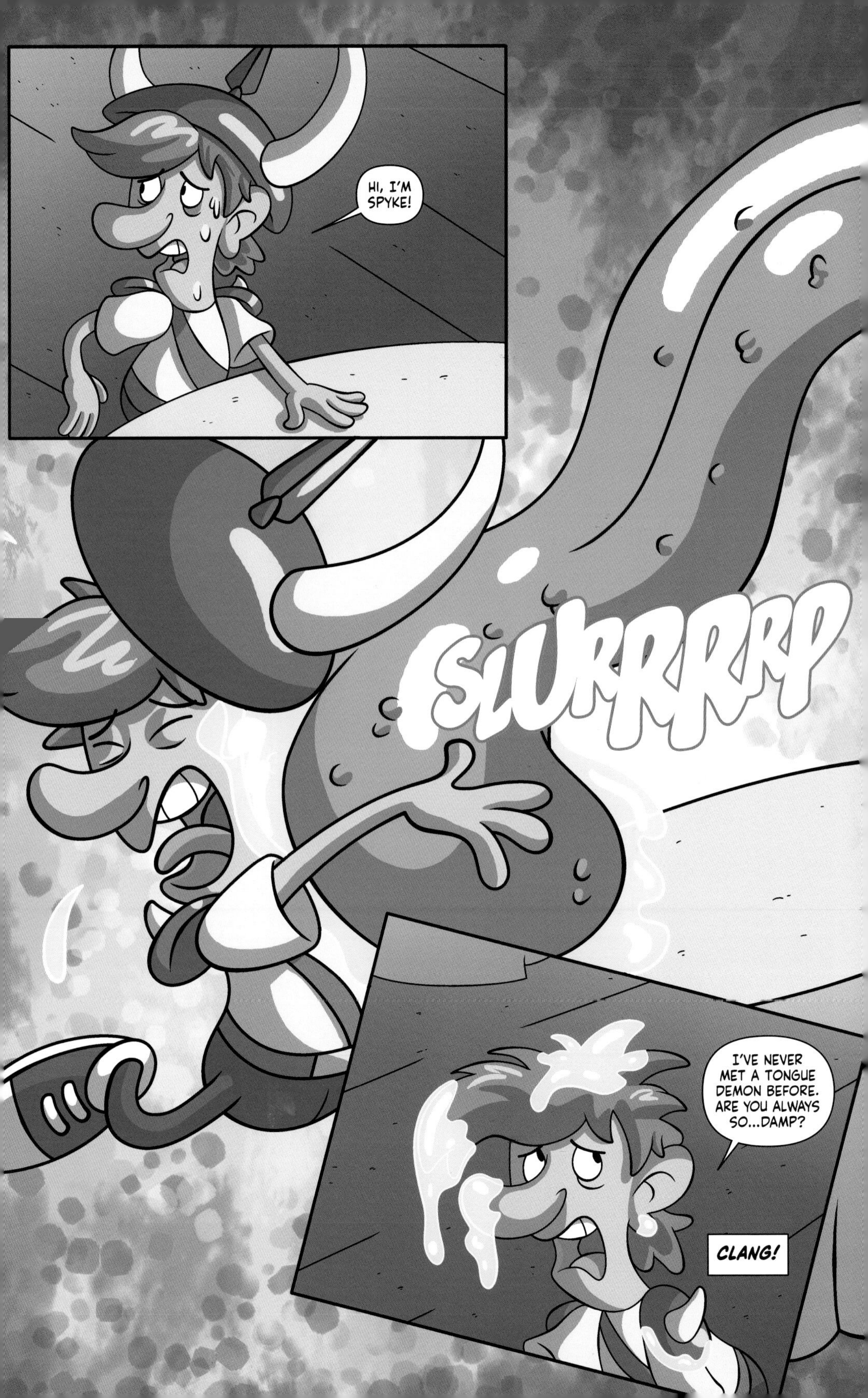
HI, I'M SPYKE!
SLURRRRP
I'VE NEVER MET A TONGUE DEMON BEFORE. ARE YOU ALWAYS SO...DAMP?
CLANG!

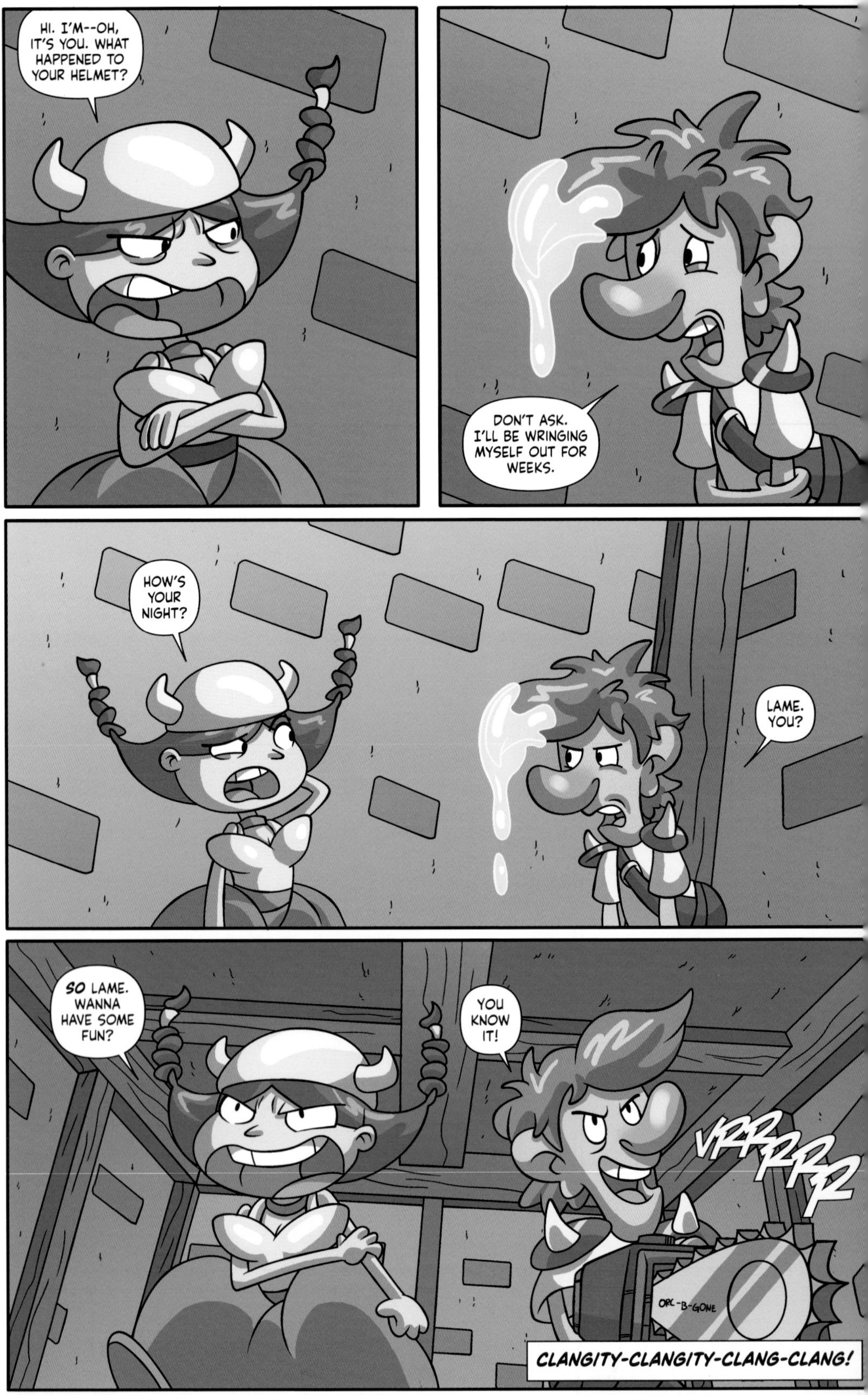
HI. I'M--OH, IT'S YOU. WHAT HAPPENED TO YOUR HELMET?
DON'T ASK. I'LL BE WRINGING MYSELF OUT FOR WEEKS.
HOW'S YOUR NIGHT?
LAME. YOU?
SO LAME. WANNA HAVE SOME FUN?
YOU KNOW IT!
VRRRRRR
ORC-B-GONE
CLANGITY-CLANGITY-CLANG-CLANG!

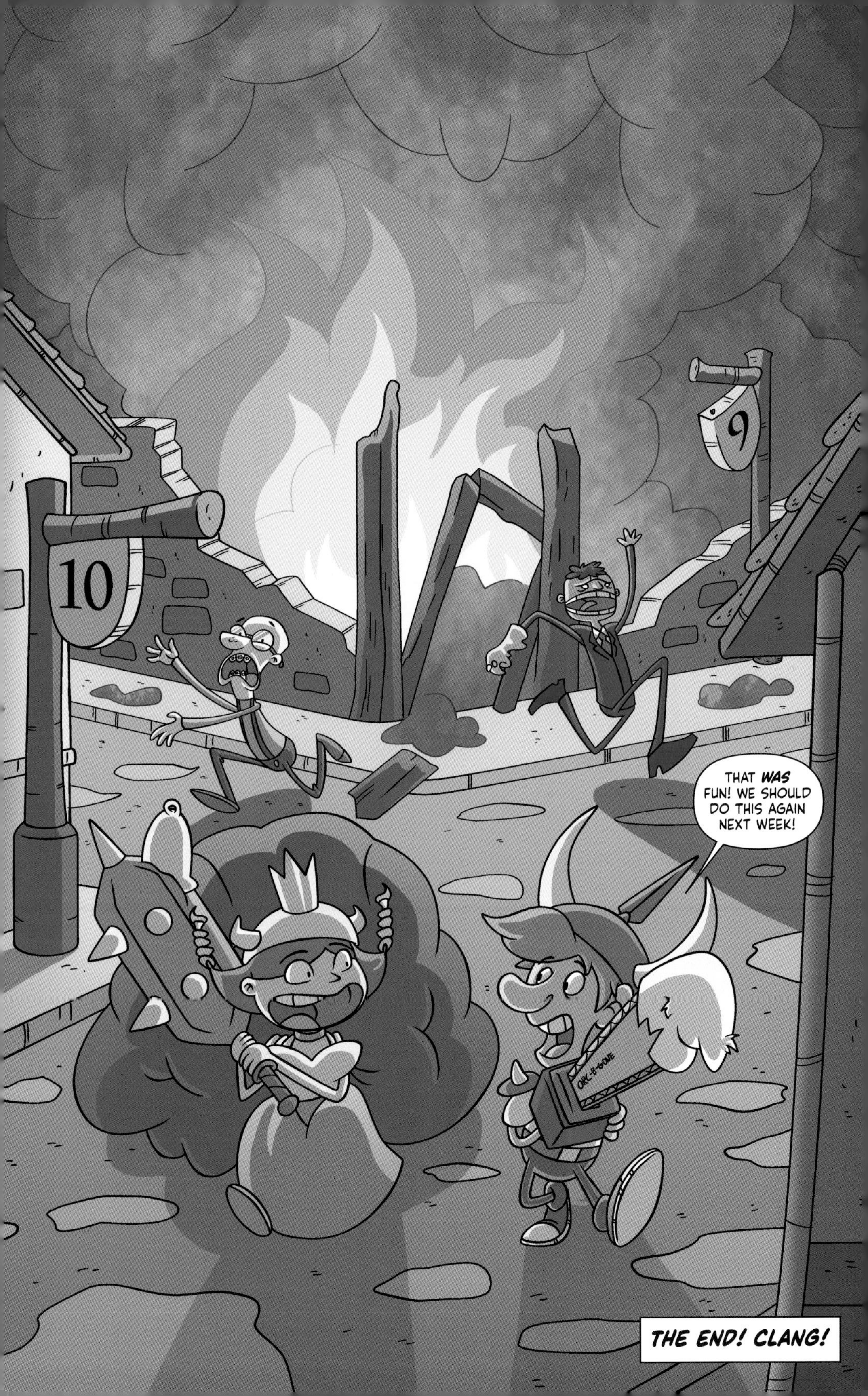
10
9
THAT WAS FUN! WE SHOULD DO THIS AGAIN NEXT WEEK!
ORC-B-GONE
THE END! CLANG!

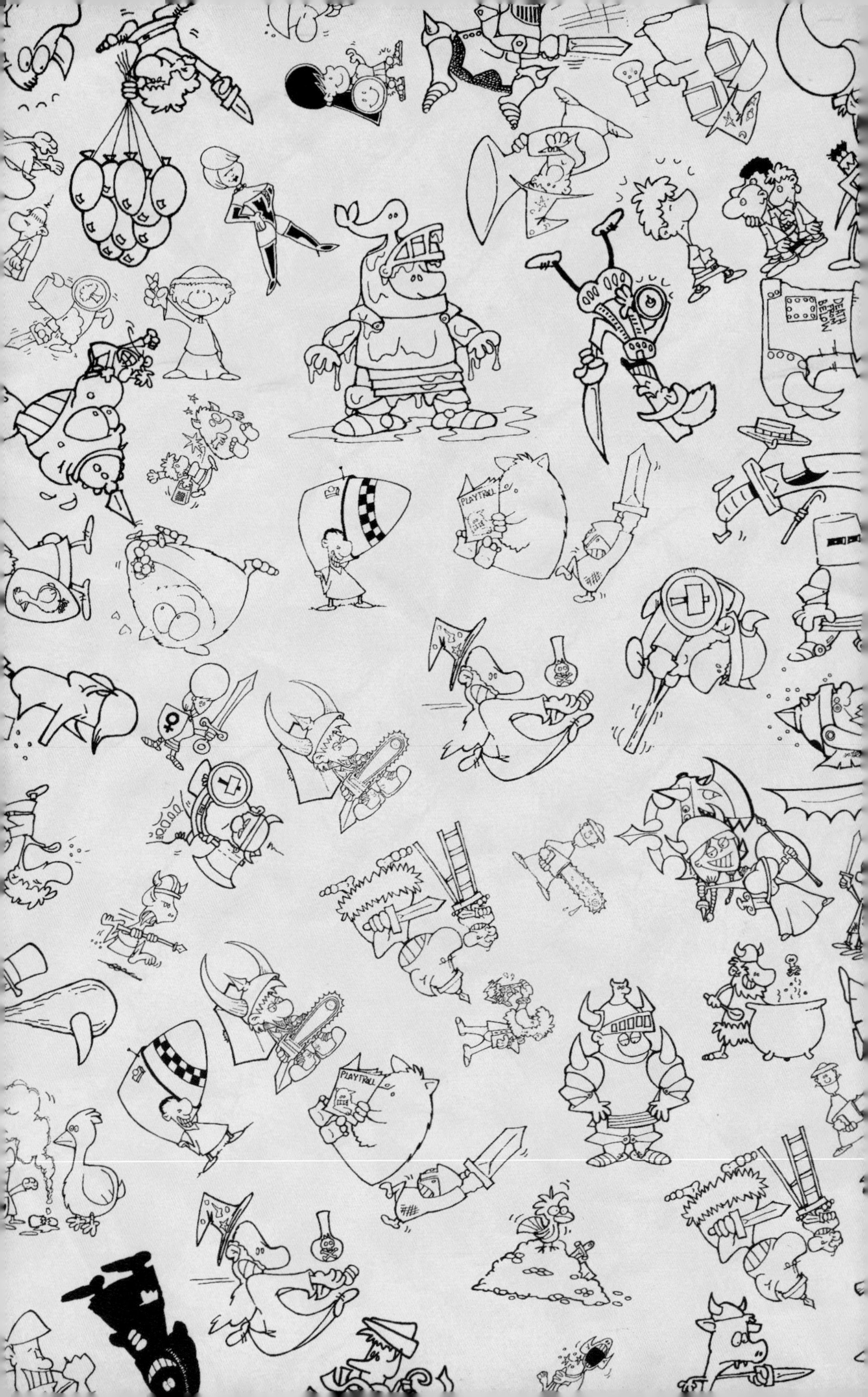
DEATH FROM BELOW
PLAYTROLL
PLAYTROLL

CHAPTER
TWENTY-FOUR

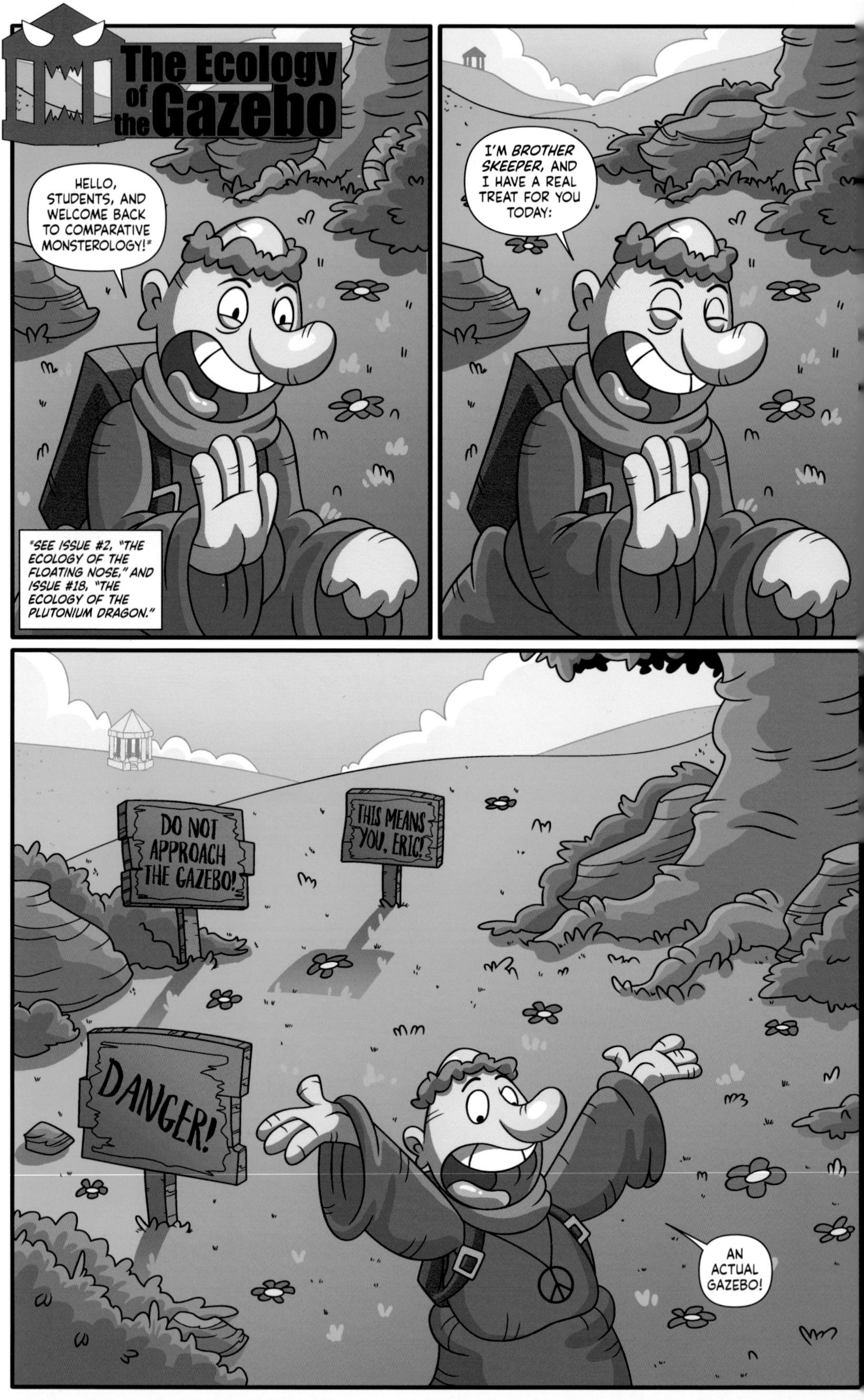
The Ecology of the Gazebo
HELLO, STUDENTS, AND WELCOME BACK TO COMPARATIVE MONSTEROLOGY!*
*SEE ISSUE #2, "THE ECOLOGY OF THE FLOATING NOSE," AND ISSUE #18, "THE ECOLOGY OF THE PLUTONIUM DRAGON."
I'M BROTHER SKEEPER, AND I HAVE A REAL TREAT FOR YOU TODAY:
DO NOT APPROACH THE GAZEBO!
THIS MEANS YOU, ERIC!
DANGER!
AN ACTUAL GAZEBO!

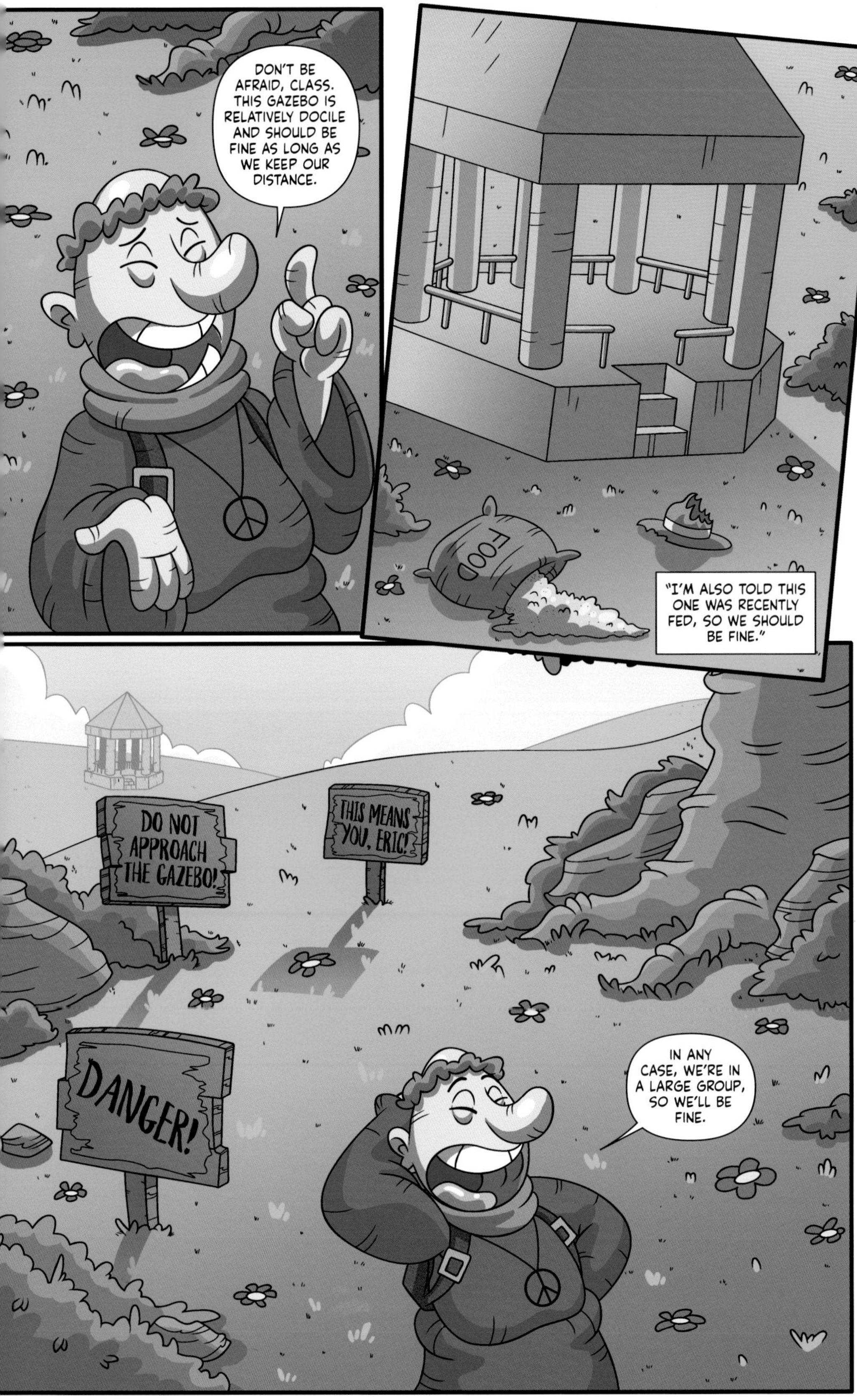
DON'T BE AFRAID, CLASS. THIS GAZEBO IS RELATIVELY DOCILE AND SHOULD BE FINE AS LONG AS WE KEEP OUR DISTANCE.
FOOD
"I'M ALSO TOLD THIS ONE WAS RECENTLY FED, SO WE SHOULD BE FINE."
DO NOT APPROACH THE GAZEBO!
THIS MEANS YOU, ERIC!
DANGER!
IN ANY CASE, WE'RE IN A LARGE GROUP, SO WE'LL BE FINE.

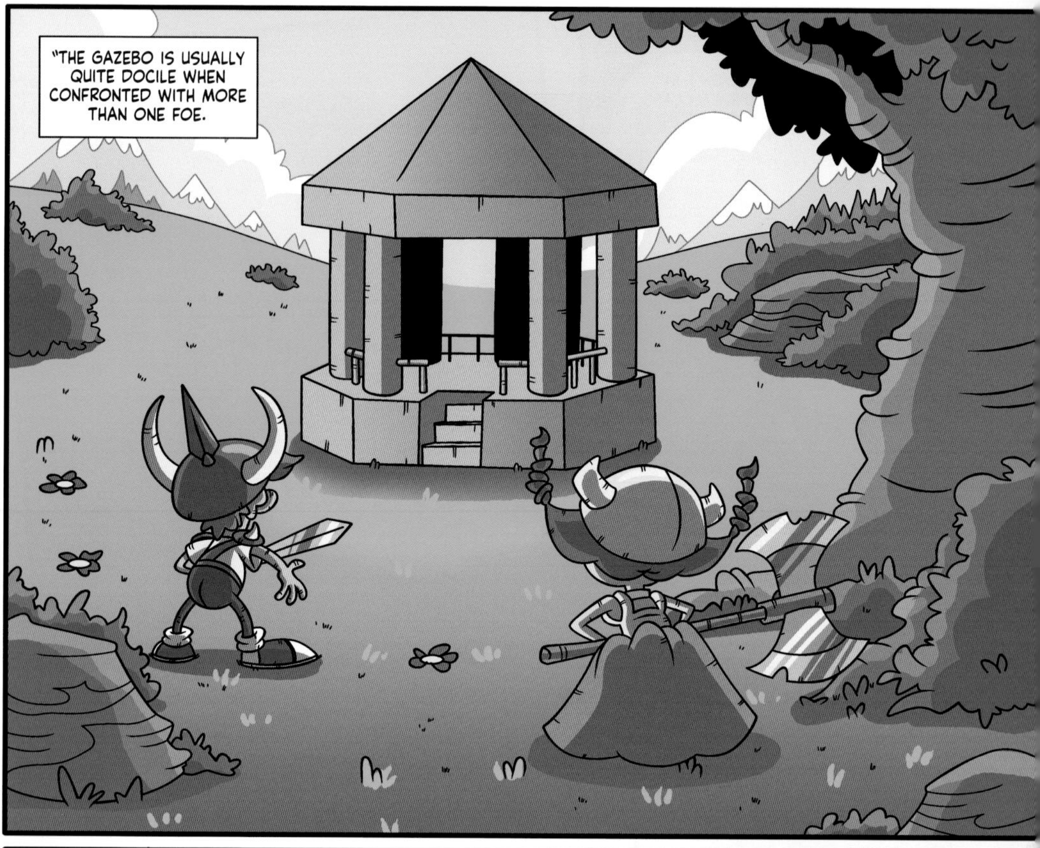
"THE GAZEBO IS USUALLY QUITE DOCILE WHEN CONFRONTED WITH MORE THAN ONE FOE.

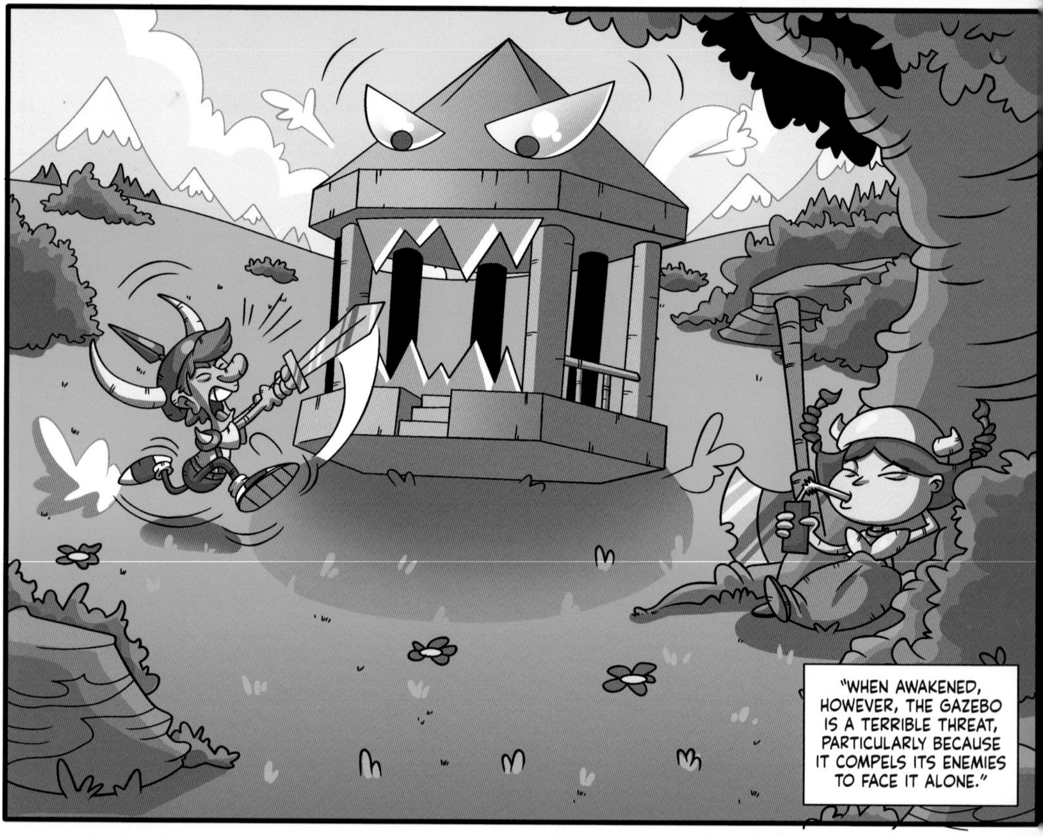
"WHEN AWAKENED, HOWEVER, THE GAZEBO IS A TERRIBLE THREAT, PARTICULARLY BECAUSE IT COMPELS ITS ENEMIES TO FACE IT ALONE."

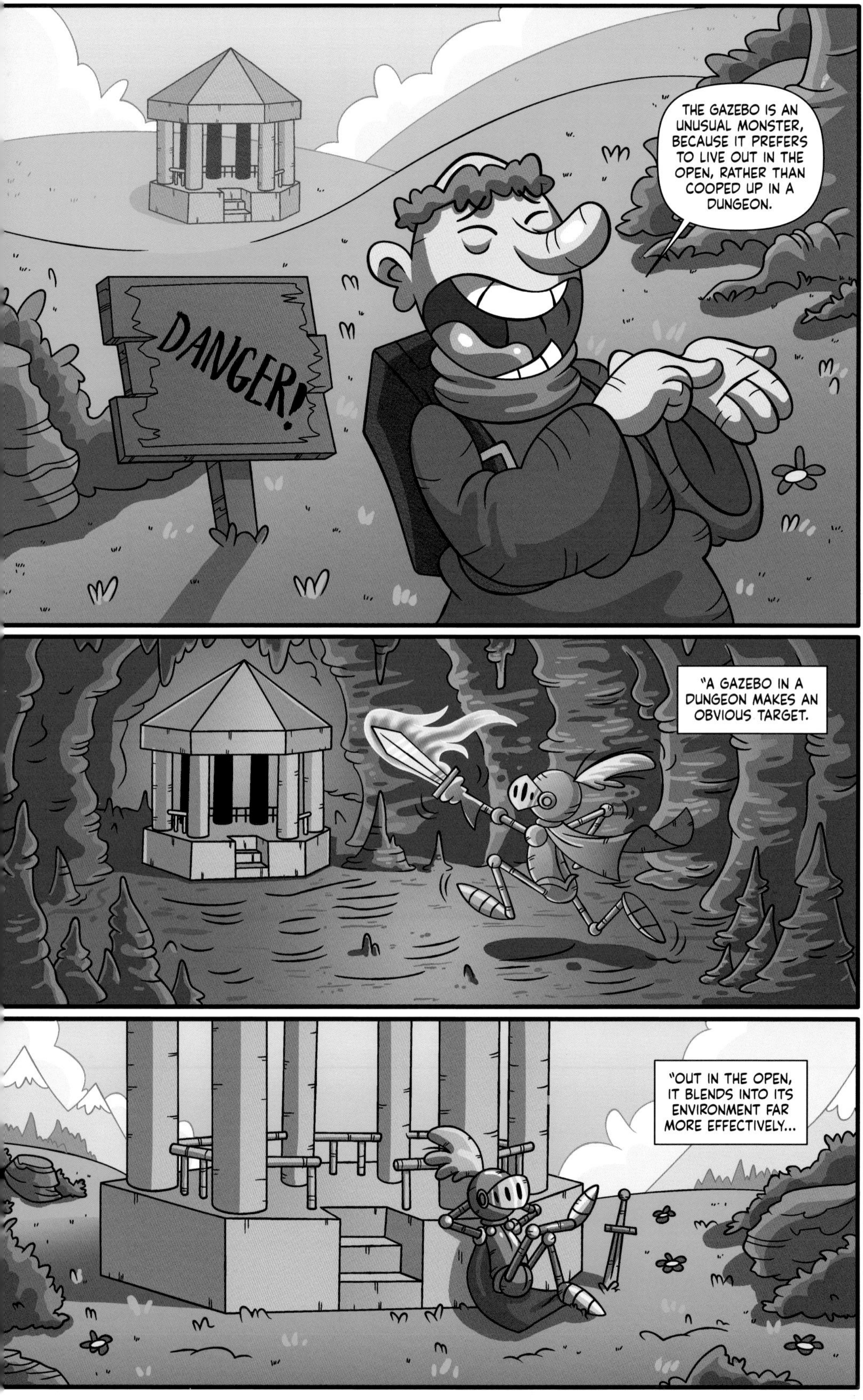
THE GAZEBO IS AN UNUSUAL MONSTER, BECAUSE IT PREFERS TO LIVE OUT IN THE OPEN, RATHER THAN COOPED UP IN A DUNGEON.
DANGER!
"A GAZEBO IN A DUNGEON MAKES AN OBVIOUS TARGET.
"OUT IN THE OPEN, IT BLENDS INTO ITS ENVIRONMENT FAR MORE EFFECTIVELY...

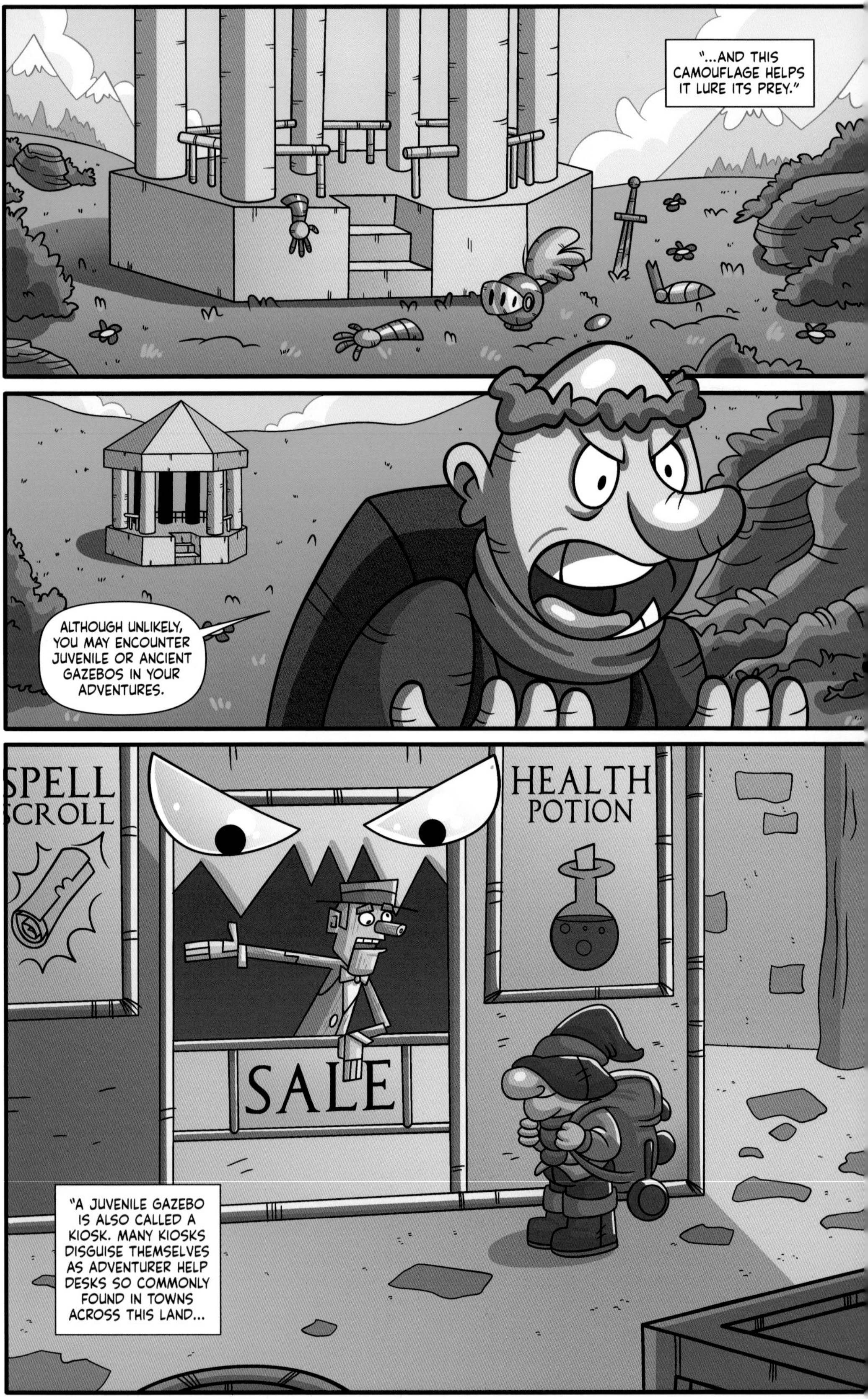
"...AND THIS CAMOUFLAGE HELPS IT LURE ITS PREY."
ALTHOUGH UNLIKELY, YOU MAY ENCOUNTER JUVENILE OR ANCIENT GAZEBOS IN YOUR ADVENTURES.
SPELL SCROLL
HEALTH POTION
SALE
"A JUVENILE GAZEBO IS ALSO CALLED A KIOSK. MANY KIOSKS DISGUISE THEMSELVES AS ADVENTURER HELP DESKS SO COMMONLY FOUND IN TOWNS ACROSS THIS LAND...

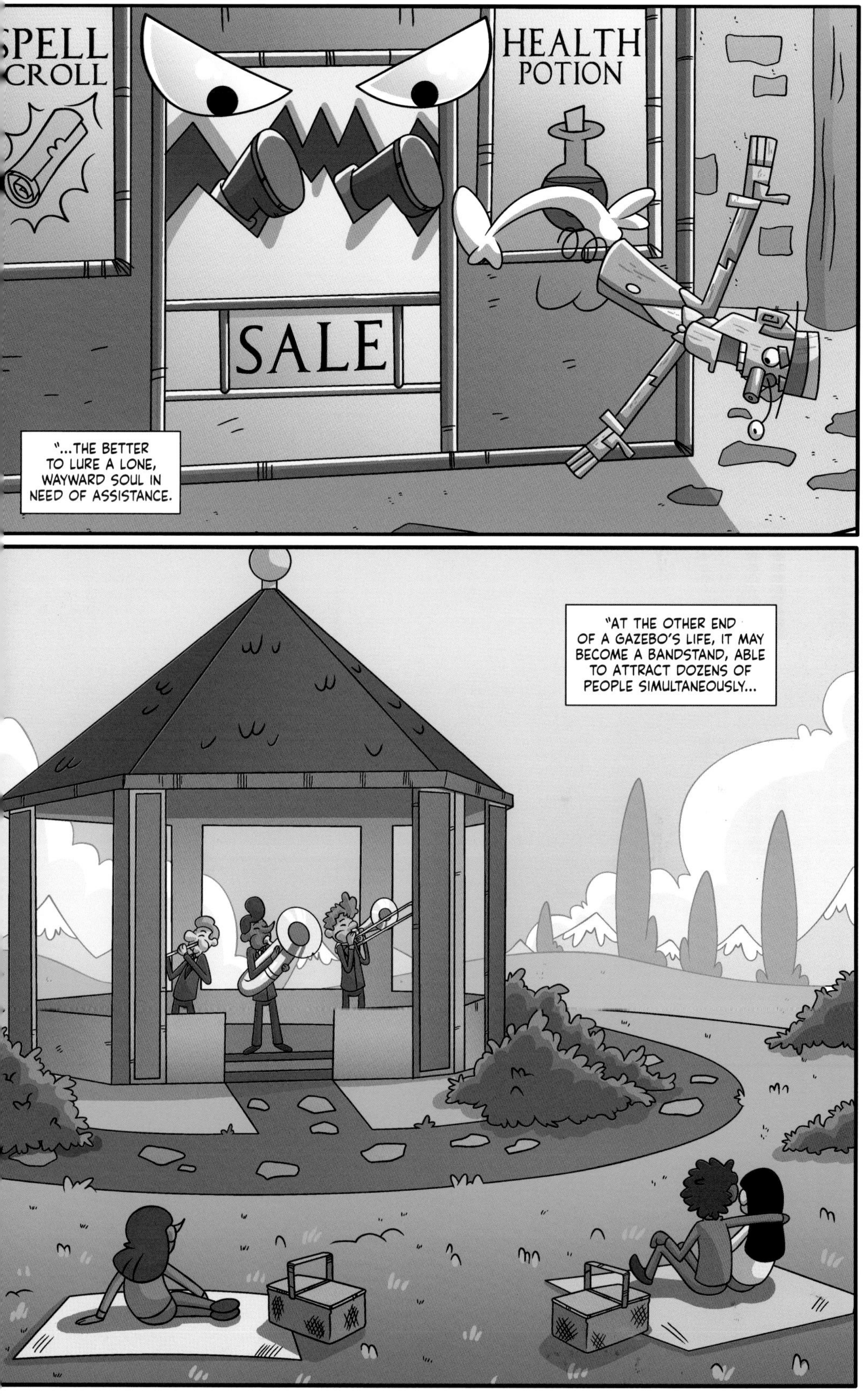
SPELL
CROLL
HEALTH
POTION
SALE
"...THE BETTER TO LURE A LONE, WAYWARD SOUL IN NEED OF ASSISTANCE.
"AT THE OTHER END OF A GAZEBO'S LIFE, IT MAY BECOME A BANDSTAND, ABLE TO ATTRACT DOZENS OF PEOPLE SIMULTANEOUSLY...

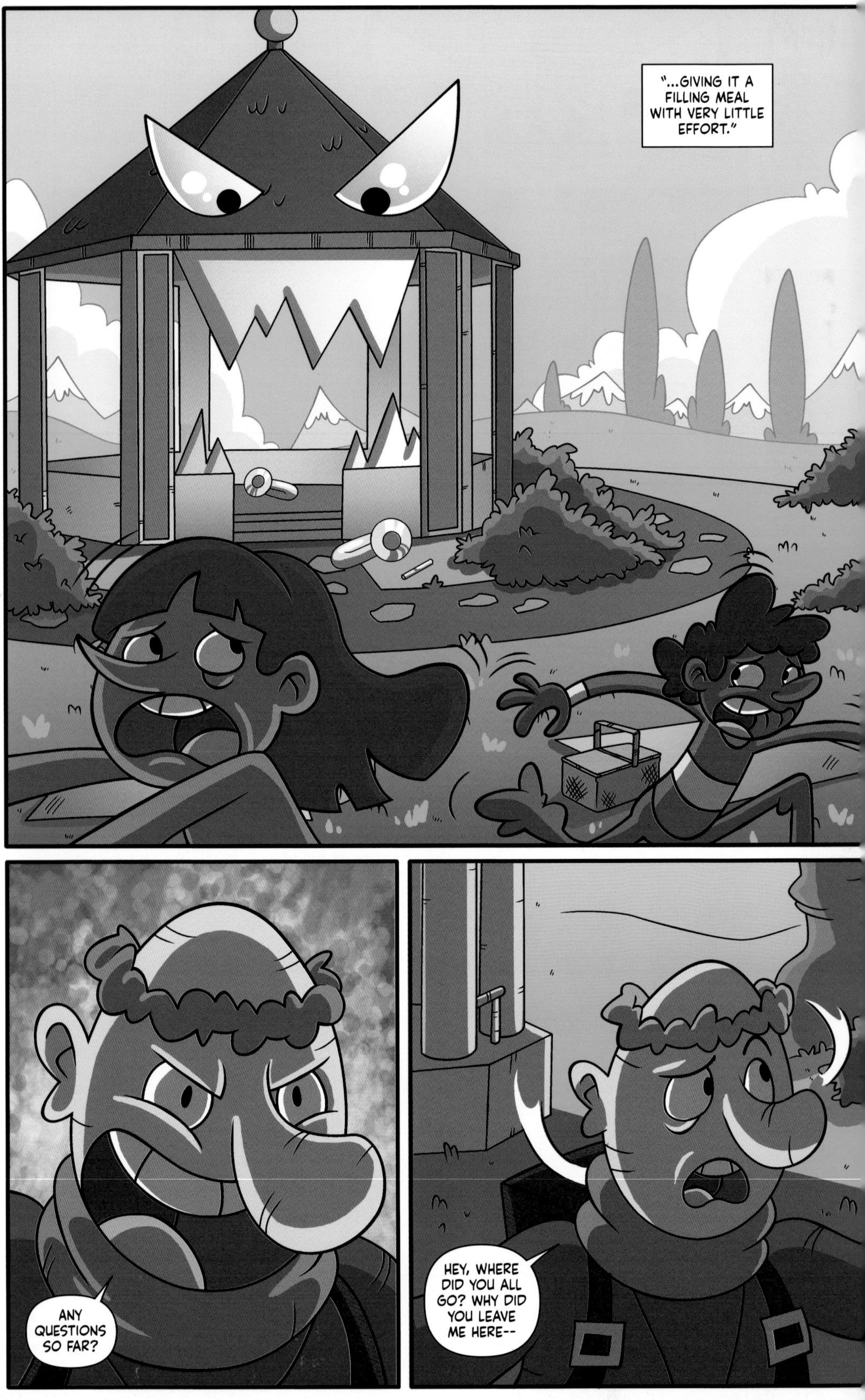
"...GIVING IT A FILLING MEAL WITH VERY LITTLE EFFORT."
ANY QUESTIONS SO FAR?
HEY, WHERE DID YOU ALL GO? WHY DID YOU LEAVE ME HERE--

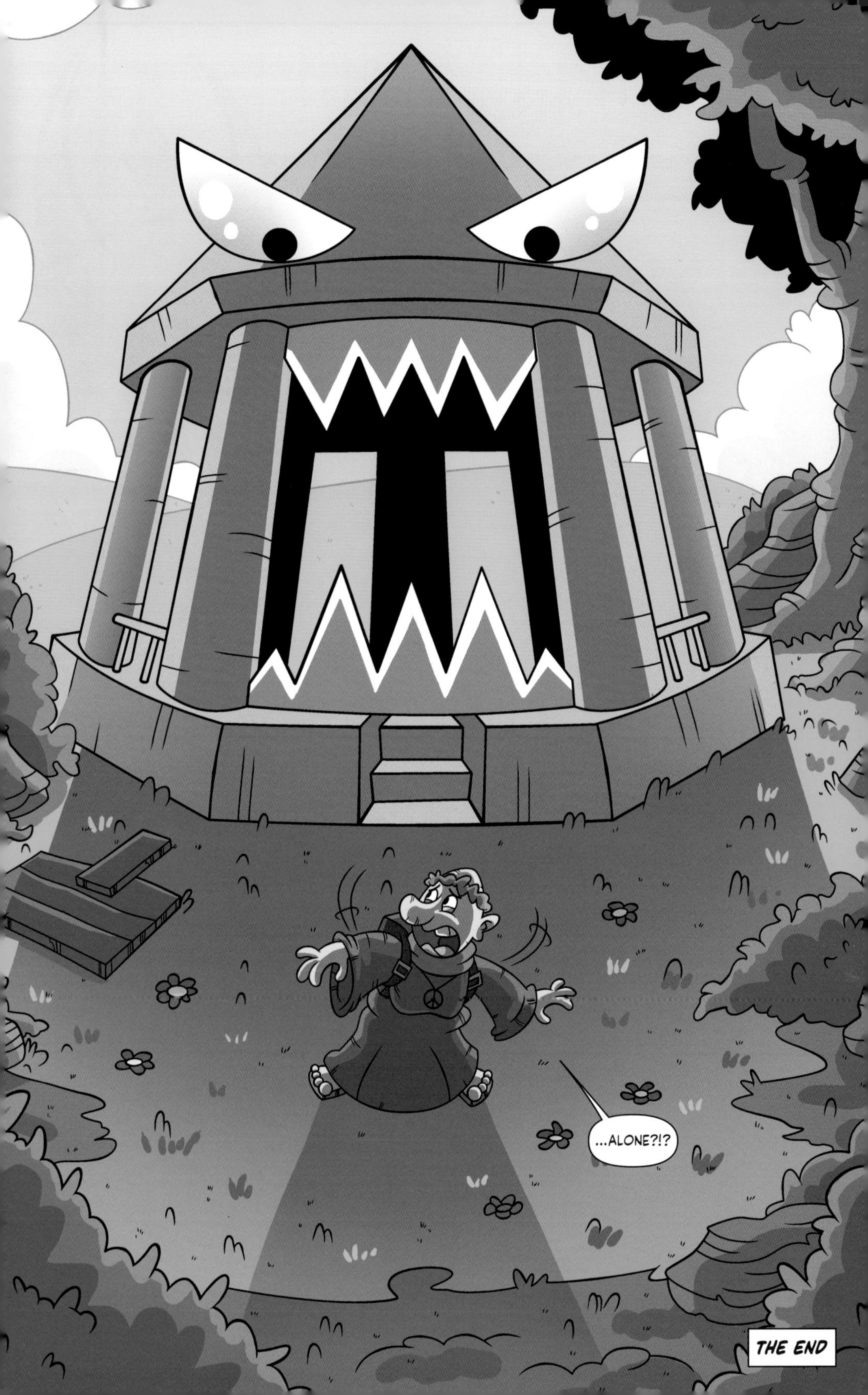
...ALONE?!?
THE END

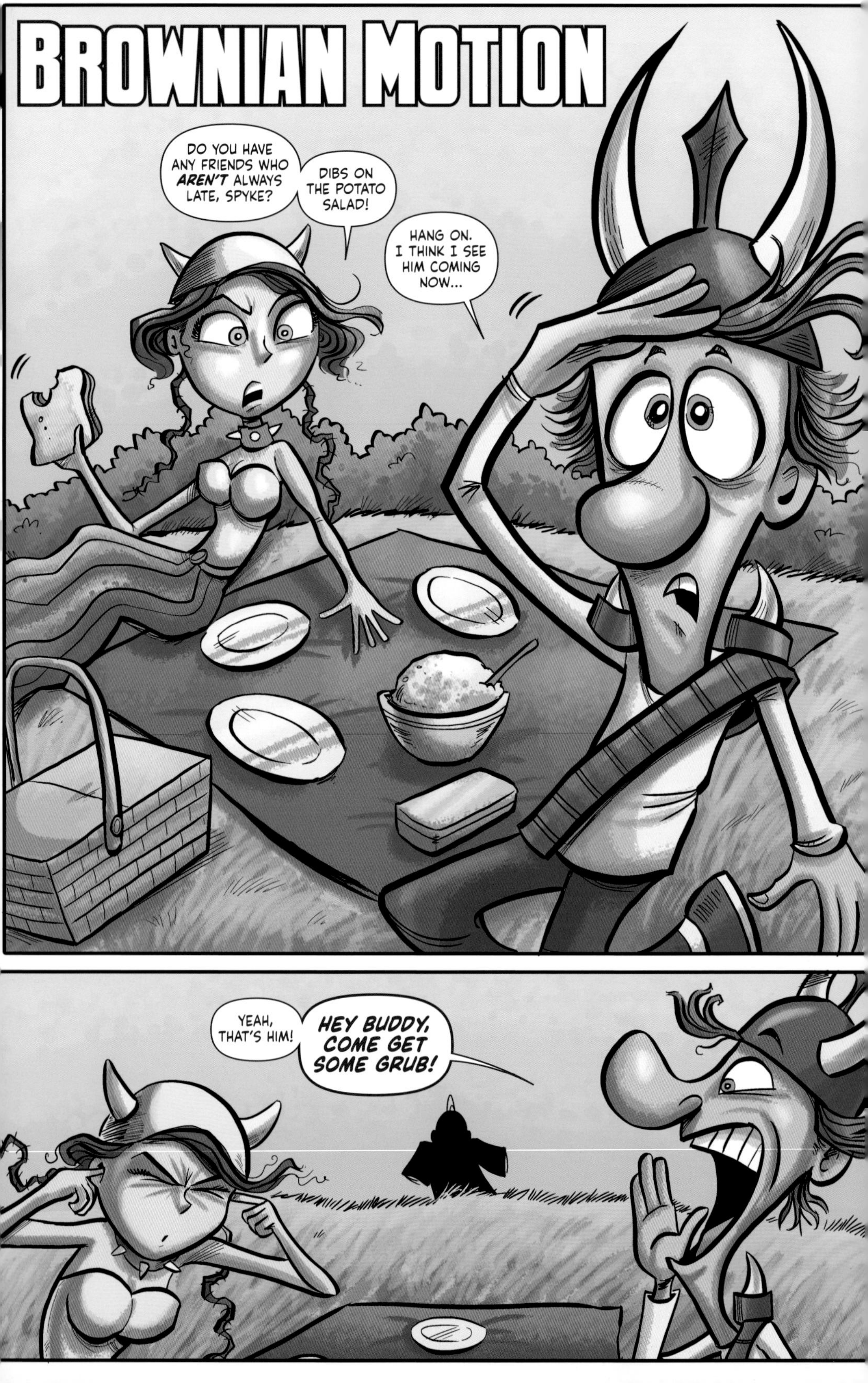
BROWNIAN MOTION
DO YOU HAVE ANY FRIENDS WHO ***AREN'T*** ALWAYS LATE, SPYKE?
DIBS ON THE POTATO SALAD!
HANG ON. I THINK I SEE HIM COMING NOW...
YEAH, THAT'S HIM!
HEY BUDDY, COME GET SOME GRUB!

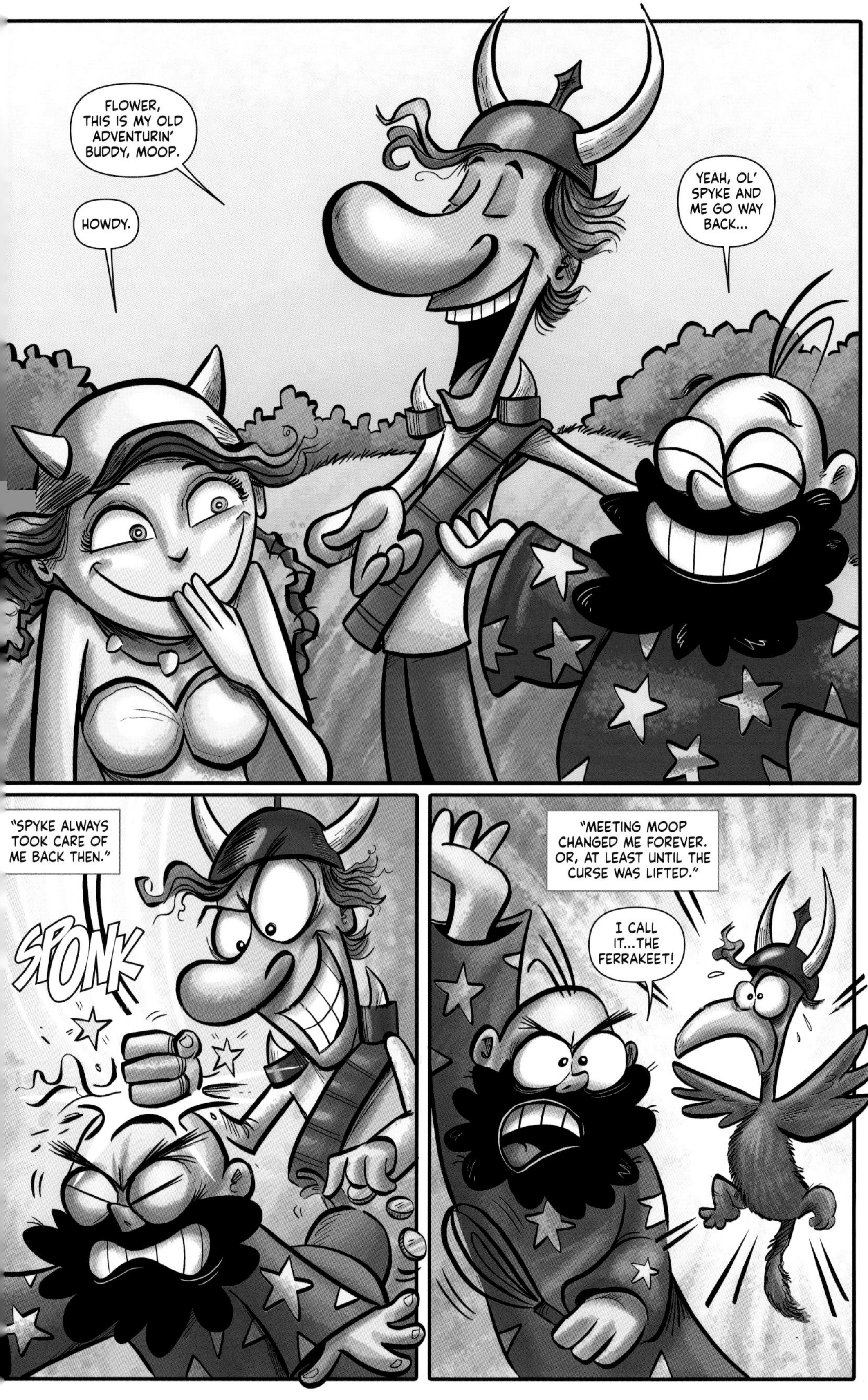
FLOWER, THIS IS MY OLD ADVENTURIN' BUDDY, MOOP.
HOWDY.
YEAH, OL' SPYKE AND ME GO WAY BACK...
"SPYKE ALWAYS TOOK CARE OF ME BACK THEN."
SPONK
"MEETING MOOP CHANGED ME FOREVER. OR, AT LEAST UNTIL THE CURSE WAS LIFTED."
I CALL IT...THE FERRAKEET!

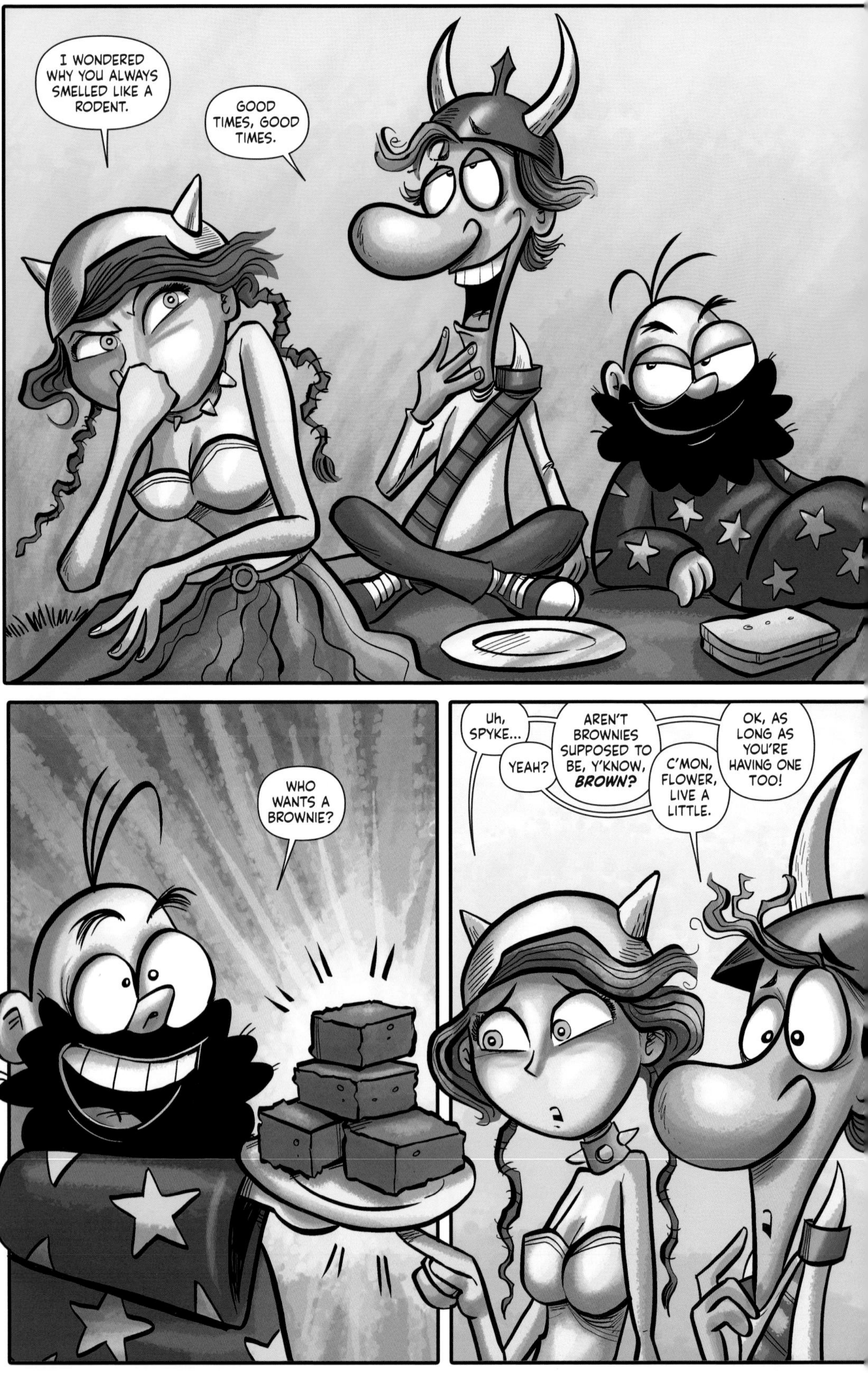
I WONDERED WHY YOU ALWAYS SMELLED LIKE A RODENT.
GOOD TIMES, GOOD TIMES.
WHO WANTS A BROWNIE?
Uh, SPYKE...
YEAH?
AREN'T BROWNIES SUPPOSED TO BE, Y'KNOW, **BROWN?**
C'MON, FLOWER, LIVE A LITTLE.
OK, AS LONG AS YOU'RE HAVING ONE TOO!

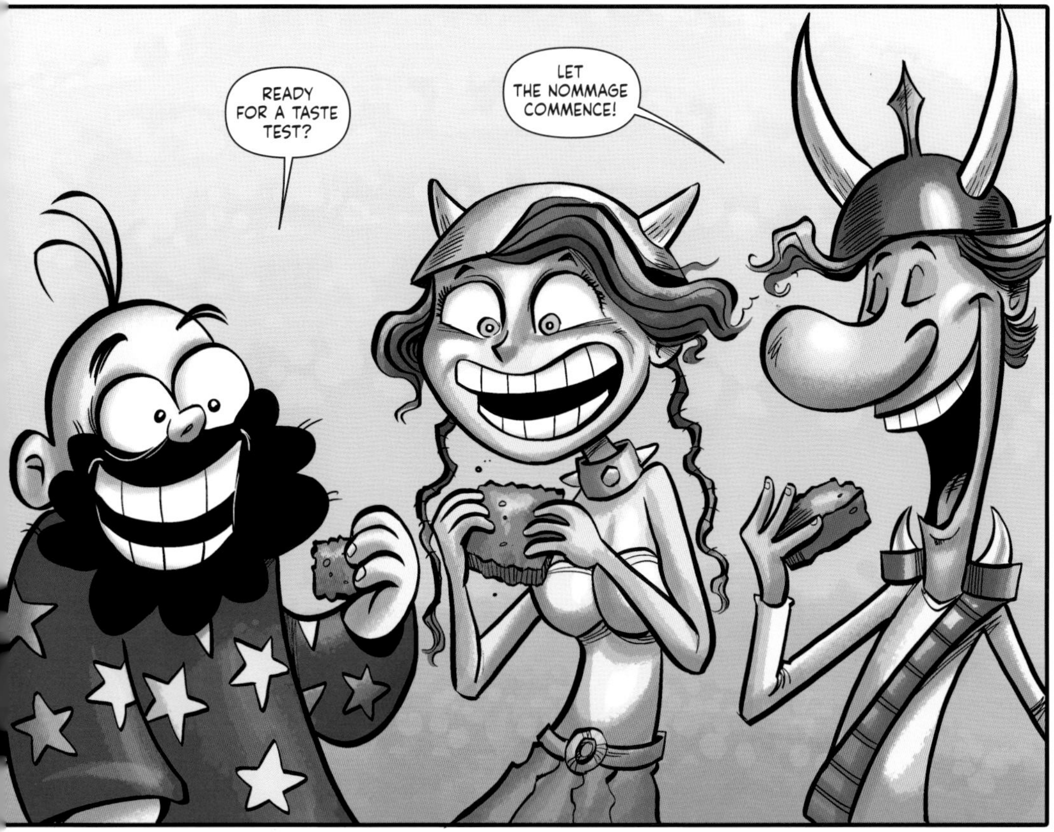
READY FOR A TASTE TEST?
LET THE NOMMAGE COMMENCE!
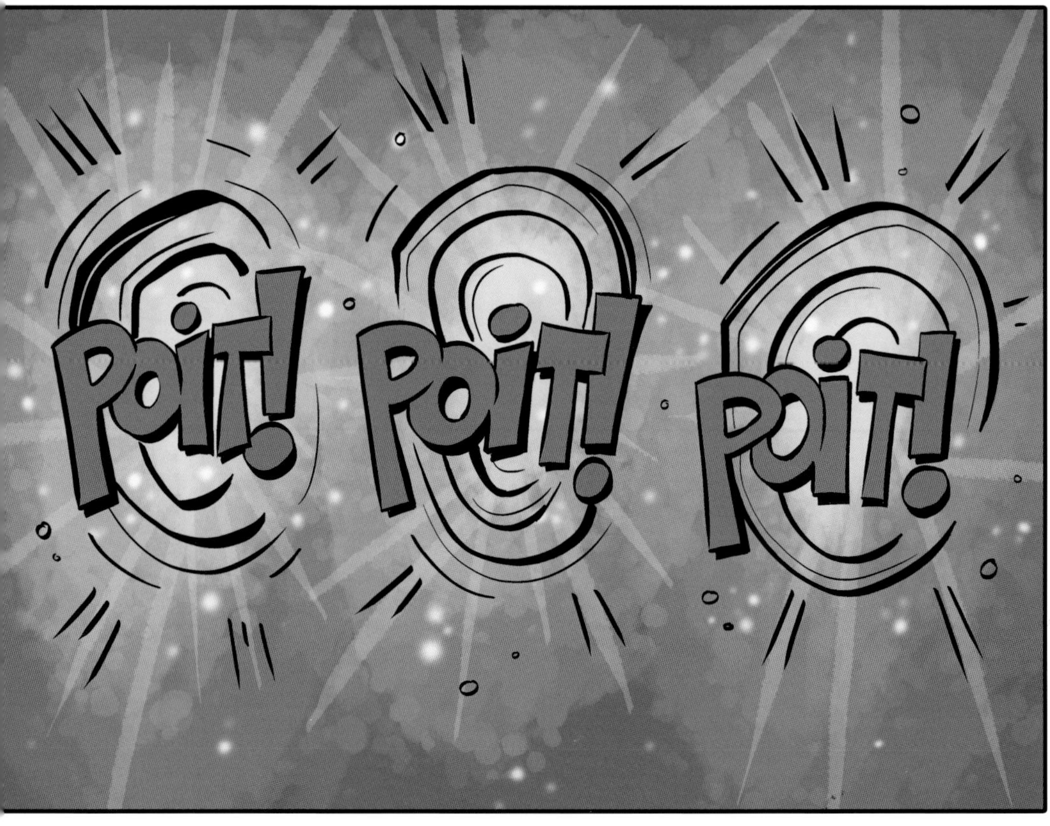
POIT! POIT! POIT!

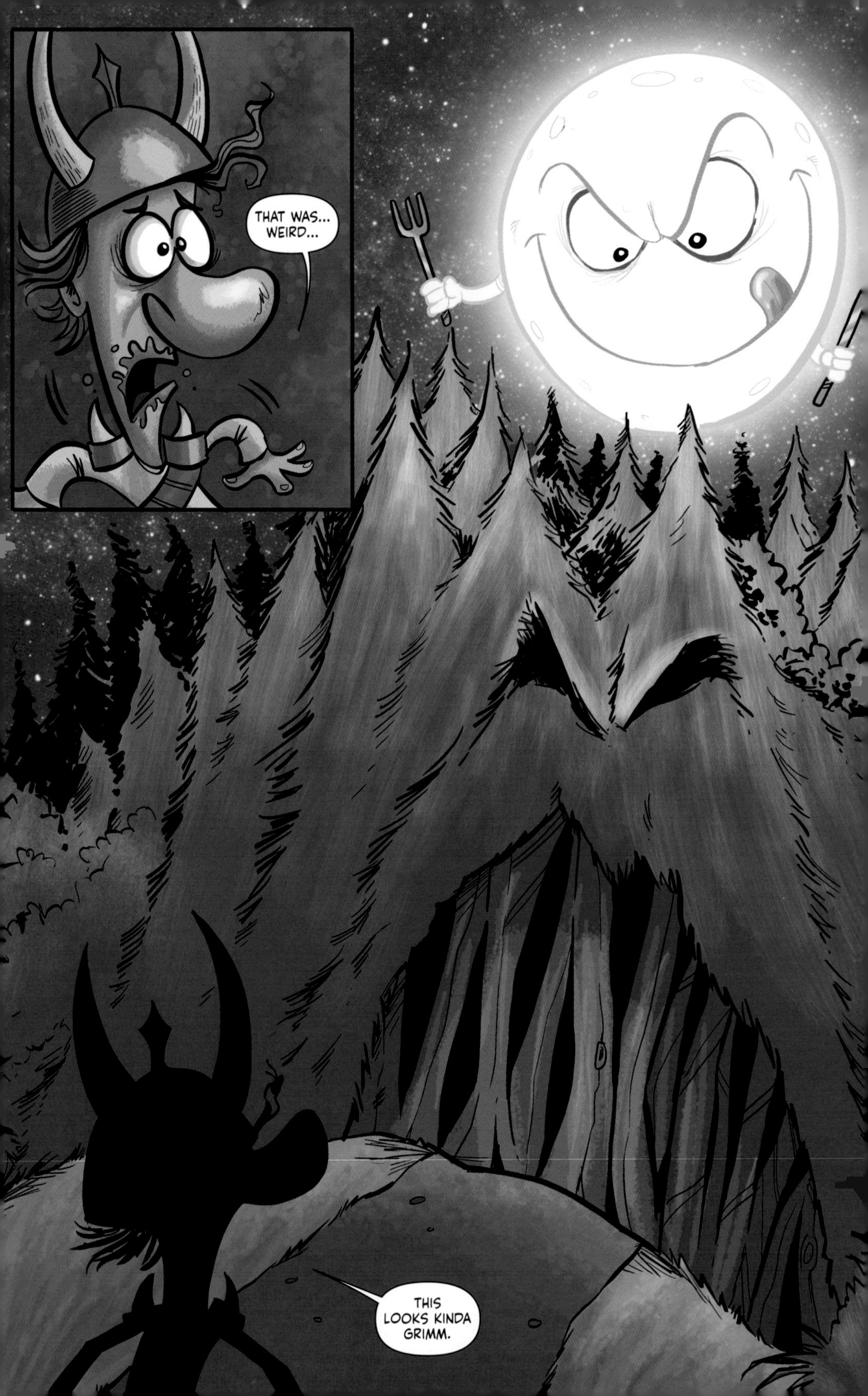
THAT WAS... WEIRD...
THIS LOOKS KINDA GRIMM.

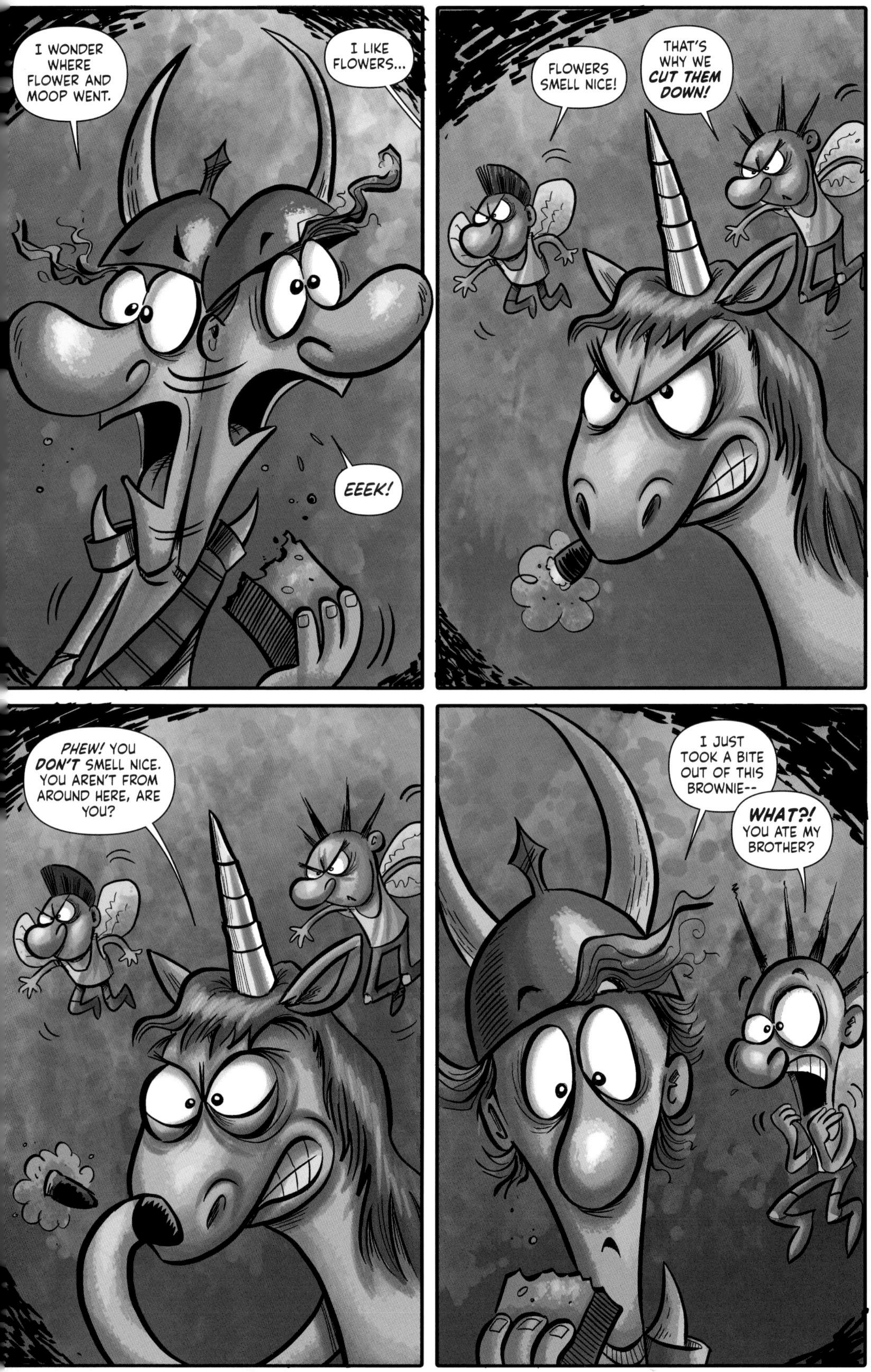
I WONDER WHERE FLOWER AND MOOP WENT.
I LIKE FLOWERS...
EEEK!
FLOWERS SMELL NICE!
THAT'S WHY WE *CUT THEM DOWN!*
PHEW! YOU *DON'T* SMELL NICE. YOU AREN'T FROM AROUND HERE, ARE YOU?
I JUST TOOK A BITE OUT OF THIS BROWNIE--
WHAT?! YOU ATE MY BROTHER?

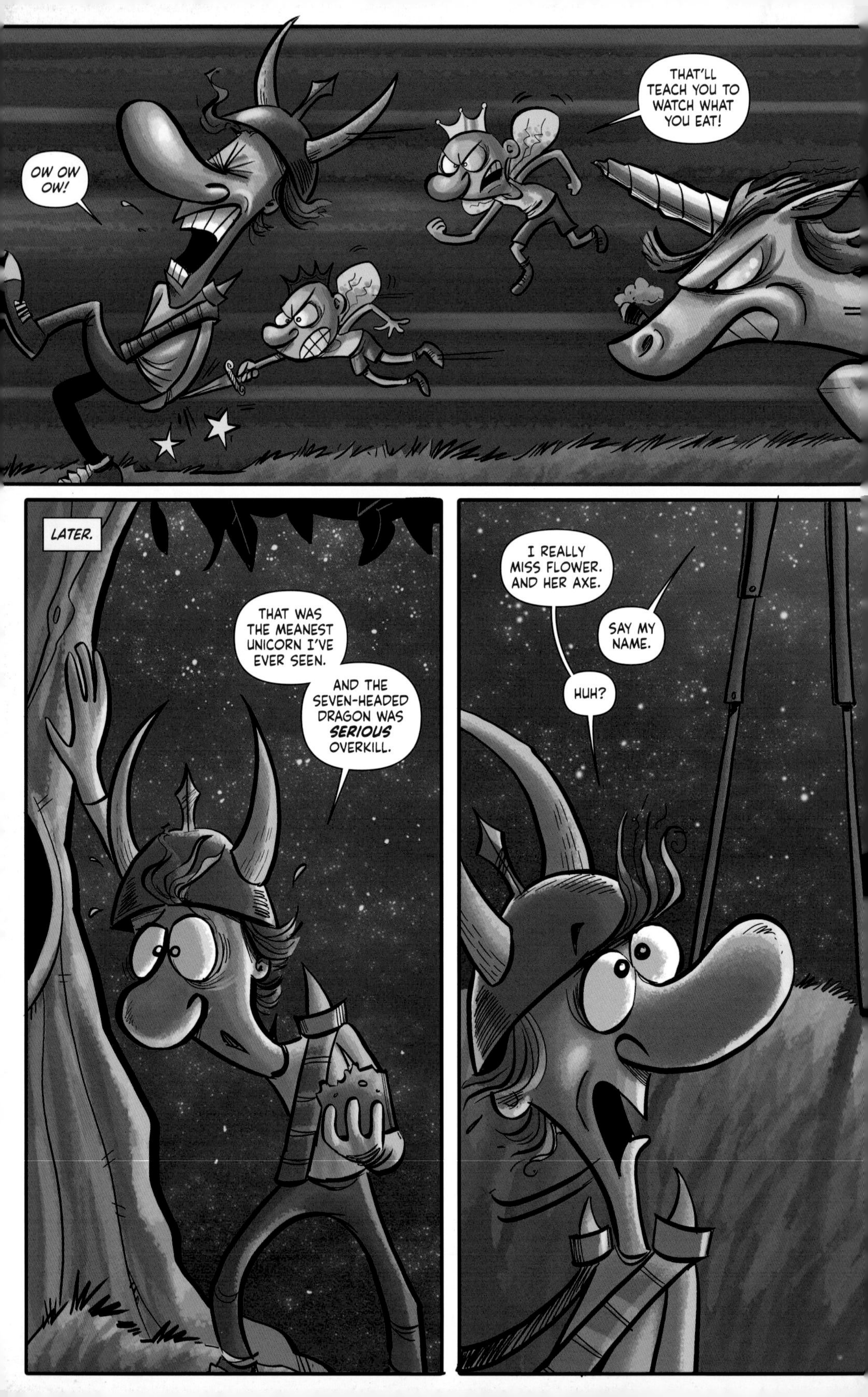
OW OW OW!
THAT'LL TEACH YOU TO WATCH WHAT YOU EAT!
LATER.
THAT WAS THE MEANEST UNICORN I'VE EVER SEEN.
AND THE SEVEN-HEADED DRAGON WAS SERIOUS OVERKILL.
I REALLY MISS FLOWER. AND HER AXE.
SAY MY NAME.
HUH?

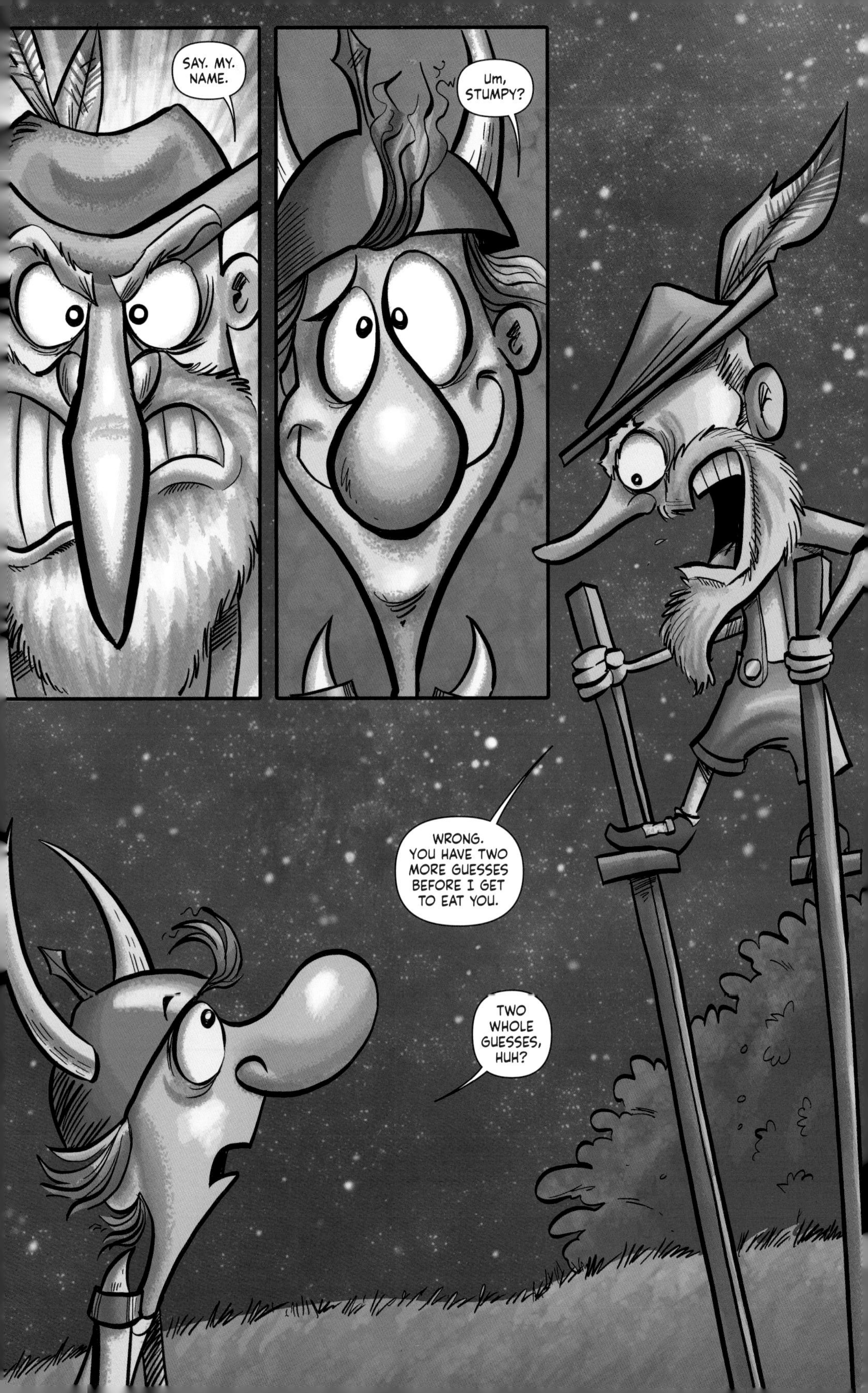
SAY. MY. NAME.
Um, STUMPY?
WRONG. YOU HAVE TWO MORE GUESSES BEFORE I GET TO EAT YOU.
TWO WHOLE GUESSES, HUH?

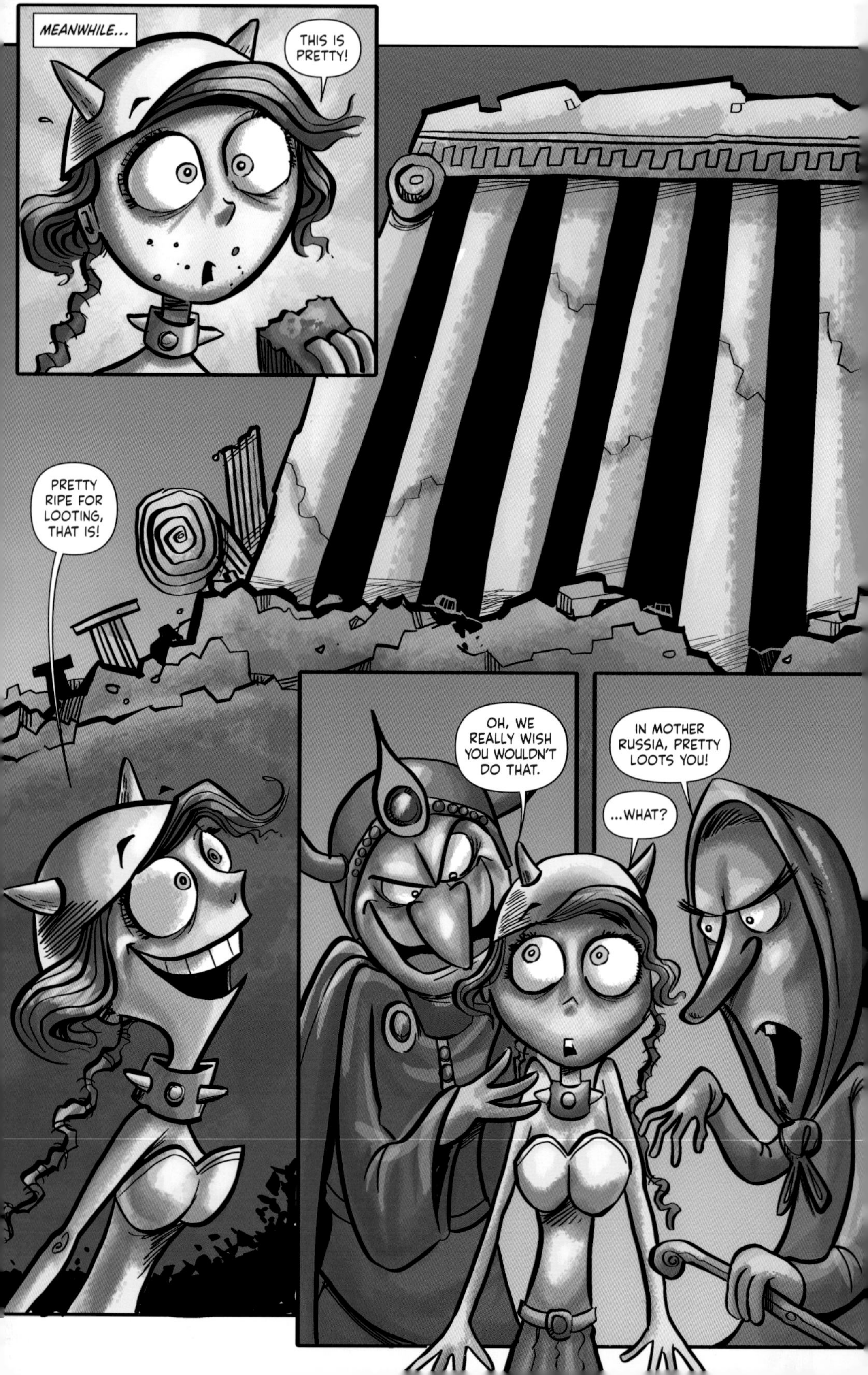
MEANWHILE...
THIS IS PRETTY!
PRETTY RIPE FOR LOOTING, THAT IS!
OH, WE REALLY WISH YOU WOULDN'T DO THAT.
IN MOTHER RUSSIA, PRETTY LOOTS YOU!
...WHAT?

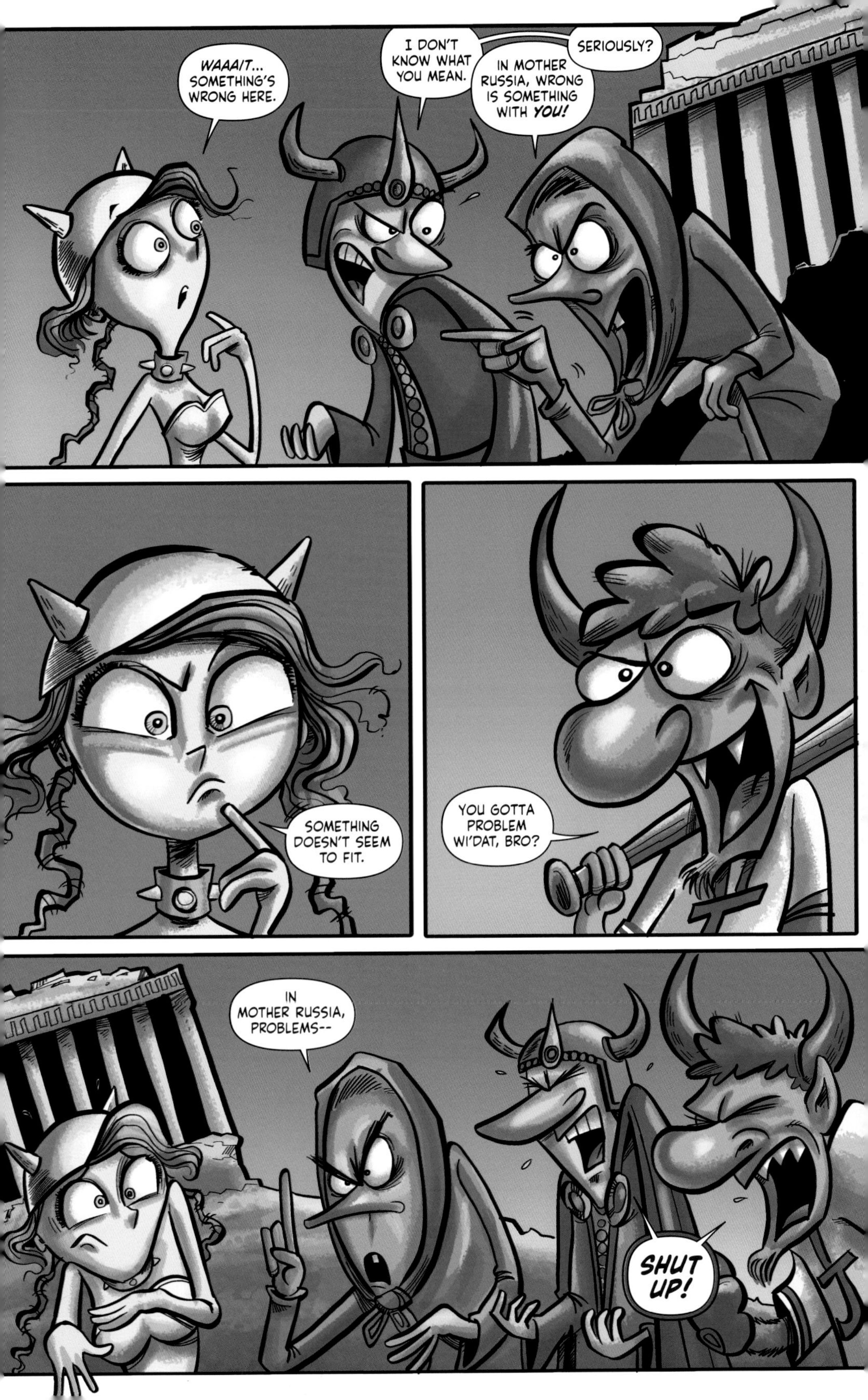
WAAAIT... SOMETHING'S WRONG HERE.
I DON'T KNOW WHAT YOU MEAN.
SERIOUSLY?
IN MOTHER RUSSIA, WRONG IS SOMETHING WITH YOU!
SOMETHING DOESN'T SEEM TO FIT.
YOU GOTTA PROBLEM WI'DAT, BRO?
IN MOTHER RUSSIA, PROBLEMS--
SHUT UP!

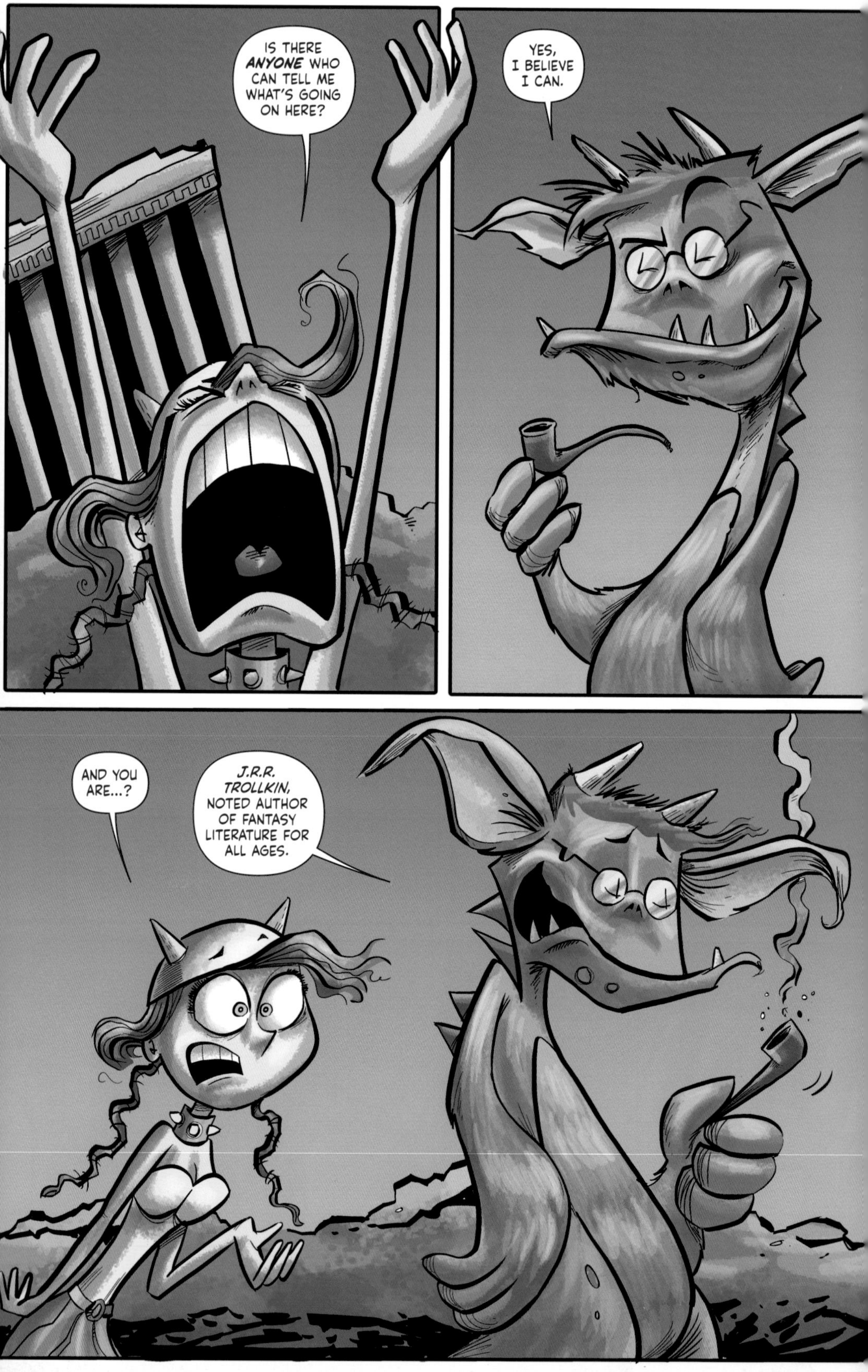
IS THERE ANYONE WHO CAN TELL ME WHAT'S GOING ON HERE?
YES, I BELIEVE I CAN.
AND YOU ARE...?
J.R.R. TROLLKIN, NOTED AUTHOR OF FANTASY LITERATURE FOR ALL AGES.

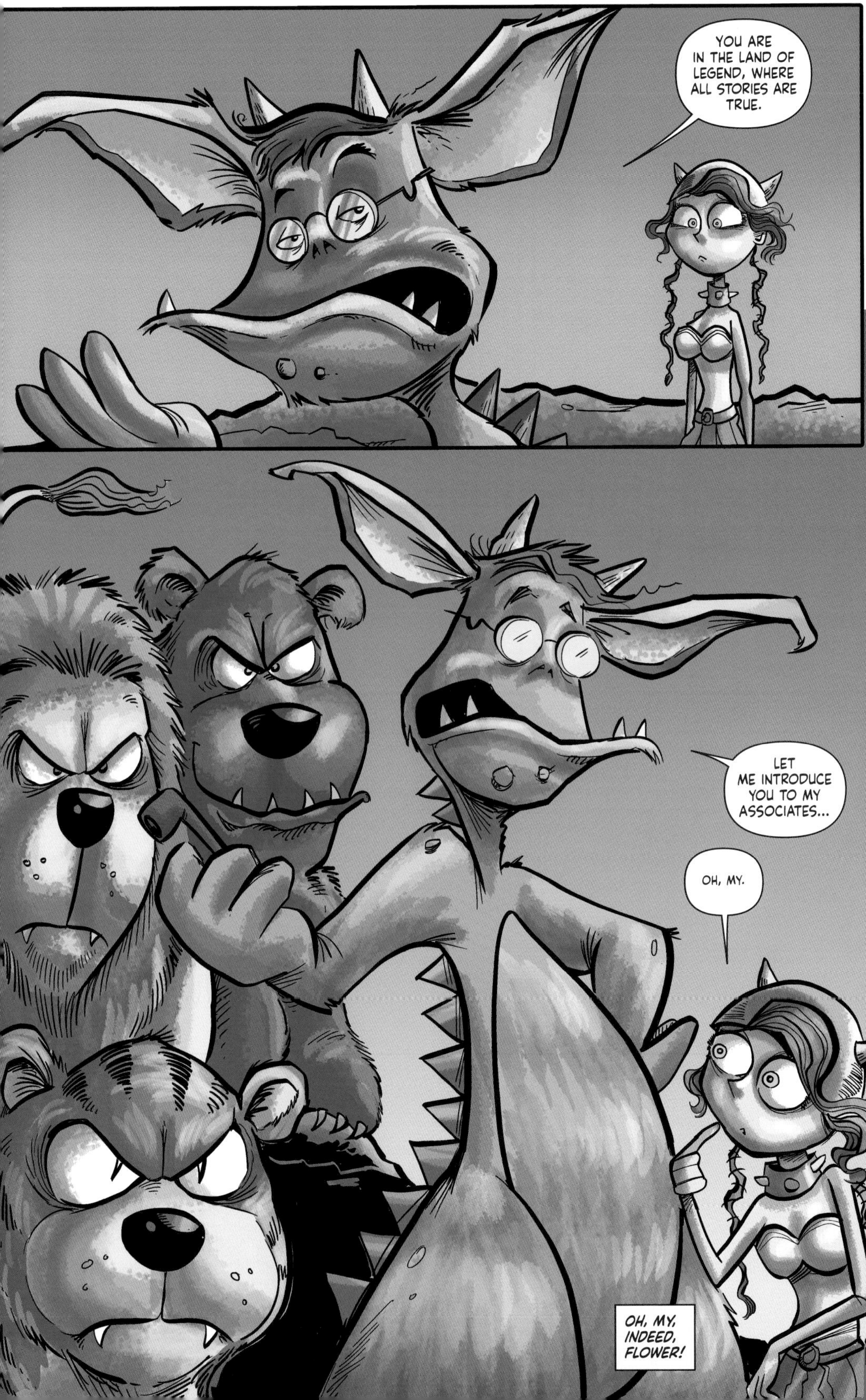
YOU ARE IN THE LAND OF LEGEND, WHERE ALL STORIES ARE TRUE.
LET ME INTRODUCE YOU TO MY ASSOCIATES...
OH, MY.
OH, MY, INDEED, FLOWER!

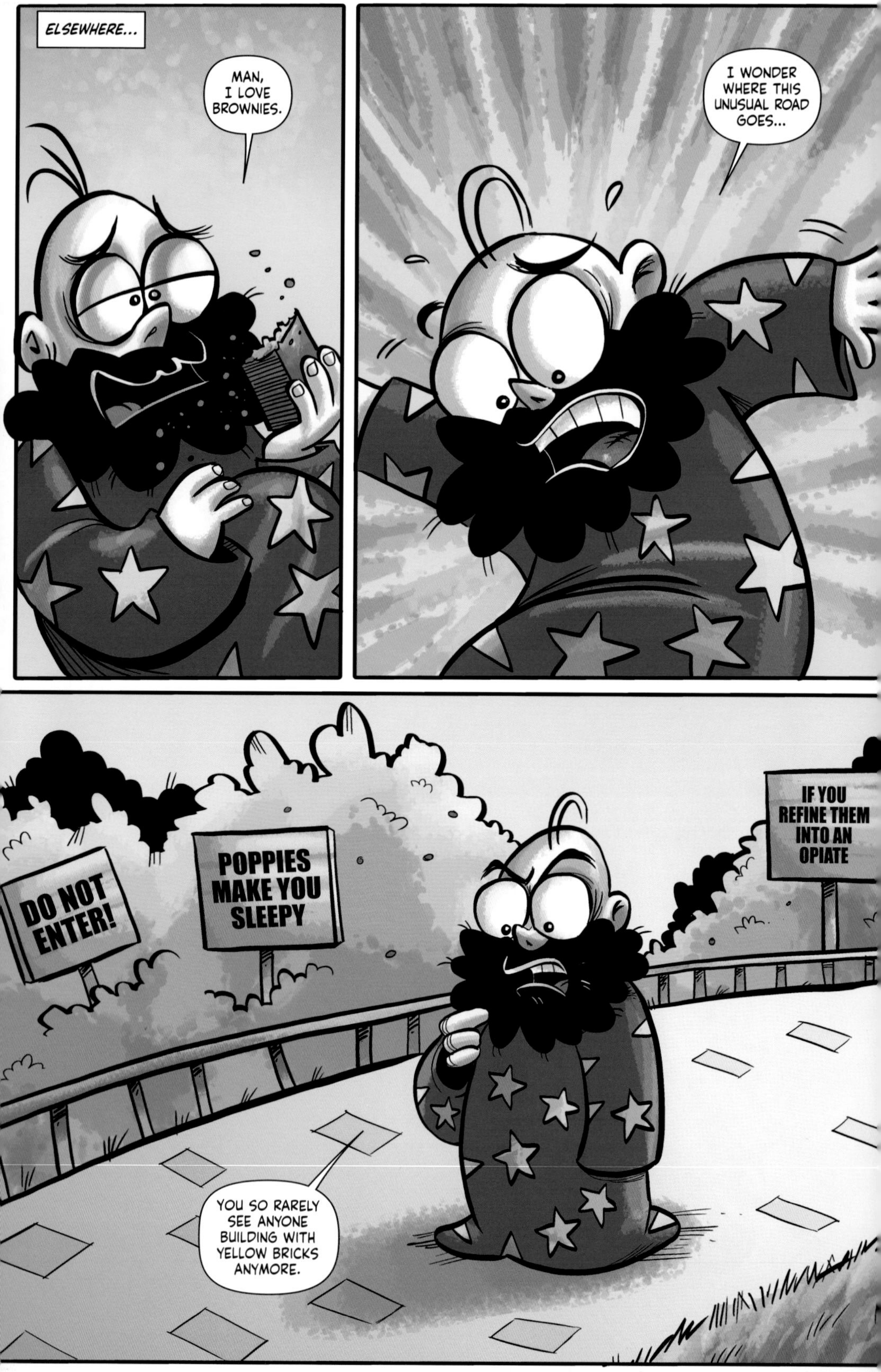
ELSEWHERE...
MAN, I LOVE BROWNIES.
I WONDER WHERE THIS UNUSUAL ROAD GOES...
DO NOT ENTER!
POPPIES MAKE YOU SLEEPY
IF YOU REFINE THEM INTO AN OPIATE
YOU SO RARELY SEE ANYONE BUILDING WITH YELLOW BRICKS ANYMORE.

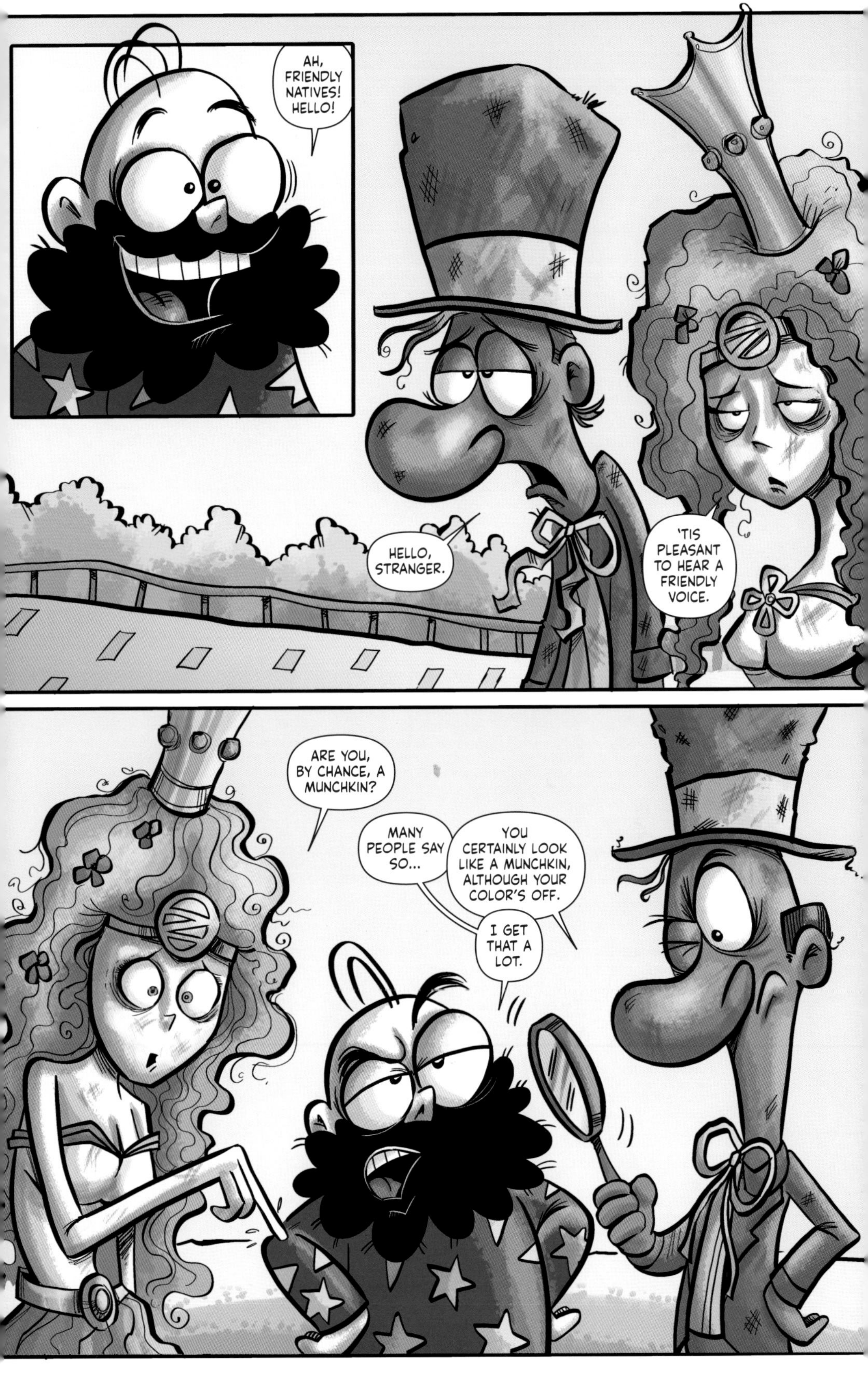
AH, FRIENDLY NATIVES! HELLO!
HELLO, STRANGER.
'TIS PLEASANT TO HEAR A FRIENDLY VOICE.
ARE YOU, BY CHANCE, A MUNCHKIN?
MANY PEOPLE SAY SO...
YOU CERTAINLY LOOK LIKE A MUNCHKIN, ALTHOUGH YOUR COLOR'S OFF.
I GET THAT A LOT.

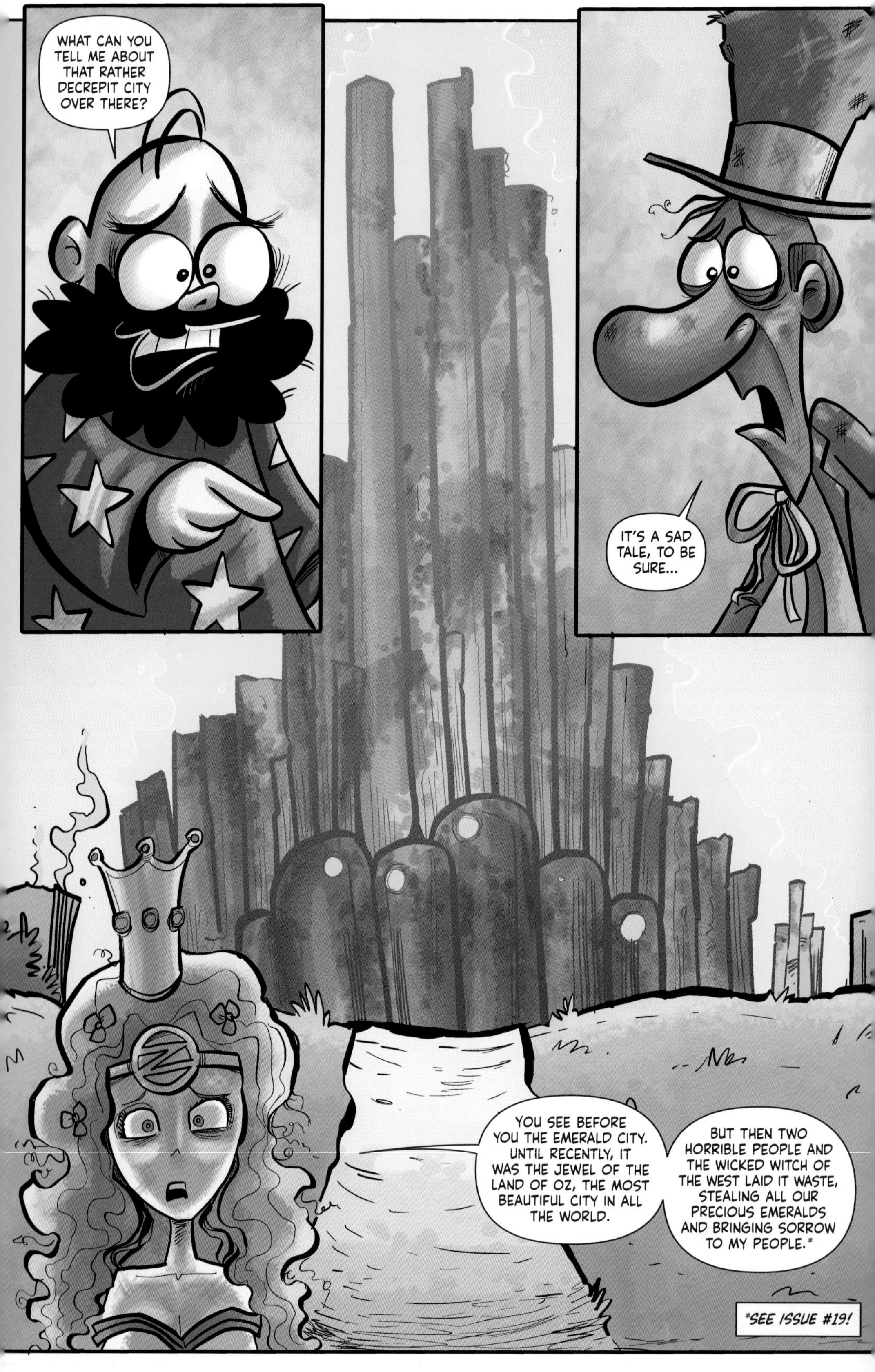
WHAT CAN YOU TELL ME ABOUT THAT RATHER DECREPIT CITY OVER THERE?
IT'S A SAD TALE, TO BE SURE...
YOU SEE BEFORE YOU THE EMERALD CITY. UNTIL RECENTLY, IT WAS THE JEWEL OF THE LAND OF OZ, THE MOST BEAUTIFUL CITY IN ALL THE WORLD.
BUT THEN TWO HORRIBLE PEOPLE AND THE WICKED WITCH OF THE WEST LAID IT WASTE, STEALING ALL OUR PRECIOUS EMERALDS AND BRINGING SORROW TO MY PEOPLE.*
*SEE ISSUE #19!

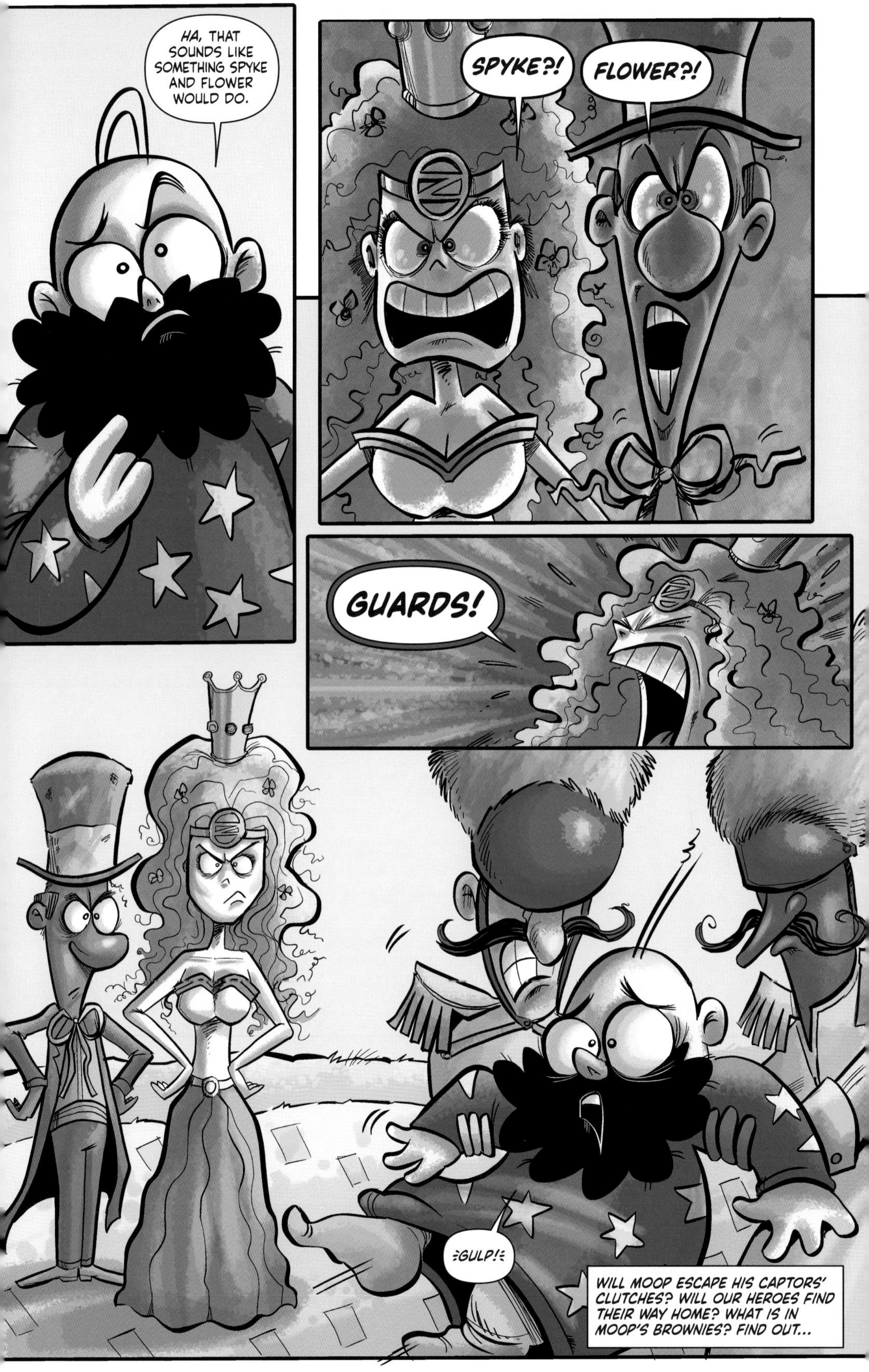
HA, THAT SOUNDS LIKE SOMETHING SPYKE AND FLOWER WOULD DO.
SPYKE?!
FLOWER?!
GUARDS!
GULP!
WILL MOOP ESCAPE HIS CAPTORS' CLUTCHES? WILL OUR HEROES FIND THEIR WAY HOME? WHAT IS IN MOOP'S BROWNIES? FIND OUT...

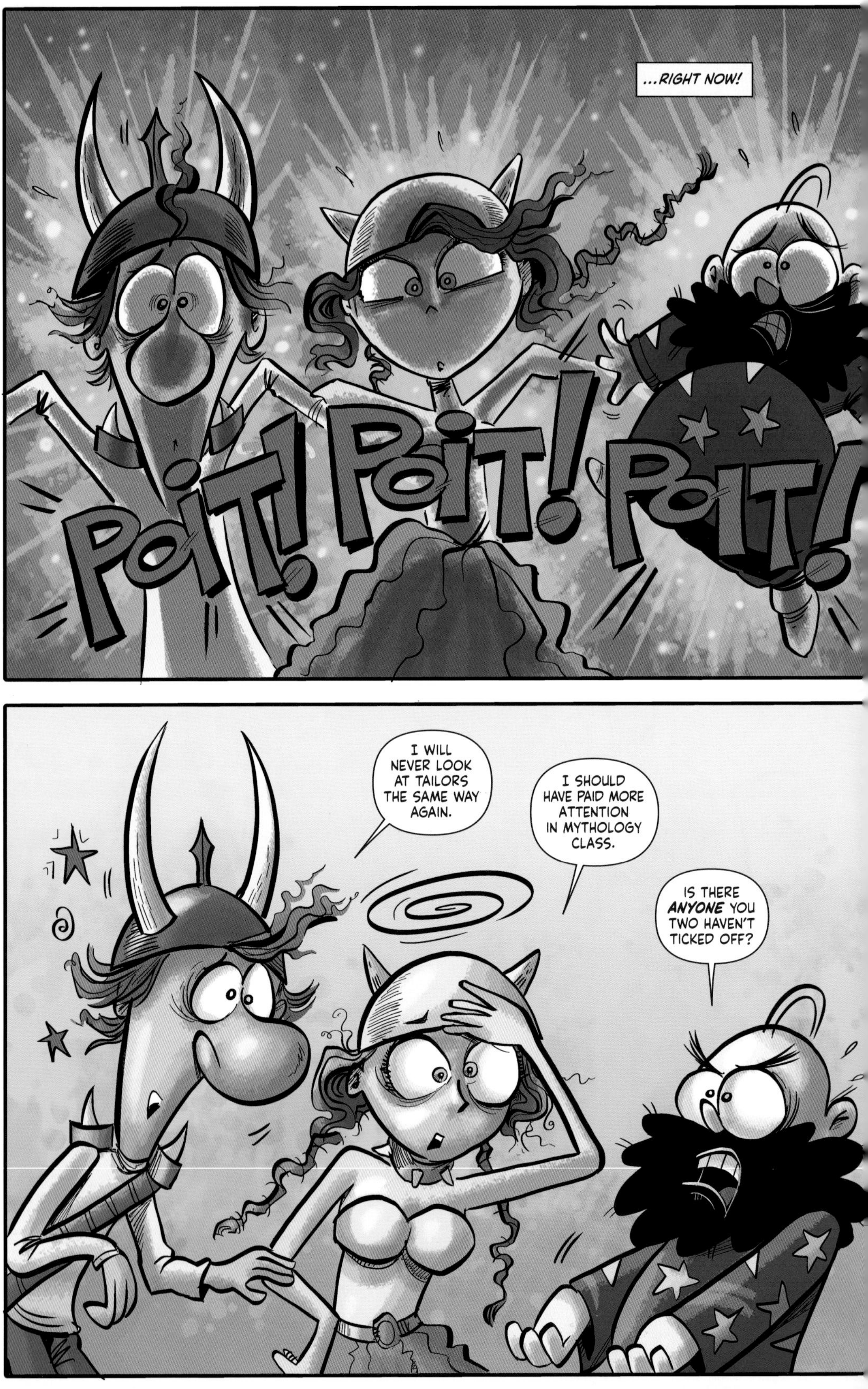
...RIGHT NOW!
POIT! POIT! POIT!
I WILL NEVER LOOK AT TAILORS THE SAME WAY AGAIN.
I SHOULD HAVE PAID MORE ATTENTION IN MYTHOLOGY CLASS.
IS THERE **ANYONE** YOU TWO HAVEN'T TICKED OFF?

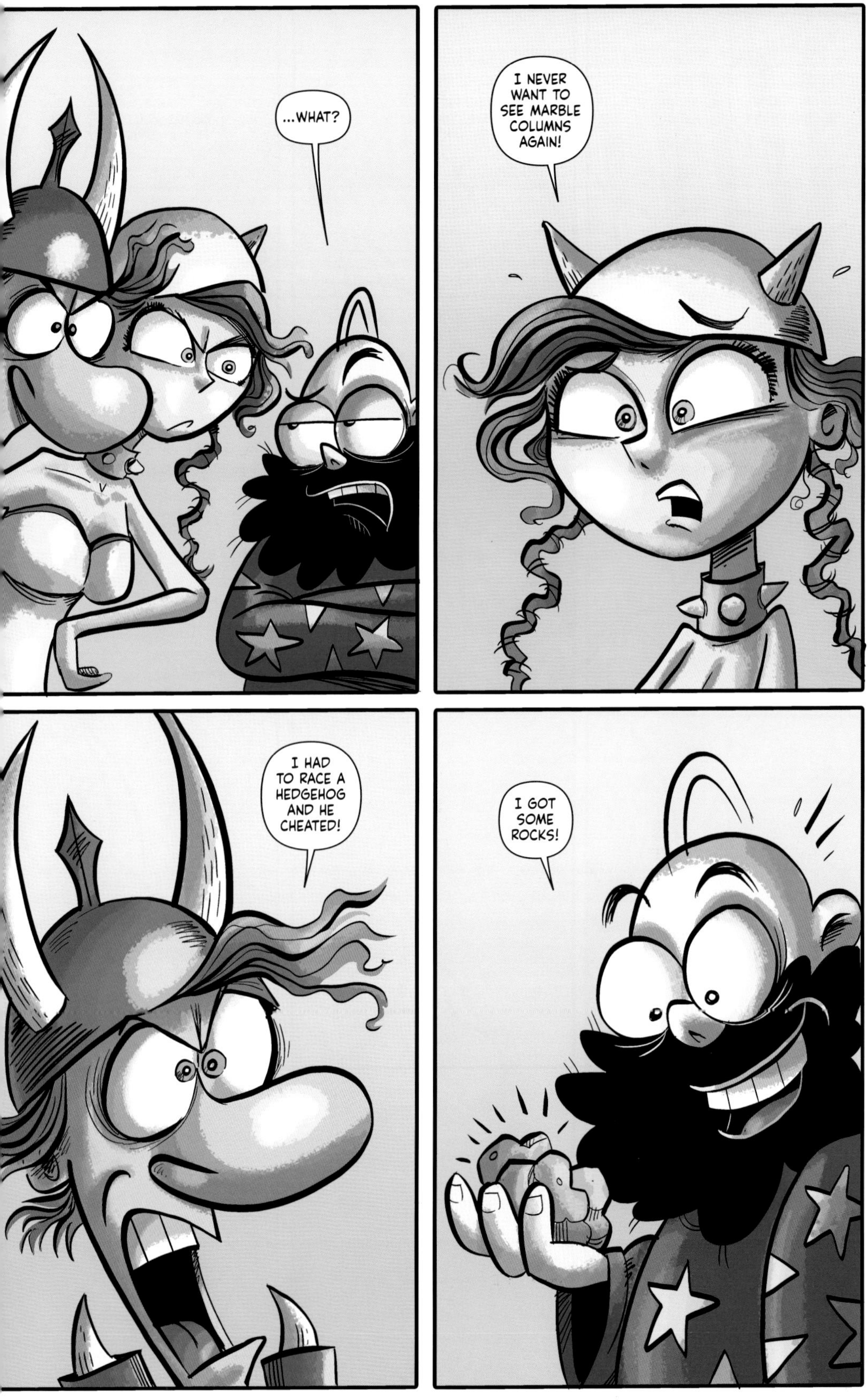
...WHAT?
I NEVER WANT TO SEE MARBLE COLUMNS AGAIN!
I HAD TO RACE A HEDGEHOG AND HE CHEATED!
I GOT SOME ROCKS!

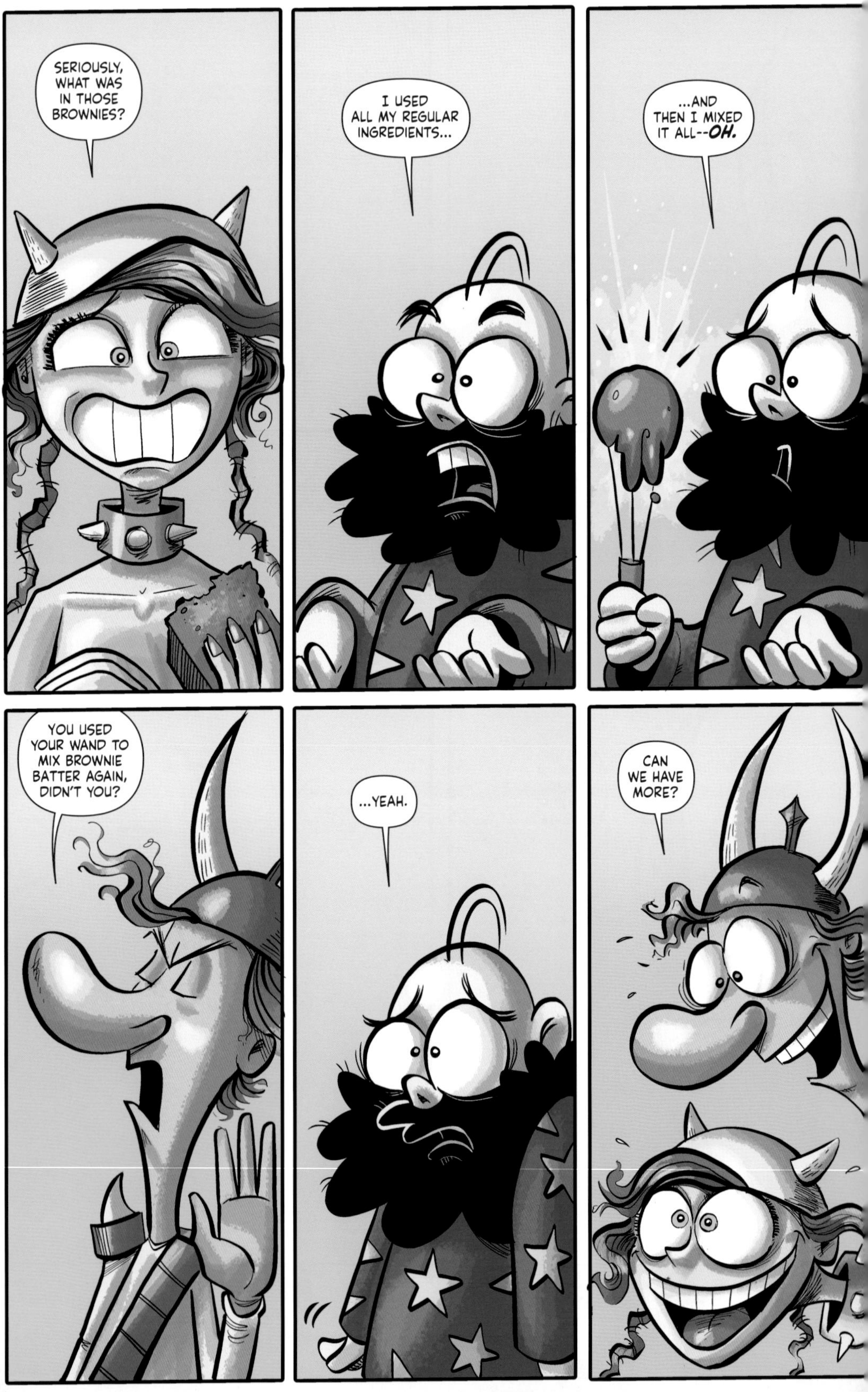

SERIOUSLY, WHAT WAS IN THOSE BROWNIES?
I USED ALL MY REGULAR INGREDIENTS...
...AND THEN I MIXED IT ALL--OH.
YOU USED YOUR WAND TO MIX BROWNIE BATTER AGAIN, DIDN'T YOU?
...YEAH.
CAN WE HAVE MORE?

THANKS FOR FOLLOWING SPYKE, FLOWER, AND ALL THEIR FRIENDS ON THESE ADVENTURES!

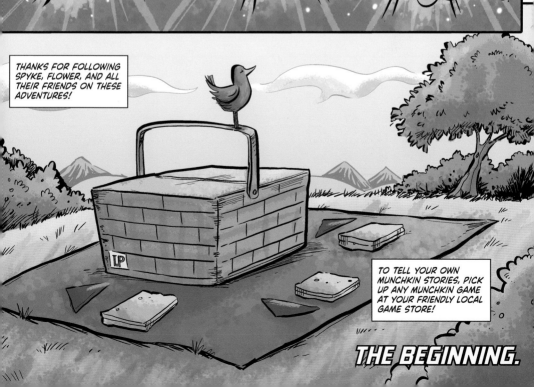

TO TELL YOUR OWN MUNCHKIN STORIES, PICK UP ANY MUNCHKIN GAME AT YOUR FRIENDLY LOCAL GAME STORE!

THE BEGINNING.

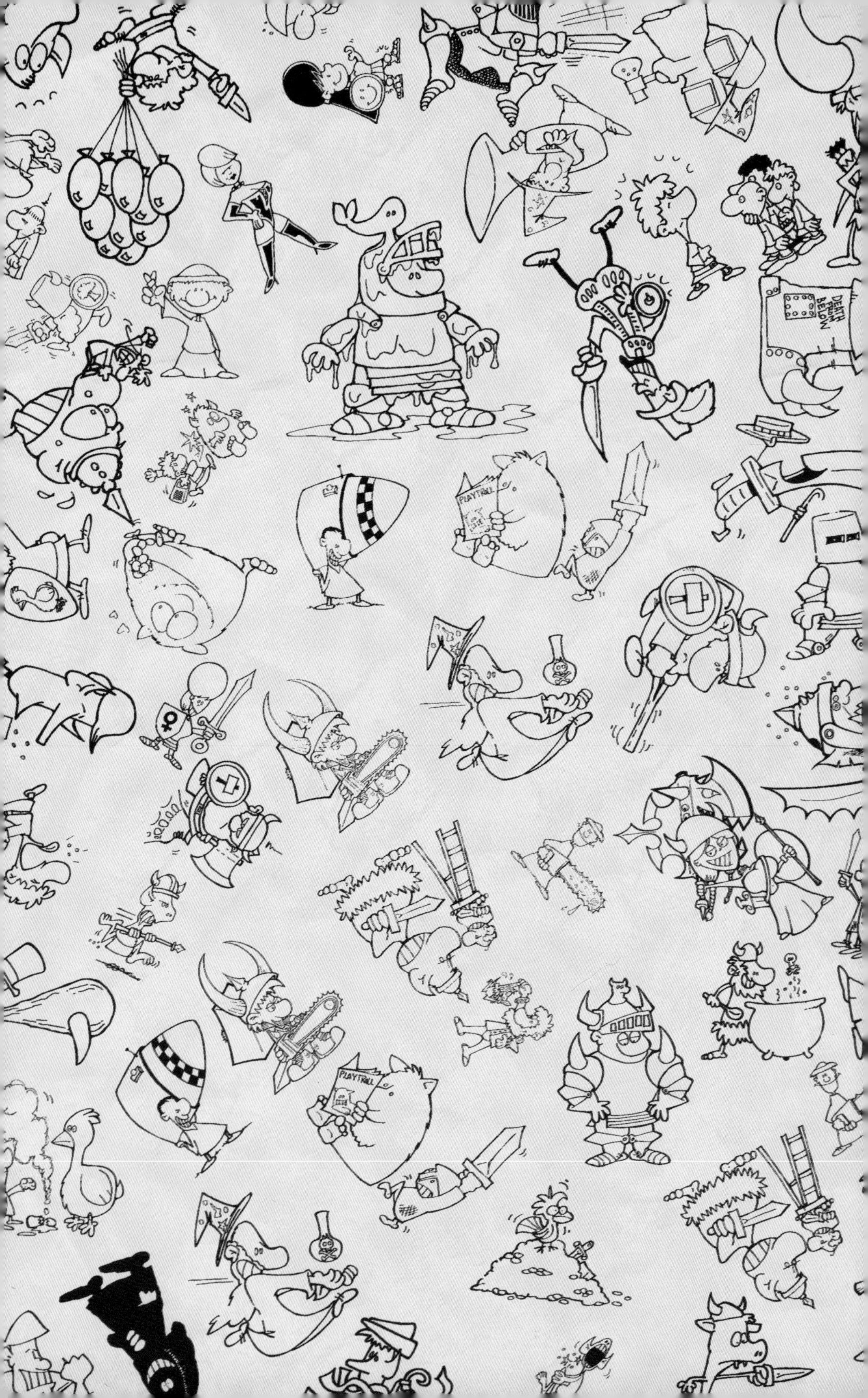
DEATH FROM BELOW
PLAYTROLL
PLAYTROLL

COVER GALLERY

Issue 21 Cover by
Mike Luckas

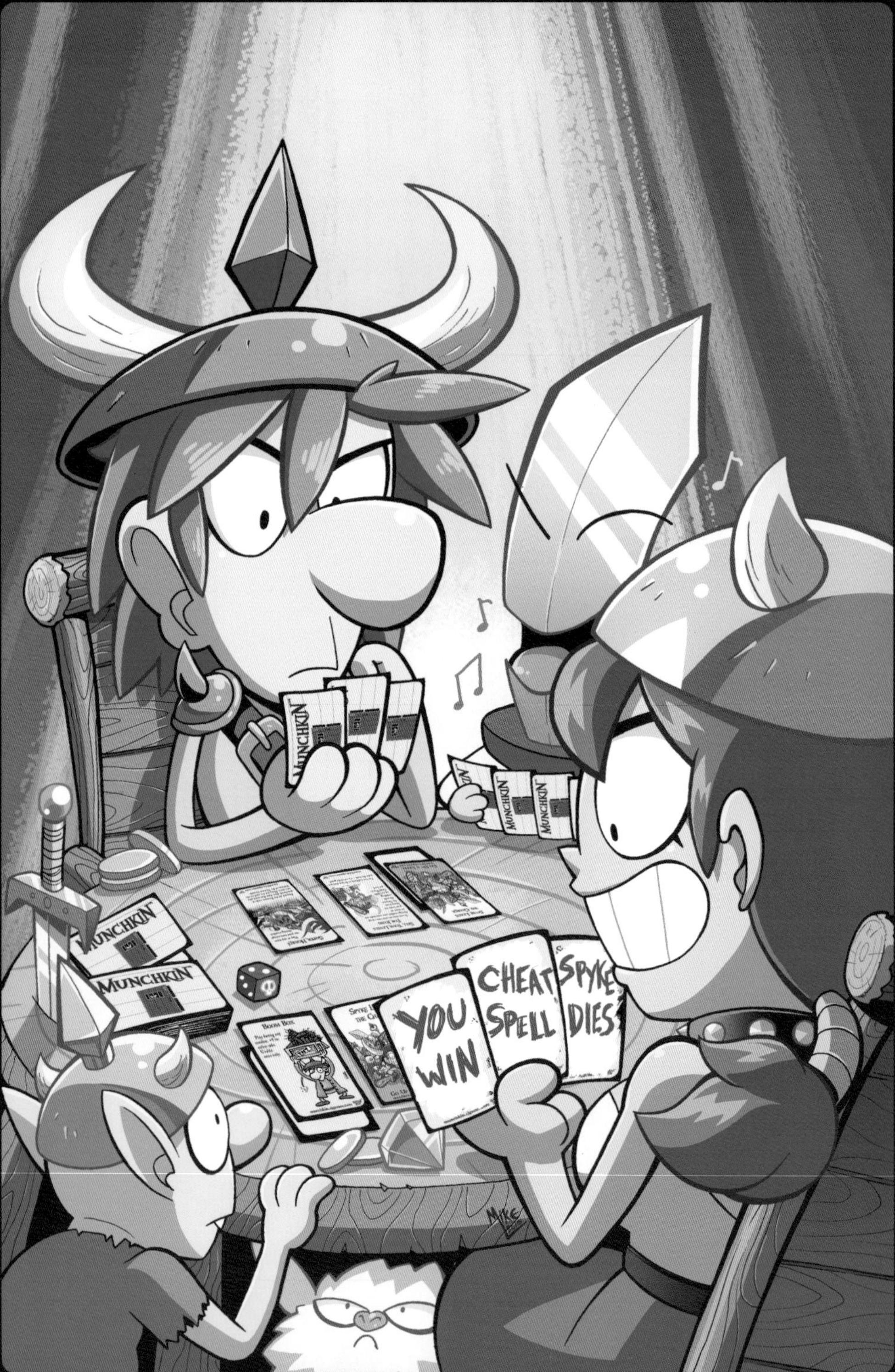
MUNCHKIN
MUNCHKIN
MUNCHKIN
MUNCHKIN
MUNCHKIN
YOU WIN
CHEAT SPELL
SPYKE DIES
MIKE

Issue 22 Cover by
Greg Hyland

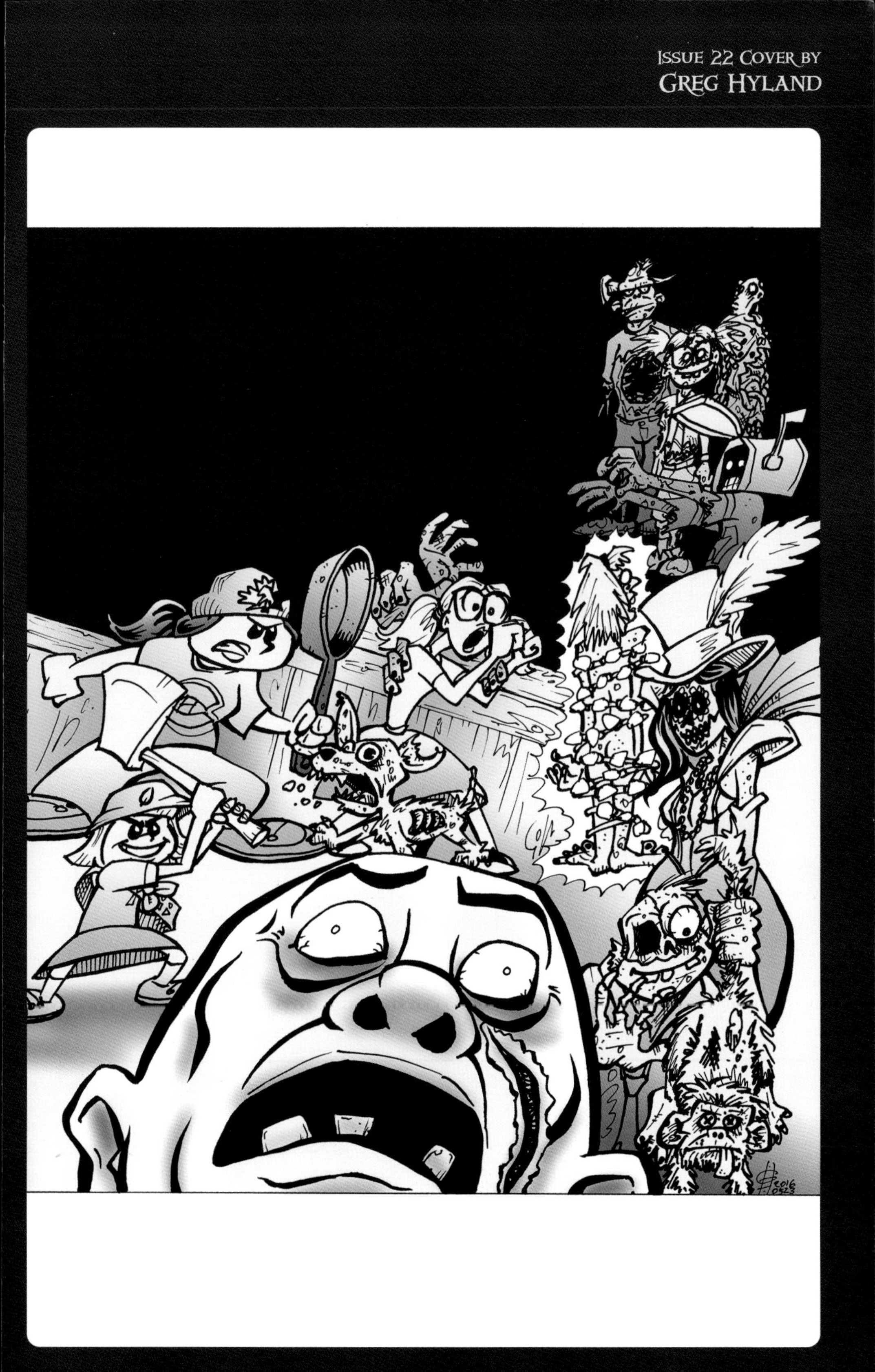

Issue 23 Cover by
Mike Luckas

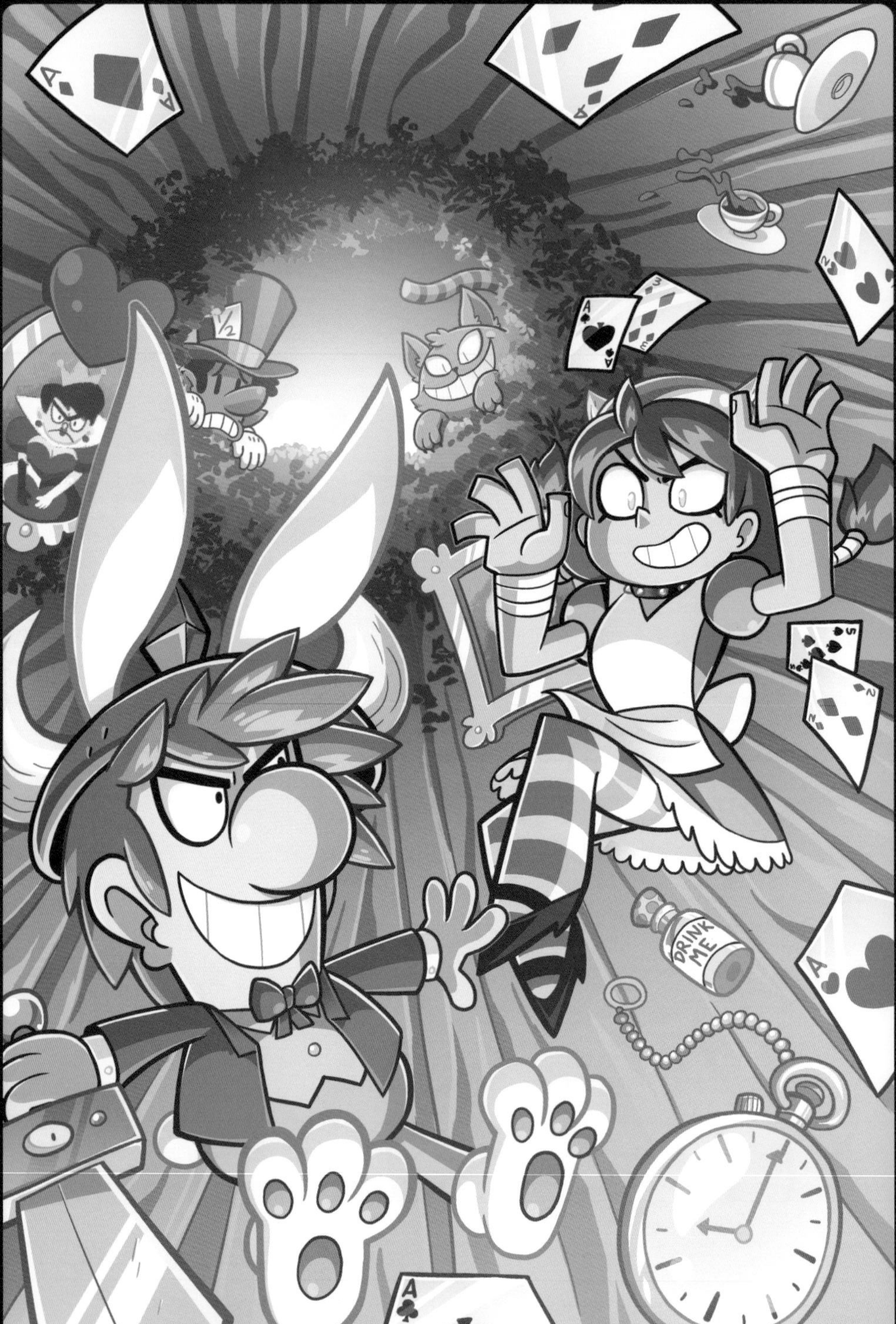
DRINK ME

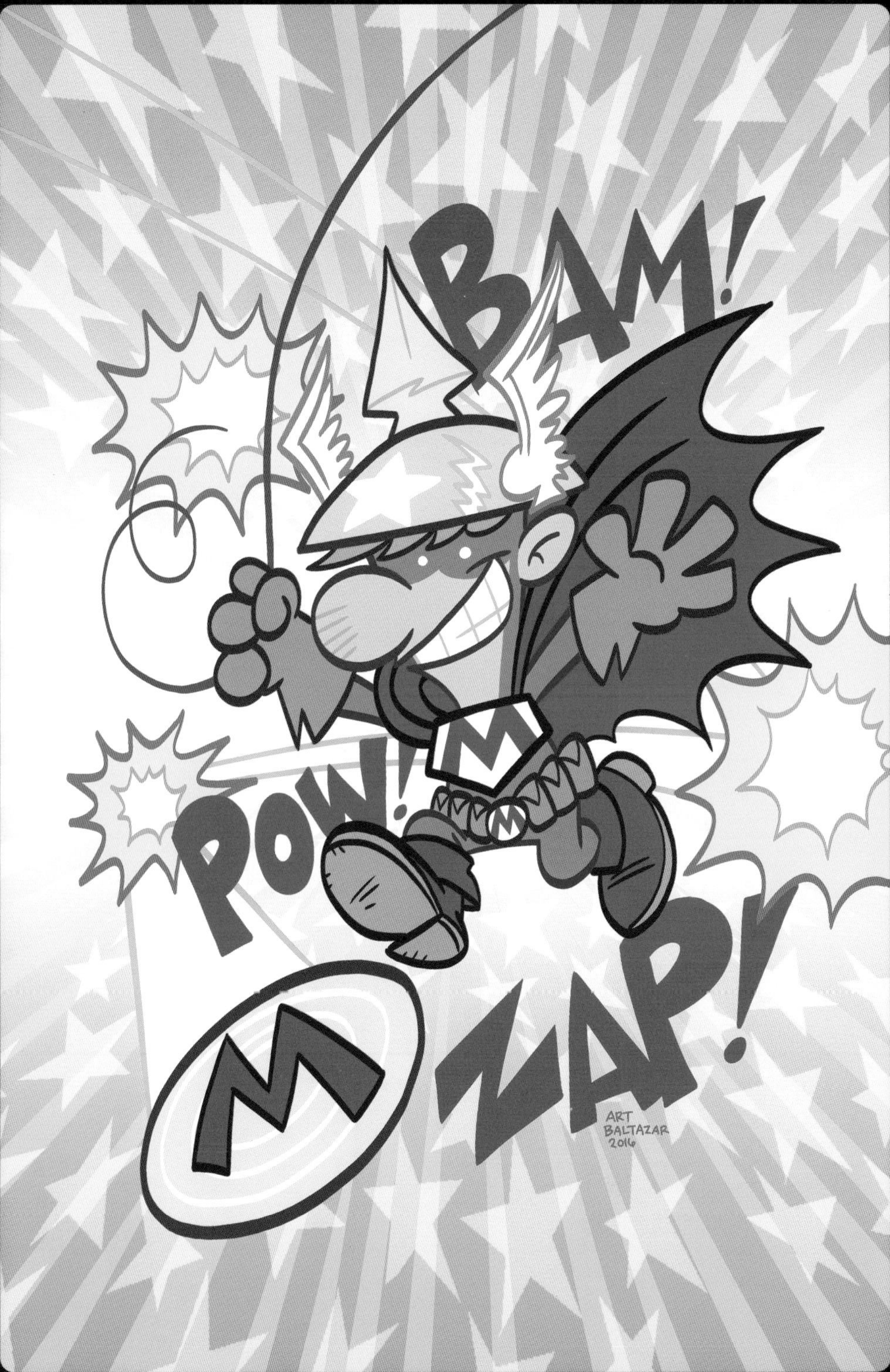
BAM!
POW!
ZAP!
ART BALTAZAR 2016

Issue 25 Cover by
Ian McGinty

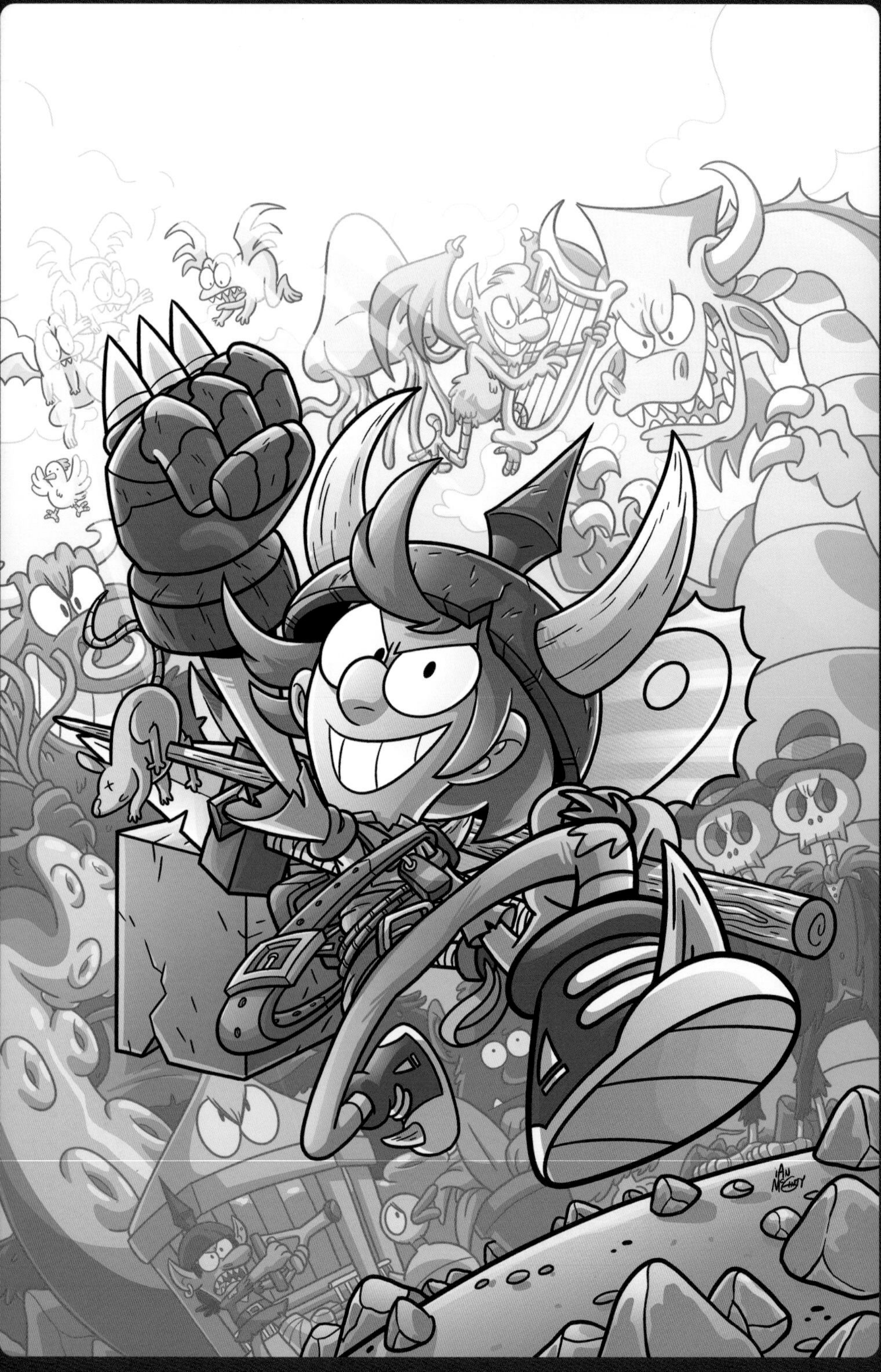

Issue 25 variant Cover by
Derek Fridolfs

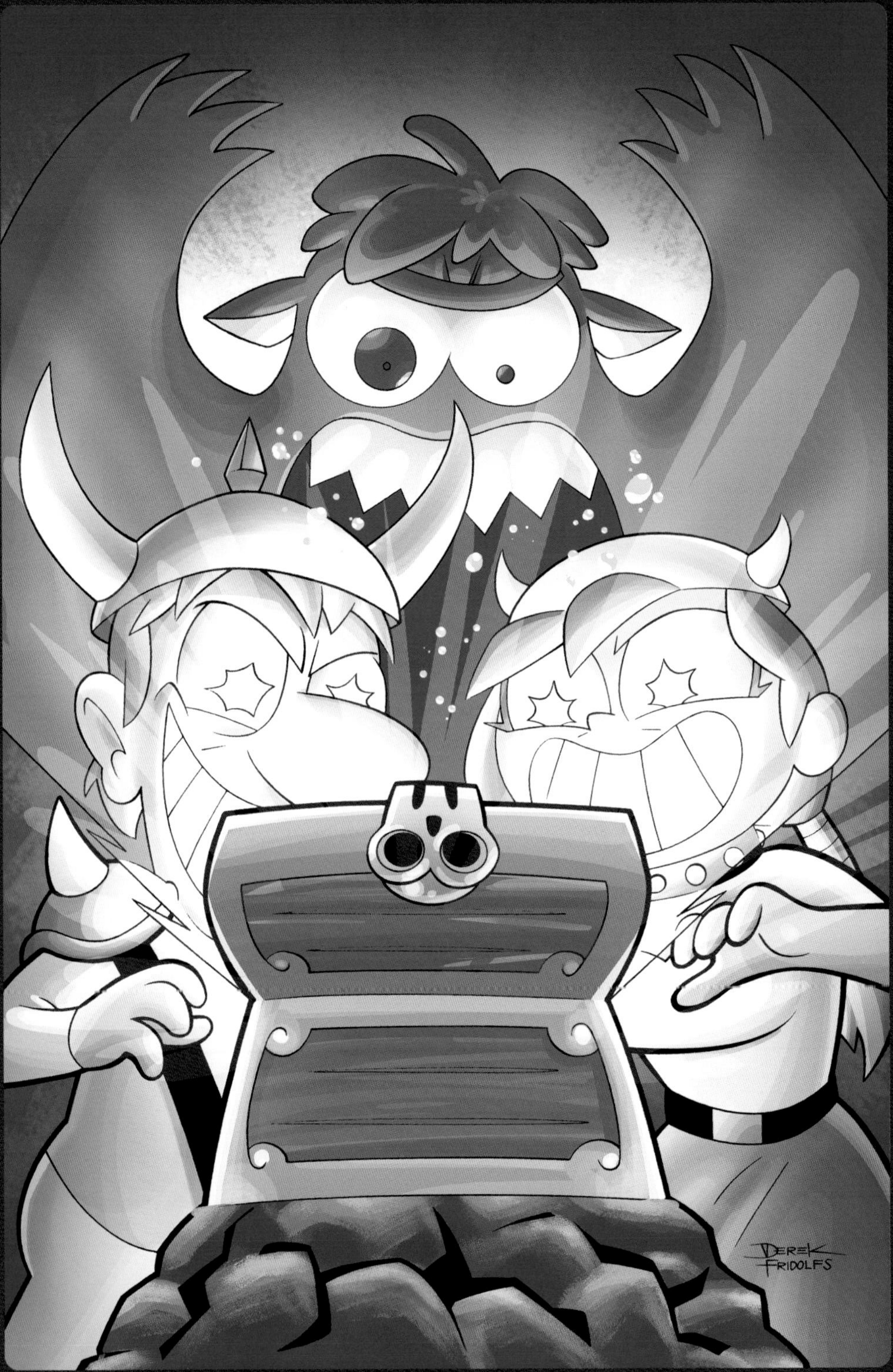
DEREK
FRIDOLFS

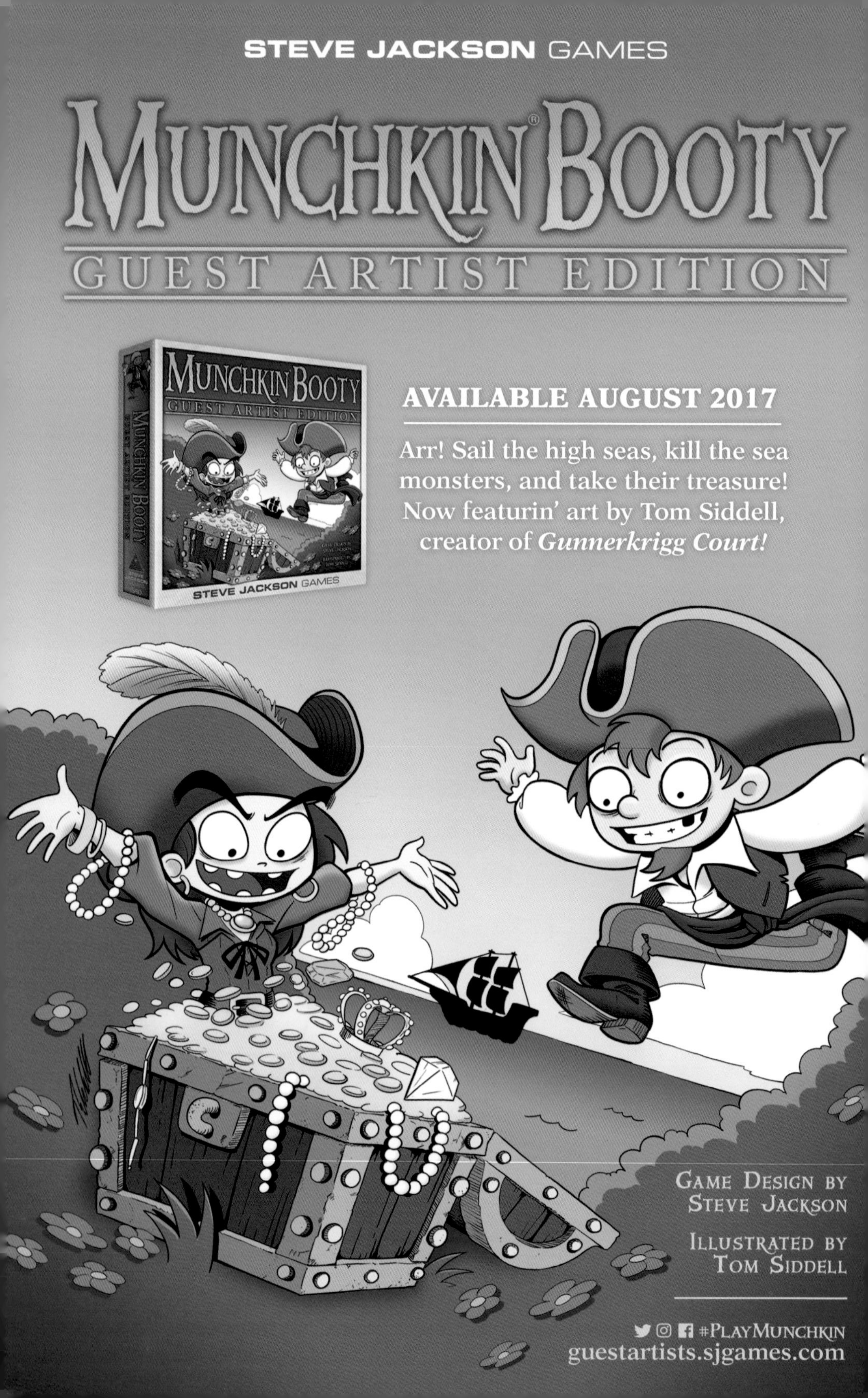
STEVE JACKSON GAMES
MUNCHKIN® BOOTY
GUEST ARTIST EDITION
AVAILABLE AUGUST 2017
Arr! Sail the high seas, kill the sea monsters, and take their treasure! Now featurin' art by Tom Siddell, creator of *Gunnerkrigg Court!*
GAME DESIGN BY STEVE JACKSON
ILLUSTRATED BY TOM SIDDELL
#PLAYMUNCHKIN
guestartists.sjgames.com

DISCOVER
ALL THE HITS

STEVENSON • ELLIS • WATTERS • ALLEN
LUMBERJANES
BEWARE THE KITTEN HOLY
NEW YORK TIMES BESTSELLING SERIES

Allison + Treiman + Cogar
GIANT DAYS
VOLUME ONE

From a writer of Disney's Moana
RIBON • FISH • PEER
SLAM!
VOLUME ONE

Hope Larson • Brittney Williams • Sarah Stern
GOLDIE VANCE
"Scoot over Nancy Drew..." —Los Angeles Times
Volume One

THE BACKSTAGERS

TYSON HESSE'S
DIESEL
IGNITION

BOOM! BOX

AVAILABLE AT YOUR LOCAL COMICS SHOP AND BOOKSTORE

To find a comics shop in your area, call 1-888-266-4226

WWW.**BOOM-STUDIOS**.COM

Lumberjanes
Noelle Stevenson, Shannon Watters, Grace Ellis, Brooke Allen, and Others

Volume 1: Beware the Kitten Holy
ISBN: 978-1-60886-687-8 | $14.99 US

Volume 2: Friendship to the Max
ISBN: 978-1-60886-737-0 | $14.99 US

Volume 3: A Terrible Plan
ISBN: 978-1-60886-803-2 | $14.99 US

Volume 4: Out of Time
ISBN: 978-1-60886-860-5 | $14.99 US

Volume 5: Band Together
ISBN: 978-1-60886-919-0 | $14.99 US

Giant Days
John Allison, Lissa Treiman, Max Sarin

Volume 1
ISBN: 978-1-60886-789-9 | $9.99 US

Volume 2
ISBN: 978-1-60886-804-9 | $14.99 US

Volume 3
ISBN: 978-1-60886-851-3 | $14.99 US

Jonesy
Sam Humphries, Caitlin Rose Boyle

Volume 1
ISBN: 978-1-60886-883-4 | $9.99 US

Volume 2
ISBN: 978-1-60886-999-2 | $14.99 US

Slam!
Pamela Ribon, Veronica Fish, Brittany Peer

Volume 1
ISBN: 978-1-68415-004-5 | $14.99 US

Goldie Vance
Hope Larson, Brittney Williams

Volume 1
ISBN: 978-1-60886-898-8 | $9.99 US

Volume 2
ISBN: 978-1-60886-974-9 | $14.99 US

The Backstagers
James Tynion IV, Rian Sygh

Volume 1
ISBN: 978-1-60886-993-0 | $14.99 US

Tyson Hesse's Diesel: Ignition
Tyson Hesse

ISBN: 978-1-60886-907-7 | $14.99 US

Coady & The Creepies
Liz Prince, Amanda Kirk, Hannah Fisher

ISBN: 978-1-68415-029-8 | $14.99 US

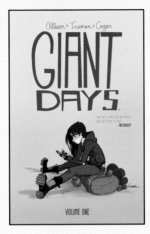

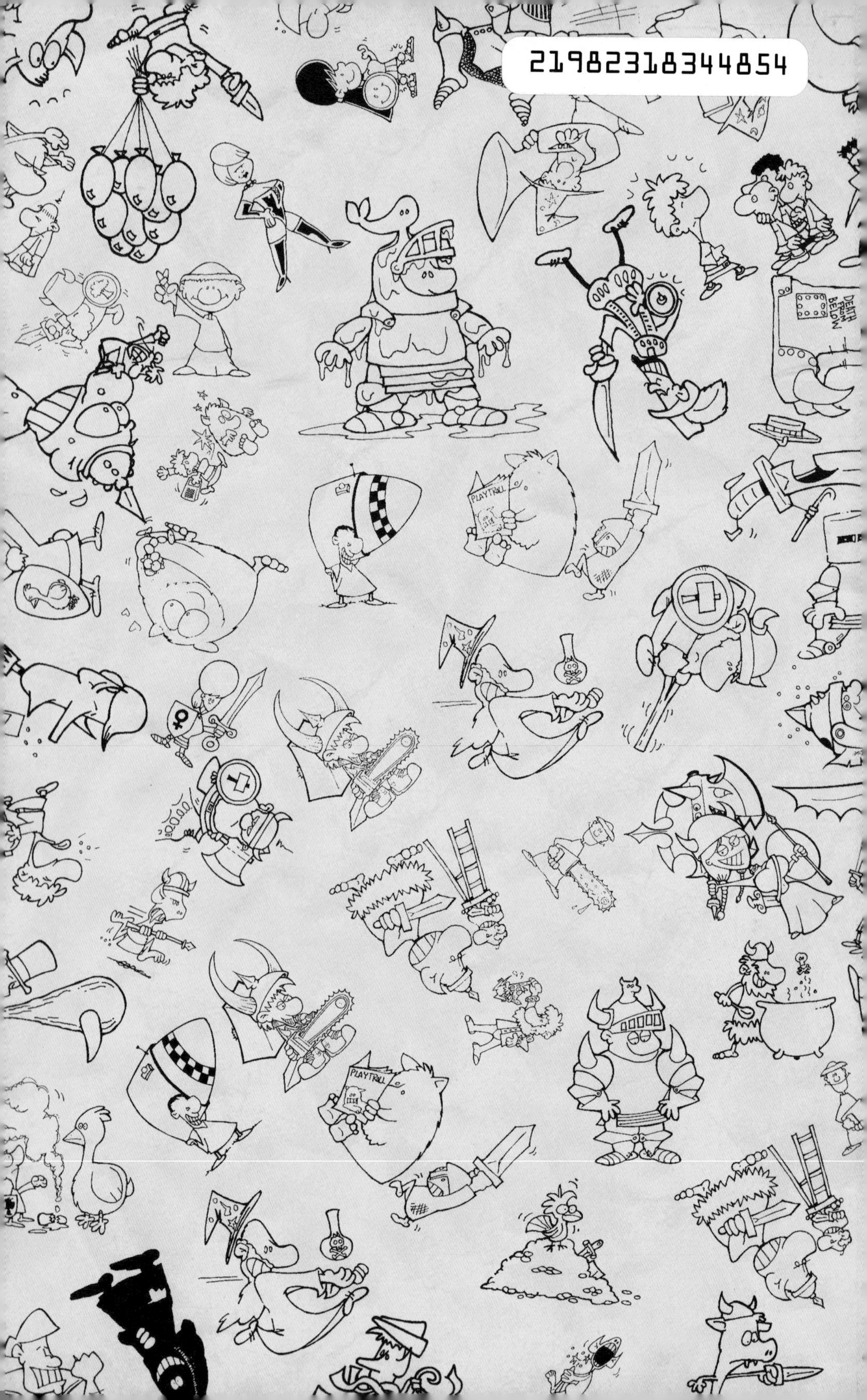
DEATH FROM BELOW
PLAYTROLL
PLAYTROLL